IMMIGRATION
TO
NEW YORK

IMMIGRATION TO NEW YORK

Edited by
William Pencak
Selma Berrol
and
Randall M. Miller

A New-York Historical Society Book

Philadelphia: The Balch Institute Press

London and Toronto: Associated University Presses

Associated University Presses
440 Forsgate Drive
Cranbury, NJ 08512

Associated University Presses
25 Sicilian Avenue
London WC1A 2QH, England

Associated University Presses
P.O. Box 39, Clarkson Pstl. Stn.
Mississauga, Ontario,
L5J 3X9 Canada

The paper used in this publication meets the requirements
  of the American National Standard for Permanence of Paper
  for Printed Library Materials Z39.48–1984.

Library of Congress Cataloging-in-Publication Data

Immigration to New York / edited by William Pencak, Selma Berrol,
  and Randall M. Miller.
      p.   cm.
    Includes bibliographical references.
    ISBN 0-944190-09-X
    1. Immigrants—New York (N.Y.)—Congresses.   2. New York
(N.Y.)—Emigration and immigration—Congresses.   3. New York
(N.Y.)—Social conditions—Congresses.   I. Pencak, William, 1951- .
II. Berrol, Selma Cantor.   III. Miller, Randall M.
IV. New-York Historical Society.
JV7048.I55   1990
304.8'7471—dc20   89-13757
                                                                 CIP

Printed in the United States of America
⊗

Contents

Acknowledgments
xi

General Introduction
WILLIAM PENCAK
xiii

PART ONE
The Old Immigration

Introduction
WILLIAM PENCAK
3

— 1 —
Labor's Decline within New York City's
Democratic Party from 1844 to 1884
ANTHONY GRONOWICZ
7

— 2 —
Bishop John Timon, Archbishop John Hughes, and Irish
Colonization: A Clash of Episcopal Views on the Future
of the Irish and the Catholic Church in America
LEONARD R. RIFORGIATO
27

— 3 —
From the Barricades of Paris to the Sidewalks of New York:
German Artisans and the European Roots
of American Labor Radicalism
STANLEY NADEL
56

PART TWO
Early Twentieth-Century Immigration

Introduction
SELMA BERROL
83

— 4 —
Mobilization and Conflict:
The Background and Social History of the
Norwegian Colony in Brooklyn to 1910
DAVID C. MAUK
86

— 5 —
'. . . The Adoption of the Tactics of the Enemy':
The Care of Italian Immigrant Youth in the
Archdiocese of New York During the Progressive Era
MARY ELIZABETH BROWN
109

— 6 —
The Fall of the German-American Community:
Buffalo 1914 to 1919
ANDREW P. YOX
126

— 7 —
European Immigrant/Ethnic Theater
in Gilded Age New York:
Reflections and Projections of Mentalities
JAMES H. DORMON
148

PART THREE
The Post-World War II City

Introduction
RANDALL M. MILLER
175

— 8 —

Recent Third World Immigration
to New York City, 1945 to 1986:
An Overview
DAVID M. REIMERS
179

— 9 —

The Migration Division of Puerto Rico and
Puerto Ricans in New York City, 1948 to 1969
MICHAEL LAPP
198

— 10 —

Portal of Portals: Speaking of the United States
"As Though It Were New York"—and Vice Versa
ELLIOTT R. BARKAN
215

Contributors
243

Index
245

Acknowledgments

As with the previous three conferences, our greatest thanks go to Dr. James Bell, former Director of the New-York Historical Society. It was his inspiration which linked the Society's conference theme for 1986 with its museum exhibition celebrating the centenary of the Statue of Liberty. His dedicated leadership and generous support made the conference a success and the publication of half of its twenty papers possible. Sheryl Jarvis worked wonders in preparing the program, registering the participants, organizing the reception, and in general co-ordinating the essential planning. To her, to Janet Nicolai, to the staff of the New-York Historical Society, and to Roberta Grobel Intrater, who provided a tour of her photograph exhibition "Liberty's Legacy: Photography of New York's Ethnic Festivals" we extend our heartfelt thanks. James Mooney, Librarian of the Society, and Marilyn McShane, its Publications Coordinator, have worked indefatigably to see the volume through to completion.

The superb comments which sparked the conference's stimulating discussions were supplied by (in order of appearance): Sean Wilentz, David Gerber, James Bergquist, Alan Kraut, Salvatore LaGumina, Mimi D'Aponte, Maxine Seller, Lydio Tomasi, Betty Boyd Caroli, Carol Groneman, Dennis Clark, Humbert Nelli, and Thomas Curran.

William Pencak, Abington, Pennsylvania
Selma Berrol, New York, New York
Randall M. Miller, Philadelphia, Pennsylvania

WILLIAM PENCAK

General Introduction:
Immigration to New York

In 1986, as a refurbished Statue of Liberty emerged from its cage of
scaffolding to herald the nation's year-long celebration of its immigrant
heritage, New York was for the third time riding the crest of a wave
of newcomers to the United States. New York has been the port of
entry for about a third of the nine million immigrants legally entering
the country since quotas were liberalized in 1965.* This figure is dwarfed,
however, by New York's share of America's first two great migrations.
About seventy percent of the Irish-German (1840–1860) and Southern
and Eastern European (1890–1924) immigrants entered through New
York State, mostly New York City. In each period, millions remained
in the Empire State. More than any great city in modern times, if not
world history, New York over the past century and a half has been populated, shaped, and built by successive waves of immigrants.

The essays gathered here were first presented as papers at a conference held by the New-York Historical Society to celebrate Lady Liberty's
Centennial. Eight deal exclusively with New York City while two look
at the Irish and Germans in the state's second city of Buffalo. The Historical Society is proud to publish as the first modern scholarly collec-

---

* This figure excludes Puerto Ricans, who are American citizens. However, as their
experience in New York is in many ways similar to and comparatively illuminates
that of immigrants, we have included one essay on Puerto Ricans.

tion on immigration to New York a volume which deals in nearly equal proportion with each of the great immigration eras. The books discusses Hispanics, Asians, and Norwegians, the more familiar Irish, German, and Italian immigrants, and popular images of newcomers.

Diversity and complexity are at the heart of New York's immigration experience. But unifying elements exist. If immigrants have been welcomed symbolically by the Statue of Liberty, New Yorkers' initial reception has usually been less than gracious. Immigrants therefore formed their own churches, charitable societies, political clubs, and cultural institutions which provided them with an identity apart from an establishment primarily interested in maintaining order and exploiting their labor. But immigrants and their institutions also bargained with native Americans and older immigrant groups. They eventually obtained varying degrees of economic mobility, political power, and social dignity. The essays in this volume tell of how immigrants walked a tightrope between the need to assimilate into and advance in an alien society while maintaining the sense of self-worth all too frequently denied them by more entrenched elements, sometimes including earlier immigrants from the same nation.

This paradox of assimilation versus ethnic affirmation lies at the heart of American history. On the one hand, older Americans have sought to incorporate minorities culturally, but on the other hand have tried to keep them at arm's length politically, economically, and socially. By asserting their cultural distinctiveness while seeking political power, better jobs, and social equality, the minorities have turned the tables. As a consequence, the United States celebrates ethnic pluralism as a bastion of national unity. Like the factions described in James Madison's Tenth Federalist, the late twentieth-century nation has become so diverse ethnically and mobile geographically that we are all minorities. Mutual bargaining leading to mutual toleration has become the foundation of political stability.

PART ONE

The Old Immigration

WILLIAM PENCAK

Introduction:
The Old Immigration

New York City grew from a predominantly native city of 33,000 in 1790 to a metropolis of 813,000 in 1860. On the eve of the Civil War, most Manhattanites were recent immigrants or their American-born children. Since 1840, seventy percent of some four million immigrants, including 1.8 million from Ireland and 1.4 million from Germany, entered the United States through its foremost Atlantic port. The half million who remained in the Empire City had to confront the xenophobic Native American ("Know Nothing") movement and more generalized hostility from long-term residents fearful of being taken over by foreigners.

The essays in this section describe three characteristic institutions the "Old Immigrants"—as historians refer to those of the mid-nineteenth century—transformed in their process of adjustment to the New World. Anthony Gronowicz examines the supposedly Irish political machine, Leonard Riforgiato the Roman Catholic church, and Stanley Nadel the radical political culture brought to New York by German refugees. If each institution helped the immigrants survive in their new habitat, it did so more through separation than assimilation. In effect, the newcomers created niches where they could coexist separately if unequally and uneasily with native Americans.

According to Anthony Gronowicz, the myth that the "Irish machine" ran late nineteenth-century New York to the general detriment of public welfare and private morals was a nativist, Progressive slander. He finds

3

far more openness to working men and immigrants in the Democratic Party at the beginning of the Irish mass migration than forty years later. Statistically comparing party activists in 1844 and 1884, Gronowicz demonstrates that by the latter date, a party shaken by the Tweed scandals and pro-Southern sentiments during the Civil War was firmly controlled by wealthy WASPS who dominated a *minority* (30 percent) of Irish public officials and the majority of immigrant and first-generation voters. The machine did provide careers in politics and patronage jobs for the Irish. But it may have preempted a distinctively Irish working-class political movement which might have challenged the supremacy of a party elite committed to the same industrial and social order as its Republican counterpart.

One implication of Leonard Riforgiato's essay is that the failure of the Irish to win control of the Democratic party may have stemmed from the anti-assimilationist attitude demonstrated in the self-segregation of the Irish Catholic church. To be sure, nativist hostility encouraged the Irish to turn inward, but Archbishop John Hughes' rejection of public schools and colonization schemes which would have dispersed the Irish among the nation's rural population also played a role. Under Hughes' irascible leadership, the Church insisted on maintaining its Irishness to the detriment of its members' geographic and educational mobility. Hughes' efforts to construct an Irish nation within a nation contrasted sharply with Buffalo Bishop John Timon's abortive efforts to colonize the Irish on mid-western farms and to integrate Irish schools and charities with those of his city's Protestant establishment. By comparing the two bishops, Riforgiato shows how Hughes' implacable hatred of WASP culture shaped the history of American Catholicism.

If the Irish brought with them a fervent Catholicism, many German political exiles in the 1840s arrived in New York with a zeal for radical political change. Much like Paris (where many of them had previously lived) or Munich, the Germans founded a bewildering array of clubs and journals, ranging from Communist to anarchist, setting the pattern still distinguishing the city's internally divided Left. But they did more than that. Unlike the unskilled Irish, the predominantly skilled German artisans laid the foundation for a post-Civil War labor movement which maintained the momentum the native Workingmen's Parties of the 1830s had failed to develop. Nadel reminds us that New York's radical and labor militancy was already traditional when the eastern Europeans with whom it is most often associated arrived at the turn of the century.

Immigrant groups usually assimilate to America—eventually. But a generation or two is often required. Natives need to be reassured that their values and polity will survive; immigrants need time to acquire economic and social respectability for hostility to abate. By examining the role of the Democratic party, the Catholic church, and radical political clubs in the pre-assimilation period for Irish and German immigrants of the mid-nineteenth century, these essays bring to life the dynamics of immigrant cultures struggling to survive and retain their integrity in an unfriendly new world.

ANTHONY GRONOWICZ

1

Labor's Decline within New York City's Democratic Party from 1844 to 1884

The Democratic party has claimed to represent working people in New York since the 1790s when the first mass-based parties emerged. It became preeminent as the city grew from thirty thousand inhabitants to four hundred thousand by 1844, and to over one million forty years later. This essay examines how the role that the working class played within this political party changed from 1844 to 1884.

Historians have yet to examine what effect actual participation by different social classes within party ranks might have had upon either party development or upon the classes themselves. Studies of the social basis of politics concentrate on determining voting preferences through analyses of election returns.[1] Yet the act of voting represents the lowest order of participation in a constitutional republic. One must also examine the role of party activists.

Two presidential election years in two different eras of the nineteenth-century New York City Democrats afford an opportunity to observe party structure and personnel under the maximum use to which local political organization is normally put. First, 1844 was a critical election year at the historic moment when "similarities and differences between the major New York parties . . . crystallized . . . and were reflected in the platforms and addresses adopted at national and state conventions," and Democrats officially designated themselves as "the American Democracy."[2] Second, 1884 was when the Democrats captured the presidency for the first time since 1856, and Grover Cleveland, former governor of New York, headed the resurgent "national democracy." His political mentor was Samuel Tilden, who had inaugurated his political career as the staunch Jacksonian head of the Democratic Young Men's General Committee in 1844. As he was also the Democratic presidential candidate in 1876, Tilden represents something of an ideological bridge between the party of 1844 and that of 1884.

By 1884, over three-quarters of the city's population was of Irish and German extraction compared to less than one-third in 1844. By comparing their representation within the party across time we can determine how effectively the party represented society.

Originally, as Jeffersonian "Republicans," the Democrats sought to develop an ethnic-craft coalition that recruited "mechanics in general . . . Taylors, Coopers, Hatters, Masons and Shipwrights." This coalition can be traced back as early as 1795.[3] The Federalists also mobilized those who earned a living using their hands and backs, like cartmen.[4] The two parties, however, distributed workers along ethnic lines. Jeffersonian Republicans with their anti-English bias appealed to newcomer Germans and Irish.[5]

As these groups came to predominate in the city, so did the Democrats. In 1844 they carried it in the presidential election, despite an earlier mayoral victory by the anti-immigrant American Republican Party which drew heavily from the Whig Party. The Whigs' support of state funds for private enterprise and state power to promote social control favored evangelical and temperance-minded Protestants and antagonized Catholic immigrants who were fleeing state oppression as well as a lack of employment opportunities.

Political power in the New York Democracy centered in a General Committee of fifty-one men elected from each of the city's seventeen wards. It overlapped with the Tammany Society which had originated in the 1780s as a secret fraternal order for the "benevolent purpose of affording relief to the indigent and distressed." Since several Tammany leaders also figured prominently in the Democratic-Republican Party, Tammany's steering committee — the Council of Sachems — which owned the building where the Party met, decided which party factions could use its facilities.[6] Paralleling the General Committee was the Young Men's General Committee, a stepping stone to the General Committee, comprised of men under thirty. The Tammany Society, the Democratic General Committee, and the Young Men's General Committee were the most important agencies of the party.

Below these groups stood the ward committees that mediated between the party elite and the mass of voters. They served as the party's organizational building blocks. At their meeting halls, people gathered to share the Democratic experience.[7] Each ward committee consisted of thirteen to twenty-five men, who, in turn, elected three representatives to the General Committee. In practice, fewer than half the General Committee members attended meetings, and a caucus of the General Committee leadership nominated party officials.

Wards in turn consisted of election districts that varied in number from two in the second and twelfth wards to eight in the eighth. The election district was the smallest political unit; each contained a polling place supervised by a voting inspector.[8] Votes were cast for ward aldermen and assistant aldermen who served on the Common Council, the city's legislative body. The chief executive, the Mayor, was popularly elected annually beginning in 1834. Each ward also elected a tax collector, two assessors, and two constables. Groups of wards constituted the four U. S. congressional seats, while in the state legislature one senator and thirteen assembly men represented the city. Assembly district boundaries differed from the wards in this period as state politicians sought to control city politics through gerrymandering.[9]

Since the wards acted as link between people and party, they possessed a complex infrastructure of subcommittees and auxiliary organizations. Subcommittees nominated candidates for primaries and carried out party directives. In addition, some forty-seven separate organizations, including such colorfully designated auxiliary clubs as the Butt-End Coon Hunters and Fearnot Club, extended the influence of the party at the grass roots level by offering both political and social activity, such as fancy dress balls held during winter months.[10]

What sort of men gave increasing amounts of time to building and maintaining "the Democracy"? Although lawyers comprised the largest group (163 out of the 1,432 men for whom occupations could be found from a universe of 2,391 individuals), clubs such as the Republican Watchmen and Lamplighters, Butchers, Cabinet Makers, Grocers, and Journeymen Printers indicate that white male artisans and tradesmen also played an active role.[11] Of 1,052 organization men, 23 percent were professionals or businessmen, 38 percent were lesser white collar, 33 percent were skilled workers, while 6 percent were unskilled.[12]

Though rate of involvement was found to be proportional to socioeconomic status, a remarkably high percentage of the most active members of the party—33 percent—were skilled workers. Twenty-five percent of civic officials were also skilled workers with all but two of these occupying medium or top-ranked positions.[13]

Of the 153 ward committee members whose occupation could be ascertained, only 16 percent were professionals or businessmen, as contrasted with 48 percent white collar, 30 percent skilled worker, and 6 percent unskilled.[14] In fact, in no other level of the party were professionals or businessmen so poorly represented. The wards favored men of modest socioeconomic status.[15]

If class determined one's rank in the Democracy, ethnicity did not. The party attracted new Americans; 22 percent had Irish surnames, almost identical to their 20 percent of the population.[16] By 1840 the Irish community of the sixth ward where Tammany Hall was located was the largest in the nation.

Irish men in the top organizational level were represented in proportion to their numbers in the population. Twenty-seven percent of the Tammany Society, General Committee and Young Men's General Committee in 1844 were Irish. Sixty-four percent were old stock Americans (British and Dutch) while 7 percent were German.[17]

The Irish role in the Democracy antagonized many old stock citizens who equated Irish presence with Irish control. Mainly Whig nativists fused with the American Republican Party in 1843 in a public campaign that linked crime, corrupt Democratic politicians, and Irish immigration to the social disintegration that they asserted was afflicting the city.

The Democrats countered by rhetorically aligning themselves with the American Republican "reformers," and staged huge rallies to proclaim their case. Banners flew high, as the Democratic *Daily Plebeian* reported:

> Municipal Reform — Great Movement of the People — The Democracy alive to the Vital Interests of the Enlightened Freemen.[18]

At this rally, Ely Moore, the city's most prominent labor leader, delivered a stirring speech.[19]

In the three-way April 1844 mayoral race the Democratic candidate received 41 percent of the vote compared to the victorious American Republican's 49 percent. The Whigs' 10 percent showing brought into serious question the party's continued existence as an independent political force. In the November presidential contest the Democratic machine carried the city for James Polk over his Whig opponent Henry Clay.

Unfortunately, a systematic voter analysis cannot be undertaken since no reliable census exists for New York City before 1850.[20] Most historians agree that the Democrats captured the immigrant vote in this period.[21] Analysis of party personnel also demonstrates that old stock Americans did not dominate the party hierarchy,[22] nor that ethnicity was associated with rate of party activity.[23] Ethnic representation here as well as in the ward committees mirrored the Irish and German proportion in the population at large,[24] though the Irish were more strongly represented at the top of the party structure than at the bottom, indicating perhaps the value of visibly displaying the party as champion of immigrant interests.

Old stock Democrats were, however, more likely to be present in citywide party associations than the Irish, a reflection perhaps of their broader and growing corporate business ties.[25] Among those Democrats holding elective or appointive office, ethnic affiliation was somewhat more important[26] though, as noted, men of rank clearly dominated the party's upper reaches.

Newspapers are rich in information that confirms these findings, telling us something more about grass-roots party activity. They reveal a sophisticated network of occupational as well as ethnic groupings that made the party a social as well as a political movement."[27]

In the days before gaslight, the different Democratic clubs promised "brilliant illuminations" at their outdoor evening meetings.[28] Potential voters, many of whom did not regularly read newspapers, became aware of the party's presence on the streets. Meetings like the one conducted on September 23 by the ninth ward for "Associations, Clubs, Cartmen, Butchers, and Democrats generally,"[29] focused public attention upon the party's concern for tradesmen, while a Corresponding Committee of the Democratic Party General Committee made itself available in the Democratic Republican Reading Room to "answer any and all friendly questions" that immigrants and tradesmen might have concerning the party's stand on various issues.[30]

Party newspapers also catered to specific groups. On September 18 the *Daily Plebeian* published a petition by ninety-nine shoemakers who attacked the tariff as a "special privilege to a few overgrown capitalists to the detriment of the country."[31]

Analysis of contemporary political remonstrances indicates that crafts threatened by industrialization and victimized by monopolistic practices sought political guidance from the proslavery agricultural interests that dominated the Democratic Party on the national level. Slavery in Southern agriculture posed little economic threat to Northern small-scale manufacturing. The latter was rooted in the Jeffersonian tradition that feared the tariff as a national pricing mechanism aiding the growth of monopolies, and depriving the planter of national political hegemony by sapping his economic power through raising the cost of the many imported goods that the South utilized.[32]

Though commerce was becoming more important to New York City's economy, it occupied the energies of but 10 percent of the workers. A third of the labor force engaged in manufacturing, while the service sector commanded the major share as had been the case in colonial times.[33]

Half the country's imports and a third of its exports went through New York City, bounded in 1844 by Fourteenth Street on the west side of Manhattan island, and Eighth Street on the east. Cotton made up half the exports.[34] The Merchants comprised less than one percent of the city officials and only five percent of the Democratic Party activists, but gave powerful ideological support for slavery.[35]

Slavery proved to be the most divisive issue within the party in 1844. Five years earlier ex-President Martin Van Buren had opposed the annexation of slave-holding Texas. To trumpet his availability for another presidential term his supporters had organized Van Buren Associations in each of the city's wards. But New York's most powerful political leader since Alexander Hamilton lost the nomination at the national convention due to his position on Texas.

The Empire Club led by Captain Isaiah Rynders actively supported the annexation of Texas. Its members hooted down speakers and physically attacked rival political processions on horseback, in a style that combined pageantry with cowboy machismo.[36] Later commentators have stigmatized Rynders as an early example of the unsavory tie between New York City politics and organized crime, for he was the "political boss of the Sixth Ward and as such King of the Five Points gangsters."[37] Yet Rynders was accepted by the party, and he was the only 1844 Democratic leader still in the party forty years later—and by this time, a revered, mythic figure.[38]

The Empire Club, less reform-minded than the independent Spartans led by the demagogic Mike Walsh, strove to channel the hostility that arose from oppression in Ireland and New York City into a fighting force for the Democratic Party—one that could be used against the party's political opponents or against antislavery Mexico. The night before the presidential election, Rynders flexed his political muscle in leading the cries of "Polk and Dallas, Texas, Oregon, and Fifty-four forty, or fight."[39]

The other political organization the press identified as mainly working class was Walsh's Spartan Club. A public image of political militancy rendered Walsh attractive to the newly arrived, exploited Irish immigrant. It also appealed to the Democratic Party which assisted Walsh's followers in securing their share of the political spoils. However, in 1849 Walsh's anti-black attitudes helped split the party and led to a Whig mayoral victory.[40]

More popular and broad-based were the Young Hickory associations that staged rallies centering around the planting of hickory trees. Elected party officials, who customarily responded to a petition emanating ostensibly from among the ward's young Democrats, authorized their formation.[41] So many were created that a coordinating body, the Young Men's Central Hickory Association, was established.[42] The tree plantings involved intricate ceremonies under supervision of the "committee appointed to serve and conduct the raising"[43] that linked the party in the public's mind with the aggressive frontier image of "Old Hickory," Andrew Jackson.

The most spectacular political rallies the city had ever seen took place just prior to the presidential election of 1844. They were marked by campaign rhetoric that combined appeals to material interests with notions of racial superiority and the need for national expansion.[44]

One such rally held in and around Tammany Hall on the evening of September 16 was billed as "the largest political assemblage ever convened in this city." Since the crowd spread further than the range of the human voice, speakers simultaneously addressed separate gatherings in front of City Hall, the Registry office, and even Whig Horace Greeley's *Tribune* headquarters.[45] In all, there were ten groupings to this huge assemblage, including one composed exclusively of four to five thousand Germans. At one of these gatherings the crowd displayed its talent for song by mocking Clay:

> O coony, coony, Clay
> O coony, coony, Clay
> You never can be President
> So all the People say

While the crowd was thus enjoying itself, the *Daily Plebeian* reporter observed:

an attempt was made to submerge an exquisite who, with an open glass in hand, was scrutinizing the personal appearance of the chairman with sundry Whig explanations. The gentlemen Whig, however, escaped without injury, except a wet foot and slight soiling of one of the ruffles of his shirt.

The largest gathering of all — some 6,500 persons — massed in front of Tammany Hall for Thomas Carr's attack on the Whig's Texas position:

[the Whigs] opposed it because they mistook the popular will . . . Then [Henry Clay] was in favor of it "niggers and all. . . ."

The *Daily Plebeian* reported further that Carr boldly defended annexation on grounds of economic self-interest:

> . . . Texas was a cotton country (cheers) . . . England had a direct interest in procuring that country (cheers) . . . she could coerce the United States by commercial regulations with the assistance of Texas if she should remain an independent country (cheers) . . . Texas would furnish a market for Northern manufacturers and Northern agricultural products.[46]

Clinton De Witt then pointed out that a National Bank would contribute to inflation and lower living standards for "every poor man." He concluded "with a most pathetic appeal to the working classes in favor of the working man's candidate, James K. Polk of Tennessee," the dark horse unknown prior to his nomination.

In the final days of the election, the level of violence rose. People were beaten up and windows broken at party headquarters.[47] The party did little to cool the situation. One auxiliary, the Butt-End Coon Hunters, even announced a *Grand National Coon Hunt*.

> Resolved . . . the Butt-End Coon Hunters . . . join in the general chase . . . to take place in November next . . .

> Resolved, that we go for Oregon because she is ours; and for Texas because she wants to be; and if California and Canada wish to join us, we shall not object; because the old Coon Hunters of the Revolution deemed it Democratic to *enlarge the boundaries of Freedom*.

> Resolved: that each hunter keep his flint picked, his powder dry, and when they see the white of the eye — *let split*!

> Resolved, that the Coon will be so dead in November next that all the *resurrectionists* in the Union can't bring him to life.

This combativeness also extended to local edicts. A Common Council resolution of September 22, "prohibiting the Democracy from celebrating Democratic victories with cannon in the Park," under penalty of a fifty-dollar fine, "will not occasion much inconvenience, for if we can't fire there, *we'll go and fire outdoors*." Captain John Order was thanked "for his present to the Club of three hundred 'Young Hickory' walking sticks, intended for use of the members when on chase of the 'varmint'."[48]

The week of the election, the *Daily Plebeian* carried an article headed by a picture of an upraised arm clenching a hammer by which the people were "confirming" the nomination at Tammany Hall. This was followed by the "grand Democratic Torchlight Procession" or "Seven Miles of Democrats" featuring "mechanics and Workingmen." The slogan was martial —"Polk and Dallas, Oregon and Texas, and Down with the British"—and effective—as Polk beat Clay.[49]

The Democrats rebounded from their resounding defeat earlier in the year with a stunning victory. They had fashioned a political organization in which significant numbers of Irish and German workers participated as party activists and civic officials. Their continued participation within the party was linked to a politics that reflected the nature and scale of production.

An artisan politics corresponded to artisan-scaled production. So long as economic enterprise remained relatively small, decentralized, technologically backward, and resting to a high degree upon skilled labor, the "Democracy" could be called democratic for adult white males. In a day when many artisans and tradesmen lived where they worked, the wards were ideally suited as local political sounding boards.

The presence of slavery posed no economic threat to these white workers so long as it was confined to the South, and so long as the slaves were primarily involved in the growing of cotton. In fact this sectional labor segmentation benefited New York laborers. They were engaged in other activities associated with the cotton trade as well as in the manufacture of goods destined for the South. Their tasks complemented and reinforced the slave system.

This delicate but cruel social balance was reflected in Democratic Party ideology, an ideology that might be termed planter-artisan republicanism. It would soon come apart, however, as technology advanced, production became centralized and larger in volume and scope, and hordes of unskilled immigrants became New York citizens. But in 1844, in this transitional political phase, no political party in the world could match the Democrats in terms of their heterogeneous class and ethnic make-up.

Such was not the case with the Democratic Party of 1884. There were now five separate party organizations—each with its own headquarters and leadership—all competing for sole legitimacy at the state level. These were the three halls—Tammany, Irving, and Apollo (also known as O'Brien's Democracy)—the County Democracy, and the New York Democracy. Nonetheless, because the party's voting appeal had remained strong with labor, almost any two of the factions commanded more electoral support than the main opposition party, the Republicans.

Other changes appeared. In 1844 inter-party struggles crystallized around the national issue of slavery; in 1884 politics revolved around allegations of corruption and boss rule directed against Tammany Hall by other party factions. Whereas the party organization had dwarfed any single business enterprise in 1844, the reverse was true in 1884. Large corporations like the Erie Railroad exercised crucial political influence and had become agents for the unparalleled corruption in post-Civil War America such as the Tweed scandal among Democrats and the Whiskey Ring scandals of Republican President Ulysses S. Grant's administration. In both cases, corporate capitalist involvement was great. Tweed had been given a directorship on the Erie Railroad, where he assisted Jay Gould and Jim Fiske against Cornelius Vanderbilt.[50] Yet no responsible business executive was sent to prison, only politicians like Tweed.

Tammany was now more than ever equated with the Irish, and corruption with both. In 1882 Theodore Roosevelt characterized "the average Catholic Irishman of the first generation, as represented in the Assembly," as a "low, venal, corrupt and unintelligent brute."[51] Roosevelt's charges, continuously echoed in the press especially after Tweed's downfall, made easier the task of setting up rival political organizations. The Panic of 1873 also brought established political practice into question. Scapegoats had to be found and alternatives proffered.

By 1884 the party's social composition no longer reflected the city's social order. Instead, its internal organization more accurately reflected the distribution of power in the economy. Old stock in the party regardless of faction exercised great influence over party affairs, whatever the level of organization or event. Within the most important "primary" organizations, comprised in 1884 of the steering organs of the various Democratic factions,[52] old stock held 58 percent of the positions, the Irish only 29 percent and the Germans 10 percent.[53] Yet the Irish and Germans made up over three quarters of the city's population in 1880.

In terms of overall Irish involvement in the party, the figures are even more striking. In 1884, 30 percent of all the party's activists were Irish, while the Irish comprised over 40 percent of the general population.[54] By way of contrast, in 1844 the Irish comprised 31 percent of the party while their share of the total population was less than one quarter. Clearly, the structural impact of the Irish upon the party was less in the 1880s than in the 1840s.

Newspapers included the names of 1,971 men who participated in party activities in 1884. Of those Democrats for whom an occupation could be ascertained, 57 percent were professionals or businessmen, 41 percent were white-collar and only 2 percent skilled; 7 men were unskilled.[55] Seventy-seven percent of professionals or businessmen were engaged in four or more organizations, while among white collar, skilled and unskilled, the percentages were 20, 2 and 2, respectively. In other words, upper-class white males dominated the party not only relatively but also absolutely.[56]

Breaking these statistics down according to faction, the New York Democracy responsible for the blue-blood Committee of Seventy and other reform-minded groups possessed the highest percentage of professionals or businessmen (83 percent), with only 15 percent white collar and 2 percent workers of any kind among its constituency. Republicans who had turned Democratic to support New York Governor Grover Cleveland, who was responsive to corporate interests, yielded the next highest proportion of professionals and businessmen, with 69 percent of upper-class background, 31 percent white collar, and not one member of the working classes. Tammany and the County Democracy had almost identical percentages with roughly 60 percent in each faction from the professional and business class; one-third were white-collar, and only 6 percent workers.[57]

Thus, the working class had been largely shut out of active participation within the party and elective office. Henry George's remarkable mayoral insurgency in 1886 almost succeeded, precisely because workers had been structurally excluded from the Democratic Party and were now in labor unions independent of party control. Among the top-ranked political organizations, professionals or businessmen held 69 percent of all positions, 28 percent were white-collar, and skilled and unskilled were calculated at 2 and 1 percent, respectively.[58] In 1844, the percentages had been 30, 41, 27, and 2 respectively for the four categories.[59]

Among the second-ranked organizations for 1884 (various reform front organizations emanating from the New York Democracy which furnished 37 men), not one worker, skilled or otherwise, could be found.[60] Tertiary organizations which consisted mostly of business clubs and also the Young Men's Democratic Committee and the Young Tammany Democrats, produced only 18 workers out of a sample of 1,478 men. None of these workers occupied any of the 177 top positions in the various organizations.[61]

Among the lowest-ranked organizations which included all Cleveland and Hendricks clubs, ethnic or otherwise, as well as other Democratic clubs, one might have expected a greater proportion of workers. This was not the case. Only 6 percent or 20 out of 321 men engaged in manual labor.[62] In terms of social status then, the Democracy had become much less democratic.[63] So too had the party activists' ethnic composition.

In 1884 New York City's population was overwhelmingly Irish and German with the Irish commanding the largest share at over 40 percent. Yet the Irish held only 14 percent of all positions within the party, compared to the Germans' 16 percent, and the old stock's 64 percent.[64] Breaking this down further, we find a curious anomaly. Whereas the Irish occupied 29 percent of the positions in primary organizations as opposed to the old stock's 58 percent,[65] not one Irish man held any position in the "reformist" secondary organizations; 80 percent were held by the old stock while the remainder were German.[66]

That the Irish were virtually excluded from the New York Democracy, the "reform" wing, suggests ethnic divisions within the party that are a function of the segmentation of the labor force according to skill, cultural origin, and time and circumstance of arrival in New York City. Among tertiary organizations, mainly the numerous Democratic business clubs, the proportion of Irish dropped to 8 percent while old stock were at 70 percent.[67] Within the lowest level organizations, the old stock component came to 52 percent as contrasted with the Irish and German shares of 20 percent each.[68]

The Irish yielded the highest percentage at 30 among Democratic civic officials, not among party members or activists *per se*. Still, old stock predominated, holding half of all elected offices. However, of the 101 top-ranked civic officials, 42 percent were Irish and 38 percent old stock, thereby giving the Irish their only plurality in any sector of the party.[69]

It is significant that the Irish did not dominate any of the factions. But, since the most publicly visible sector of the party was predominantly Irish, the opposition press could readily focus upon Irish men as powerful misshapers of urban policy.

The party had become a "machine" that gave jobs to those appropriately obedient to the dictates of its boss. Gone were the ward committees, which for all their procedural faults, had actively engaged the energies of and reflected the political needs of men who believed in some day owning the land or small shop that would guarantee individual autonomy. The old ward politics were no longer suited to the dynamic national needs of industrial capitalism.

Politics had become a big business as big business had come to rule the country. As industrial capitalists began to redefine forcibly the status of most men, party personnel had become less typical of the population as a whole. Ever since slavery had divided the local party in 1844, there had been no further changes in party name nor advances made in democratizing its internal structure. Proletarianized journeymen and apprentices were not formally included within the party structure. 1884 activists yielded only 2 percent who could be considered working class.

No man symbolized the turnabout in attitude towards political participation by the working class more than Samuel J. Tilden, an original Jacksonian. In 1877, the year after just barely losing the presidency in the electoral college, but clearly winning the popular vote, he headed a commission that called for restricting the franchise of the working class and reorganizing city government along the lines of the industrial corporation.[70]

To explain corruption as the result of mass participation, the concept of Jacksonian Democracy was first employed in the 1880s by incipient Progressives like Theodore Roosevelt. They portrayed Jackson and his followers as boors whose political strength lay in rank appeal to the masses.[71] Urban political corruption was blamed on bosses sustained by the immigrant vote. The Progressive movement sprang from the upper class and made politics less democratic, if not less corrupt.[72]

This change in attitude toward the concept of democracy can be seen in comparing Alexis de Tocqueville's qualified praise for American democracy in the 1830s with James Bryce's remark published in 1895 that the most conspicuous failure in American life was the government of its big cities.[73] The cynicism of Boss Plunkitt had replaced the opportunism of Walsh.

At the same time that American workers were no longer active participants within the dominant parties, European workers were developing mass-based social-democratic parties. The locus of progress in political participation on the part of the working class had shifted from the United States to Europe.

Notes

The author thanks Walter Licht, Paul Goodman, Michael Wallace, Carl Prince, James Rogers Sharp, J. Morgan Kousser, Joel Silbey, Daniel Walkowitz, Bruce Laurie, Michael Bernstein, Allan Bogue, Sean Wilentz, Seymour Mandelbaum, Edward Pessen and Arthur Schlesinger, Jr. for their editorial advice. All of their suggestions were seriously entertained, if not gratefully utilized.

1. The reasons for this neglect are sufficiently complex so as to preclude discussion in this essay. One cause stems from acceptance of the notion that voting behavior is mainly a function of ethnic and religious factors. The methodological and theoretical inadequacies of this ethno-cultural approach are effectively critiqued in

Richard L. McCormick's "Ethno-Cultural Interpretations of Nineteenth-Century Voting Behavior," *Political Science Quarterly*, 89 (June 1974), 351-377.
2. Lee Benson, *The Concept of Jacksonian Democracy* (Princeton, 1963), 219, 226.
3. *Public Advertiser*, July 7, 1807 [quote]; *New York Journal and Patriotic Register*, July 9, 1795. Since the Democrats retained little archival material of value, it is fortunate that in the nineteenth century newspapers typically served as party informational and ideological organs with managing editors often assuming party leadership roles. Partisanship, however, did not diminish reliability, since even partisan newspapers were obliged to record regular party business.
4. *Evening Post*, April 22, 1795.
5. *New York Journal and Patriotic Register*, July 9, 1794, August 25, 1798, December 15, 1798.
6. Edwin P. Kilroe, *Saint Tammany and the Origin of the Society of Tammany or Columbian Order in the City of New York* (New York, 1913), 12-13. A full rank ordering of organizations, events, positions in the aforementioned, elective or appointive officials, and occupations can be found in Anthony Gronowicz's "Revising the Concept of Jacksonian Democracy: A Comparison of New York City Democrats in 1844 and 1884" (Ph.D. dissertation, University of Pennsylvania, 1981), 127-150.
7. Even Karl Marx's New York emissary, Joseph Weydemeyer, organized his New York Workingmen's alliance along ward lines. Robert Ernst, *Immigrant Life in New York City, 1829-1863* (New York, 1948), 118-119.
8. Since voter fraud was conducted by both major parties, voting inspectors were reinforced with party stalwarts. The *Daily Plebeian* "warned" its readers on October 14, 1844:

> The Whig leaders have no hope of electing Clay in a fair fight — the weapons they rely on are falsehood and fraud. Protect your Organization — Guard the Ballot Boxes.

9. In June ward electors met separately to select representatives who nominated candidates on September 27 to the Senatorial, Congressional, and Assembly Conventions. These representatives numbered 3 for the senatorial, 5 for the assembly, and 7 for the congressional elections from each ward. *Daily Plebeian*, September 29, 30, 1844.

At a County Convention held in August at Tammany Hall, 3 delegates from each ward chose 13 men to go to the Syracuse State Convention held on September 4. There candidates for governor, lieutenant governor, and presidential electors were nominated. *Daily Plebeian*, August 21, 28, 1844.

10. The term "organizational" has been employed to describe routine ongoing party business, while non-routine activity is classified as an "event."

For example, though the "committee to nominate charter officers" chosen by the ward committees was active in all wards, it is classified as an "event" due to its exclusive association with a non-routine "activity"— the mayoral primary elections. Since its power was directly related to the role it played in the selection of candidates, it ranks higher than clubs or associations that fulfilled more of a social function.

When classifying, it is useful to assign first-rank status to those men summoned to perform specific one-time party tasks on the broadest geographical level. These ultimately consisted of district electors and state and national convention delegates. Delegates to statewide institutions or conventions are accorded secondary importance (4 such groupings). In third place are those engaged in city-wide political occurrences (30 events); in fourth place everyone else (56 events).

Assigned third-rank among 1844 political organizations are city-wide organizations like the Empire and Polk clubs that were active in party functions. All other other organizations, principally at ward or below ward level as well as the more obscure least mentioned city-wide organizations, are relegated to last place.

It is also necessary to rank positions within organizations and events. Four broad classifications emerge: "top," to which 17 positions like "president" are assigned; "middle," composed of 35 groups (e.g., general committee member); "work-horse," 33 separate groups (e.g., treasurer); "body" (e.g., attender).

Also required is a hierarchy of civic officials. The latter category includes those holding elective or appointive positions within the authoritative political structure outside the formal party apparatus. Included are all men running for office, those merely mentioned as a possible candidate, or those who formally hold that office. They are divided into 4 categories related to their administrative duties and labeled top, medium, high white collar, and low white-collar. "Top" (e.g., governor) is broken down into 12 classifications: "middle" (e.g., judge) 29; "lower middle" (e.g., keeper) 22; "low" (e.g., flour inspector) 29. Once a hierarchy of organizations and events is established, theoretically each of the 2,391 men gleaned from the 1844 party newspapers can be ranked as to his individual importance.

11. In classifying the population in terms of role played in the economy, it is useful for statistical as well as analytical purposes to divide the work force into 4 categories. Bankers, capitalists, owners, managers, preferred professions, and trades comprise the first category (80 classifications); less preferred professions and trades the second (225 classifications); skilled craftsmen or workers the third (124 classifications); and finally unskilled or low skilled workers (30 classifications).

LABOR CATEGORIES (IN PERCENTAGES)	I	II	III	IV
1844 population-at-large occupational structure	16	19	50	15
Democratic Party occupational structure	23	37	33	7
Total # of men belonging to distinct organizations	23	38	33	6
Total # of men belonging to distinct events	28	35	31	6
Party members of one political organization	52	58	68	79
Party members belonging to two or three political organizations	33	31	25	18
Party members belonging to four or more political organizations	15	11	7	3
Party members participating in one political event	55	55	67	76
Party members participating in two or three political events	29	29	24	24
Party members participating in four or more political events	16	16	8	0

The fundamental class division lies between categories II and III – between those who sell their labor power versus those who are in a position to employ other labor to support themselves. In general though, the 4 broad categories do not differ to any significant degree from occupation tables drawn up by Stuart Blumin, Robert Dockhorn, Clyde Griffen, Theodore Hershberg and Michael Katz. See Stuart Blumin, "Mobility and Change in Ante-Bellum Philadelphia," Stephan Thernstrom and Richard Sennett, eds., *Nineteenth-Century Cities* (New Haven, 1969), 165-208; Clyde Griffen, "Occupational Mobility in Nineteenth-Century America: Problems and Possibilities," *Journal of Social History*, 5 (Spring 1972), 310-330; Robert Dockhorn and Theodore Hershberg, "Occupational Classification," *Historical Methods Newsletter*, 9 (March-June 1976), 59-98; and Michael B. Katz, "Occupational Classification in History," *Journal of Interdisciplinary History*, 3 (Summer 1972), 63-88.

12. Among those involved in political events and not in organizational work, the corresponding figures were 28 percent (245), 35 percent (314), 31 percent (274), and 6 percent (54).

The correlation between number of political events and occupation was Contigency Coefficient = .16 at the .001 level of significance.

The correlation between number of political organizations and occupations was Contingency Coefficient = .16 at the .001 level of significance.

The contingency coefficient measures the strength of a relationship. 1 to 1 is the best relationship. Above .3 is considered very strong; a reading below .15 is considered random. Level of significance measures the degree to which we may generalize to the population-at-large. Below .05 is considered significant, with 0.000 meaning that the significance is absolute. Thus, in the particular case cited here, one's occupation is predictive of how active one was.

13. The correlation between position, if a civic official, and occupation, was Contingency Coefficient = .34 at the .148 level of significance.

14. The correlation between position in secondary organizations (i.e., ward committees) and occupations was Contigency Coefficient = .10 at the .947 level of significance.

15. Not one woman or African-American was among the 5,391 activists in 1844 or 1884.

16. The party was comprised of 65 percent old stock, 9 percent German, 4 percent "others" (African-American, French [Catholic and Protestant], French-Canadian, Italian, Jewish [English, French, German, Polish, and Russian], Polish, Scandanavian, Slavs other than Poles, Spaniards, Greeks, Lithuanians, and unknown). The same groups were present in the general population with percentages of 72, 6, and 2, respectively.

    The correlation between number of political organizations and ethnicity was Contingency Coefficient = .07 at the .268 level of significance. The correlation between the number of political events and ethnicity was Contingency Coefficient = .08 at the .218 level of significance.

17. The correlation between position in the primary organizations and ethnicity was Contingency Coefficient = .30 at the .006 level of significance. The Irish occupied 30 percent of the top positions in these primary organizations.

18. *Daily Plebeian*, October 23, 1844.

19. The identification of early United States labor leaders with capitalist values was embodied by real estate speculator Moore, whose youthful experience as a printer gave him the minimum necessary credentials to play his later role as spokesman for labor within the Democratic Party. Walter Hugins, *Jacksonian Democracy and the Working Class* (Stanford, 1960), 63-67.

20. Ernst, *Immigrant Life*, 286.

21. The most recent full-length studies of the period, Sean Wilentz, *Chants Democratic* (New York, 1984) and Amy Bridges, *A City in the Republic* (Cambridge, 1984) concur on this point.

22. Of the 184 men involved in primary organizations, 64 percent were old stock and 27 percent Irish with the top ranked officers being comprised of 64 percent old stock and 30 percent Irish. The correlation between position in primary organizations and ethnicity was Contingency Coefficient = .30 at the .006 level of significance.

23. In absolute terms both those groups were also as active as the native white Americans. While 9 percent of the old stock participated in 4 or more organizations, 11 percent of the Germans and 6 percent of the Irish were so involved. Conversely two-thirds of all three groups were involved in only one party organization. While 12 percent of the old stock participated in 4 or more events, 7 percent of the Germans and 6 percent of the Irish were so involved. Again, roughly two-thirds of all three groups could be found in only one party event, though the Irish at 69 held a six-point spread over the old stock and Germans, respectively.

24. Among the 264 men belonging to ward committees, the figures were remarkably similar, with 62 percent and 26 percent being the shares respectively. The correlation between position in secondary organizations and ethnicity was Contingency Coefficient = .13 at the .847 level of significance.

25. Among subcommittees and auxiliary organizations, the proportion of old stock rose to 71 percent, while the Irish fell to 12 percent, a fraction of a percentage point below the Germans. The correlation between position in tertiary organizations and ethnicity was Contingency Coefficient = .17 at the .554 level of significance.

    The lowest ranked organizations yielded results of 64 percent for the old stock and 23 percent for the Irish. The correlation between position in these quartenary organizations and ethnicity was Contingency Coefficient = .06 at the .058 level of significance.

Comparison with events yielded similar results. Though only 19 men were involved in this sample, they carried 74 percent of the positions within primary activities as contrasted with 21 percent for the Irish. The correlation between position in these events amd ethnicity was Contingency Coefficient = .25 at the .866 level of significance. Comparable percentages for secondary events were 64 and 25 (Contingency Coefficient = .10 at the .961 level of significance), for tertiary events − 68 and 20 (Contingency Coefficient = .12 at the .384 level of significance), and quartenary events − 68 and 18 (Contingency Coefficient = .13 at the .092 level of significance.)

The correlation between position in primary organizations and ethnicity was Contingency Coefficient = .28 at the .001 level of significance. Here old stock men increased their presence from 63 to 66 percent going from ward to above ward levels, while the Germans and Irish decreased their percentages 7 to 5 and 30 to 20 respectively.

Tertiary organizations yielded figures of 69 to 73, 10 to 12; and 19 to 10 respectively. The correlation between level of tertiary organizations and ethnicity was Contingency Coefficient = .11 at the .320 level of significance. Again secondary organizations were ignored because analysis was solely of ward committees.

Among quartenary organizations the corresponding percentages were 66 to 58, 7 to 11, and 23 to 26. Only on the lowest levels of party organization, therefore, did new immigration increase its share. The correlation between level of quartenary organizations and ethnicity was Contingency Coefficient = .07 at the .074 level of significance.

Analogous results were obtained with events.

| | Old Stock | | German | | Irish | |
	Ward	Above Ward	Ward	Above Ward	Ward	Above Ward
Primary events	63	80	0	7	38	13
Secondary events	64	83	6	0	25	17
Tertiary events	66	71	9	9	24	13
Quartenary events	65	69	9	10	23	18

The correlation between levels of primary, secondary, tertiary and quartenary events − and ethnicity − was Contingency Coefficients = .29, .06, .18, .05, at the .341, .748, .000, .547 levels of significance, respectively.

26. Of the 202 officials for whom ethnic data has been obtained, 154 or 76 percent were old stock, 14 percent Irish and 7 percent German. A slight bias in favor of old stock was in evidence, but it was nowhere as salient as class. The correlation between position, if one was a civic official, and ethnicity was Contingency Coefficient = .16 at the .821 level of significance.

27. The sub-organizations ranged from the Irish Emigrant Society to the German Democrats to the various watch associations that patrolled the city's streets prior to the establishment of a uniformed police force in 1845. *Daily Plebeian*, June 5, 17, July 1, 4, 1844.

28. *Ibid.*, September 11, 1844.

29. *Ibid.*, September 24, 1844.

30. *Ibid.*, September 10 1844.

31. *Ibid.*, September 18, 1844. This excerpt summarizes the plight to which the skilled worker and yeoman farmer had been driven by the growth of business monopolies. It anticipated the political rallying cries of smaller farmers and factory workers in the 1870s and 1880s.

Fellow mechanics:

We have been told that the present high tariff would . . . make us less dependent upon the power of capital and capitalists. . . . *Protection to American Industry* is the horrid phrase that has been rung in our ears for the last twenty-

five years. . . . The nation that can produce the cheapest market will always
have the advantage in the market of the world. . . . The great and most
important interest of this and all other countries is the agricultural; they
are now oppressed beyond endurance. . . . Fellow Mechanics, the age of
restrictions upon the industry of man is fast passing away. Freedom of all
legitimate pursuits is the prevailing sentiment of the age in which we live.
. . . We desire no monopoly in our vocation; but we are unwilling to be taxed
for the sole benefit of the manufacturers. . . . Next to agriculture the me-
chanical industry embraces in its diversified pursuits, a large majority of
the working classes. . . *Ibid.*, September 19, 1844.

32. *Ibid.*, August 22, September 11, 1844.
33. Diane Lindstrom, "Economic Structure, Demographic Change and Income In-
equality: Antebellum New York." (Paper delivered at the New-York Historical Society Conference on New York and the Rise of American Capitalism, 1984, pp.
8–9, 15.)
34. James Henretta, *The Evolution of American Society, 1700–1815* (Boston, 1973), 201.
35. Brian Danforth, "Merchants in Politics: The Influence of Socio-Economic Factors
Upon Political Behavior: A Quantitative Look at New York City Merchants, 1828-
1844" (Ph.D. dissertation, New York University, 1973), 191. Danforth offers conclu-
sive quantitative evidence that substantiates Philip Foner's thesis in *Business and
Slavery: The New York Merchants and the Irrepressible Conflict* (Chapel Hill, 1941) that
many of the city's Democratic merchants subsisted off the profits of slave labor.
Danforth discovered that 83 percent "who traded solely with the South were overwhelmingly in favor of the Democrats," 163. "As the degree of involvement in southern
commerce decreased to one-third, support for the Democrats among these merchants declined to 39%," 164.
36. *Daily Plebeian*, August 13, September 20, 1844.
37. Herbert Asbury, *The Gangs of New York: An Informal History of The Underworld* (New
York, 1928), 115. Five Points was a crime-plagued Irish slum just north of City Hall,
whose suffering was alleviated by tearing it down to make way for federal and state
office buildings.
38. *Daily Plebeian*, September 11, 1844; *New York Times*, October 22, November 15, 1884.
39. *Daily Plebeian*, October 18, 1844.
40. The degree to which pro-slavery, anti-African sentiments permeated New York City
labor politics is considered in Michael A. Bernstein, "Northern Labor Finds A
Southern Champion: A Note on the Radical Democracy, 1833-1849" and Iver Bernstein, "The Draft Riots of 1863 and the Industrial Revolution in New York," both
in *New York and the Rise of American Capitalism*, eds. William Pencak and Conrad
Edick Wright (New York, 1988).
41. *Daily Plebeian*, June 20, September 30, August 12, 1844.
42. *Ibid.*, July 30, 1844.
43. *Ibid.*, March 23, 1844.
44. "We are the nation of human progress, and who will set limits to our onward march,"
free-soil editor John O'Sullivan proclaimed in the *Democratic Review* (November
1839) especially since "All history is to be rewritten . . . the whole scope of moral
truth . . . reconsidered in the light of the democratic principle." (October 1837)
      Often one such organization would serve as official sponsor for a rally at which
time a ranking of each organization might be yielded by its processional place-
ment. *Daily Plebeian*, June 20, 1844. Ward committees ceased meeting after September 27, 1844, as energies were shifted to getting the vote out.
45. *Daily Plebeian*, September 17, 1844.
46. *Ibid.*, September 21, 1844.
47. *Ibid.*, October 7, 1844.
48. *Ibid.*, October 29, 1844
49. *Ibid.*, November 2, 1844.

50. On Tweed and the Erie Railroad see Charles Francis Adams, Jr., and Henry Adams, *Chapters of Erie and Other Essays* (New York, 1886).

51. Elting Morrison, ed., *The Letters of Theodore Roosevelt*, II (Cambridge, Mass., 1951), 1470.

52. Organizations were ranked thusly. First rank were the Tammany Hall General Committee and the "Democracies"—County, New York, Irving, and Apollo. Second rank consisted of the Municipal Reform Committee, the Committee of 53 on City Reform, and the City Reform Club. Third place was assumed by the myriad of business clubs, the Young Men's Democratic Club; and the Young Tammany Democrats. In last place were the Cleveland and Hendricks Clubs — ethnic or otherwise — and all other Democratic clubs.

53. The correlation between primary organization position and ethnicity was Contingency Coefficient = .23 at the .007 level of significance.

54. The correlation between faction and ethnicity was Contingency Coefficient = .32 at the .000 level of significance.

55. The correlation between number of political organizations and occupation was Contingency Coefficient = .000 at the .130 level of significance. As to those engaged in political events, the corresponding figures were 597 (69 percent), 245 (28 percent), 17 (2 percent), and 5 (1 percent). The correlation between number of events and occupation was Contingency Coefficient = .05 at the .934 level of significance.

56. For events the percentages were 68, 29, 4, and 0, respectively. Among civic officials, 64 percent were professionals or businessmen, 31 percent white collar, and only 4 and 1 percent skilled and unskilled respectively. The correlation between position of a civic official and occupation was Contingency Coefficient = .19 at the .512 level of significance.

57. The correlation between faction and occupation was Contingency Coefficient = .23 at the .000 level of significance.

58. For 1884, the correlation between position in primary political organizations and occupation was Contingency Coefficient = .21 at the .128 level of significance.

59. For 1844, the correlation between position in primary political organizations and occupation was Contingency Coefficient = .27 at the .083 level of significance.

60. The correlation between position in secondary political organizations and occupation was Contingency Coefficient = .53 at the .003 level of significance.

61. The correlation between position in tertiary organizations and occupations was Contingency Coefficient = .15 at the .000 level of significance.

62. The correlation between position in quartenary organizations and occupation was Contingency Coefficient = .19 at the .250 level of significance.

63. Similar results were obtained from analyses of events. In percentages:

Events	Prof. Bus.	White Collar	Skld. Worker	Unskl. Worker	Total Number (not in percent)
Primary	67	26	6	1	123
Secondary	56	41	3	0	69
Tertiary	73	25	1	*	564
Quartenary	72	27	1	0	92

The correlation between position in primary events and an occupation was Contingency Coefficient = .10 at the .999 level of significance; for secondary events, Contingency Coefficient = .25 at the .602 level of significance; for tertiary events, Contingency Coefficient = .14 at the .313 level of significance; and for the lowest-ranked, Contingency Coefficient = .21 at the .631 level of significance.

64. The correlation between number of political organizations and ethnicity was Contingency Coefficient = .07 at the .065 level of significance. For events, the corresponding percentages were only 15 percent (148) for the Irish, 12 percent (121) for the Germans, and 69 percent (697) for the old stock. The correlation between number

of events and ethnicity was Contingency Coefficient = .07 at the .065 level of significance.

65. The correlation between position in primary organizations and ethnicity was Contingency Coefficient = .23 at the .357 level of significance.

66. The correlation between position in secondary organizations and ethnicity was Contingency Coefficient = .19 at the .700 level of significance.

67. The correlation between position in tertiary organizations and ethnicity was Contingency Coefficient = .09 at the .228 level of significance.

68. The correlation between position in quarternary organizations and ethnicity was Contingency Coefficient = .22 at the .006 level of significance.

69. The correlation between position of civic official and ethnicity was Contingency Coefficient = .25 at .022 level of significance.

70. David C. Hammack, *Power and Society: Greater New York at the Turn of The Century* (New York, 1982), 325.

71. Roosevelt, a hostile critic of Jackson, became the first scholar to link Jackson specifically with Democracy when he declared that "The Jacksonian Democracy, nominally the party of the multitude, was in reality the nearest approach the United States has ever seen to the 'one man power,' and to break with Jackson was to break with the Democratic Party," *Thomas Hart Benton* (Boston, 1886), 129.

72. A similar assessment is made by Samuel P. Hays, "The Politics of Reform in Municipal Government in the Progressive Era," *Pacific Northwest Quarterly*, 55 (October 1964), 157–169.

73. James Bryce, *The American Commonwealth* (New York, 1965), I, 637.

LEONARD R. RIFORGIATO

2

Bishop John Timon, Archbishop John Hughes, and Irish Colonization: A Clash of Episcopal Views on the Future of the Irish and the Catholic Church in America

The mid-1850s were a crucial period in the history of American Catholicism. During that time the Church reached a crossroads, faced with two conflicting models of development which would determine its future. These models were the views of two drastically different men, John Timon and John Hughes. Both were bishops who headed sees in New York State. The distance between John Timon's diocese of Buffalo and John Hughes' archdiocese of New York, at opposite ends of the state, symbolized the differences between the two men and the visions they espoused. They were polar opposites engaged in a struggle for the leadership, indeed the very soul, of American Catholicism, a struggle which culminated in the Irish Colonization Society movement of 1856. In the end Hughes' model won out with profound, and deleterious, consequences for American Catholicism.

Though Hughes and Timon were the same age, both born in 1797, their lives developed as differently as their views. Timon was an oddity among the ante-bellum American hierarchy in that he was American born. His parents, James and Margaret Timon, had emigrated from Country Cavan in northern Ireland in 1796 to settle at Conewago, Pennsylvania, a largely German Catholic settlement near the Maryland border. They brought with them a young daughter. John was born some seven months after the move to America.

The Timons belonged to the second of four distinct waves of emigration from Ireland identified by Kerby Miller in his recent study of Irish emigration, that which lasted from 1783–1814.[1] The vast majority of this wave who came from Ulster were Presbyterian with a smattering of Catholics who, because they lived in the most Anglicized and industrialized part of Ireland, had themselves achieved a measure of prosperity and acceptance by the English establishment. Though most of the Catholic emigrants were farmers and artisans, a number belonged to the business and professional classes. They had some liquid assets, enough to book passage as family units and to establish themselves in farming or commerce once settled in the New World.[2] Unlike succeeding waves of emigrants, this group came for socio-economic reasons — to achieve greater prosperity in America, which they viewed not only as a land of boundless opportunity, but as a permanent home. They therefore welcomed assimilation into the Anglo-American culture they encountered in the United States. In fact, they had already undergone such assimilation in their native Ulster, so emigration was not, for them, an extremely disruptive experience.

That the Timons belonged to this class is further attested by their move to Baltimore in 1800. There James opened a dry goods store in which his son John trained as a businessman. Such a venture obviously necessitated a certain reserve of liquid assets.

Like so many Americans, the Timons moved west. After staying in Louisville for one year in 1818, where another dry goods venture failed, the family settled permanently in St. Louis in 1819, achieving some measure of middle-class prosperity. But James Timon's third dry goods establishment failed in a financial crisis that swept the nation in 1823.[3] Still, he was able to pay off his creditors, dabble in real estate, and provide for his family, even though in reduced circumstances.

John Timon forsook the world of business to enter the Vincentian seminary at Perrysville, Missouri, where he was ordained in 1825. He spent the next ten years as a missionary in Missouri, Illinois, Indiana, and Arkansas. He encountered scattered groups of Catholics, to whom he ministered, but most of his early priestly life was spent in a Protestant environment with which he had to come to terms. He immersed himself in the task of conversion, attempting to present Catholicism both as harmonious with other faiths and as their logical fulfillment. He often preached in Protestant churches and practiced, from force of necessity, a rudimentary form of ecumenism.

In 1835 Timon became the first Visitor or superior of the newly erected American Vincentian province. He received diplomatic experience when the Pope appointed him prefect-apostolic to the Republic of Texas, a post he held from 1839 to 1841. His mission, which he successfully concluded, was to obtain Texan confirmation of original Spanish ecclesiastical land grants and reorganize the thoroughly demoralized church in Texas. Constantly championed for and nominated to episcopal office, Timon finally accepted appointment to the newly erected see of Buffalo in 1847.

John Hughes came from different roots. Like the Timons, the Hughes family stemmed from Ulster, in County Tyrone. Unlike them, however, they were not well off financially, having been impoverished tenant farmers. John Hughes had a sketchy education, which ended at age seventeen. Because of the crop failures of 1814, his labor was needed on the farm and as an assistant gardener on a Protestant estate. Within a year, two of the Hughes' children died. Because of the penal laws then in effect, a Catholic priest was forbidden to officiate at the graveyard service, a task reserved to the Episcopalian ministry.[4]

Despairing of escape from the cycle of poverty and bigotry, John Hughes' father, Patrick, emigrated with his second son to Chambersburg, Pennsylvania in 1816. He rented a house, leased some land, and resumed his status as a tenant fanmer. The following year he sent for the rest of his family. Only John came immediately. His oldest brother, sisters, and mother emigrated in 1818 after the crops were in and debts owed their landlord had been settled. In America the Hughes clan failed to achieve the financial success the Timons had found. The boys, including John, were forced to work away from the farm to supplement family finances. John himself labored in construction, gardening, and quarrying until 1819 when he gained admittance to the Sulpician seminary of Mount St. Mary's at Emmitsburg, Maryland. He was ordained in 1826 and assigned as a young priest to the diocese of Philadelphia. In 1838 he became auxiliary bishop to John Dubois, bishop of New York, whom he succeeded when Dubois died in 1842. He became archbishop in 1850.

Unlike Timon, who had never experienced English persecution,

Hughes throughout his life harbored a keen detestation of anything English or Protestant. As he once remarked: "They told me when I was a boy . . . that for five days I was on [a] social and civil equality with the most favored subjects of the British Empire. Those five days would be the interval between my birth and my baptism."[5] This bitterness would color every action of Hughes' public ministry.

John Hughes, then, belonged to what Miller has labeled the prefamine Irish exodus which lasted from 1815 to 1844. Those who came in the early part of this period, from 1815 to 1819, were, like the preceding wave, mostly Protestant, mainly from Ulster, and largely prosperous farmers, professionals, shopkeepers, or businessmen.[6] Among them, however, were a small number of Catholics, for the most part tenant farmers and impoverished laborers. As a class they could not afford to emigrate as family units, nor, lacking funds, to purchase farms once landed or begin businesses once in America. By 1820 the tide of emigration had shifted. Ulster still supplied the bulk of emigrants but they were now mostly Catholic. In 1832, for the first time, large numbers of poor Catholics from southern Ireland began to emigrate. Though poor, these prefamine emigrants were not absolutely destitute. They could afford passage but usually were unable to migrate further than the point of disembarkation, the eastern seaboard cities of America, where they found jobs as common laborers and settled in crowded ghettoes. Most important, this group of emigrants, the prefamine Irish, first viewed emigration not as a voluntary search for economic opportunity, but as involuntary exile forced on them by despotic British misrule in their homeland.[7]

In practical terms, those who emigrated as involuntary exiles carried their hostility to British oppression to the New World, reacting with equal hostility to an American culture they saw as both English and Protestant and retaining a profound nationalism. Rather than seeking assimilation, they attempted to isolate themselves and create a parallel culture in which their faith, which personified their nationalism, would remain pure and unadulterated by contaminating Protestant or secular influences. In a real sense, they deliberately sought to "ghettoize" the American Catholic church. John Hughes was the leader of this faction. A comparison of the episcopal actions of both Hughes and Timon is instructive in this light.

For his part John Timon deliberately sought to assimilate Catholics into American culture and did so in a number of ways. To a great degree he was ecumenical, enjoying amicable relations with those Protestant clergymen who were not rabidly anti-Catholic. He was, for example, friendly with William De Lancey, first Episcopal bishop of

Western New York, and his closest friend and chief financial supporter was an Episcopal layman, Dean Richmond, president of the New York Central Railroad and leader of the Democratic party's Albany Regency. As a rule he avoided public controversy of a religious nature. In 1848, while Timon was in Europe, his vicar general, the Reverend Bernard O'Reilly became involved in a bitter, protracted newspaper dispute with the Reverend John C. Lord, a Presbyterian, over state funding for Sisters' Hospital run by the Sisters of Mercy in Buffalo. When Timon returned, he rebuked O'Reilly and ended the controversy.

In matters of education the Buffalo diocese lagged behind others in providing parochial schools, for Timon saw no need to duplicate facilities provided by the city so long as the faith of Catholic children was not endangered. By quiet negotiation with an enlightened school superintendent he reached an agreement to allow Catholic pupils to use their own version of the Bible in school and to expunge anti-Catholic material from textbooks. The majority of diocesan parochial schools that did exist were attached to German parishes and supported by them because the Germans wanted to ensure their children would not lose their culture. German was not taught in the public schools though Timon eventually succeeded in changing this. Moreover, because he opposed select schools (those which charged tuition), religious orders were reluctant to operate in his diocese. The select school often provided support both for the order and the free parochial school they were also forced to conduct by Timon. The bishop, however, did support the creation of upper-level Catholic schools (secondary and collegiate), because they did not duplicate facilities already available in his diocese. Buffalo, for example, had only one public high school and no college.

Timon, then, viewed the role of the Church, in part, as a social agency providing for needs of both Catholics and Protestants. Non-Catholics were to be admitted to church-run institutions without fear of indoctrination, as, indeed, they were at Sacred Heart school which Millard Fillmore's daughter attended. In this way the Church would become an integral cog in the city's life. Even after the Baltimore Council decreed that each parish build a parochial school, Timon paid only lip service to the legislation and specifically instructed his priests not to enforce excommunication against Catholic parents who sent their children to public schools, since his diocese lacked parochial schools in sufficient numbers.

In like manner, Timon created social, church-run institutions supported by public funds in order to meet urban needs. He built the city's first hospital, which was open to all, and staffed by the doctors at the Buffalo Medical College. A lying-in home for pregnant women, a deaf-mute institute, and a home for widows followed. Only when Catholics became victims of discrimination after mid-century with the rise of "Know-Nothingism" in public facilities did he erect duplicate institutions. For example, he created orpanages because priests were not allowed to visit Catholic children in existing public ones.

In politics Timon was silent unless matters of faith were involved. He engaged in public political controversy only twice. Once he successfully aborted the chartering of a Buffalo reform school modeled on one in New York City which would incarcerate children of the poor and ship them to foster homes in the Midwest. In the second instance he fought the efforts of the trustees of St. Louis Church in Buffalo to have the state legislature pass a church property bill. Such a bill would have put ownership of all ecclesiastical property in lay hands and forbid Catholic bishops from acting as the corporation's agents.

Timon's view of the place of the Catholic church in American society is symbolized by the cathedral he built. He erected it in the heart of downtown Buffalo within a prosperous upper-class Protestant neighborhood, two blocks from the Episcopal cathedral. He intended this church to be an integral part of American life, not a closed ethnic enclave. For this reason he named it St. Joseph's after the patron saint of all working men.

John Hughes, on the other hand, viewed the Church in purely confrontational terms. For him, it was an embattled oasis of true religion surrounded by heretics and hostile bigots who must be defeated or shunned. If Timon's church was open to social interaction with non-Catholics, Hughes' was a fortress, armed and moated. There was not an ecumenical bone in Hughes' body. Not only was he perpetually engaged in controversy with Protestants, he actively sought out such confrontation. As a young priest, for example, Hughes engaged in a vitriolic and unedifying debate with a Presbyterian minister, the Reverend John Breckinridge. In a peculiar move, Hughes penned vicious anti-Catholic articles which he sent anonymously to a bigoted New York paper, *The Protestant*, only to identify himself as the author once they were published. His excuse was that he wanted to demonstrate that the paper would print any lies so long as they were anti-Catholic.

Nor was Hughes willing to compromise on the matter of education. In his celebrated fight against the Public School Society of New York, Hughes would accept no solution short of its destruction. He even rejected the Society's offer to allow Catholic children to use their own Bibles in school and to submit texts to Hughes who could purge passages he considered offensive to Catholics. These, after all, were precisely the points over which Hughes had initiated the struggle in the first place. Instead the Society was disbanded, the state took over the city's education, and the public schools were completely secularized. Hughes then built his own system of parochial schools for which he demanded public funds.[8]

In 1844 a series of nativist riots erupted in Philadelphia during which an Irish fire company, Irish homes, and several Irish Catholic churches were burned. The fact that a nearby German Catholic church was untouched by the mob suggests that the outburst, deplorable as it was, was directed against the Irish, not against Catholicism. Hughes was scornful of the passivity of Philadelphia's Bishop Francis P. Kenrick in the face of such provocation. Determined to meet force with force, as would any Gaelic warrior chieftain, Hughes warned New York's mayor that the Irish would burn the city to the ground should one of his churches come to harm. None did, but Hughes certainly did nothing to further mutual understanding between Catholics and nativists.

Nor did Hughes hesitate to dabble directly in politics to achieve his ends. During his school struggle he formed his own political club, known as Carroll Hall, to punish Democrats for not supporting his views on the issue. The Whig victory which resulted from Hughes' splintering of the Democratic vote taught party leaders to heed the bishop's dictums in the future. Again, however, in winning a victory, Hughes was losing a war. His actions only heightened nativist suspicion of Catholics as a hostile, solid, and threatening interest group.

Only Hughes, moreover, could deliver such an intemperate, imprudent, and polemical speech designed to further inflame nativists as he did in 1850. Entitled "The Decline of Protestantism and Its Causes," Hughes contrasted Protestant failure to convert North American Indians with Catholic success in Central and South America. The downfall of Protestantism was inevitable, he held, because it had become "stricken as with sterility."[9] He then cheerfully confessed that Catholics did indeed intend to convert all Americans, as the nativists claimed:

> Everybody should know that we have for our mission to convert the world, including the inhabitants of the United States, the people of the country, the officers of the Navy and the Marines, commanders of the Army, the legislatures, the Senate, the Cabinet, the President, and all.[10]

Rather than pour oil on troubled waters, Hughes perferred to ignite the oil.

Finally Hughes' cathedral stood as a symbol of his view of the Church in America. Though completed after his death, he planned it as a monument to Catholicism triumphant. It was located on the fringe of the city, alone in regal isolation, a vast gothic fortress occupying an entire city block. He named it St. Patrick's after Ireland's patron saint as an expression of Irish nationalism.

Hughes and Timon then differed drastically on the future of American Catholicism. Was it to be an assimilated church, taking its place in the nation's denominational structure in a spirit of cooperation, or was it to become an ethnic ghetto, set apart, aloof from, and hostile to American values and culture, insulating itself within a parallel society? This was the choice that faced the Church in the mid-1850s.

At first there had been no such problem. In the seventeenth and eighteenth centuries there were few Catholics in the American colonies, and they were mainly in Maryland and Pennsylvania. Pennsylvania Catholics were for the most part Germans. Like their German Reformed and Lutheran brethren they kept apart from English colonists as they labored to maintain a separate culture in the New World. Nor did denominational differences make them enemies, for their shared German language and culture sufficed to paper over religious differences. Hence Lutherans contributed to the construction of a German Catholic church in Philadelphia.

Maryland's Catholics were mostly English and shared a common culture with their Protestant neighbors. Though political disabilities existed, economic and social obstacles did not. Hence the Carrolls of Carrollton could amass a vast fortune and ultimately achieve political equality in their support for the Revolution.

All this changed in the nineteenth century after Catholic Irish emigrants began pouring into the nation. True, German Catholic immigration almost equalled Irish, but the reception accorded the two was generally quite different. On the whole the Germans were more skilled and better educated than the Irish, and they migrated in family groups and established self-supporting communities which attempted to retain their culture and language, leaving to the native-born the running of the country. Because, for the most part, German Catholics did not enter politics, they posed no threat to native dominance. They were, moreover, admired for their industry, frugality, and avoidance of reliance on public relief. Though many Germans settled along the Atlantic seaboard, even greater numbers moved into the Midwest and Great Lakes regions. As a result, the German-American population was dispersed and divided between urban and rural areas and did not form a geographically concentrated monolithic block in the eastern cities like New York which could be viewed as threatening.

The Irish immigrant, on the other hand, was frequently male, single, and concentrated in eastern seaboard cities and certain inland towns such as St. Louis, where he was highly visible by force of numbers alone. Moreover, because the Irish immigrants saw themselves as involuntary exiles from British persecution at home, they remained alienated from American culture which, to their eyes, appeared British in nature. Because they were English-speaking, they could, and did, voice this alienation in a language the native-born could understand. Also, unlike the Germans, the Irish actively sought political power, mainly through an almost monolithic adherence to the Democratic Party, which no doubt reflected in part their distrust of the Yankee-Protestant dominated Whigs.

Also unlike the Germans, the Irish immigrants were poor and ill-educated. Worse, perhaps, was the persistent stereotype of the Irish as a people given to alcoholic excesses and notorious for their tendency to engage in street brawling. Because most Irish who emigrated after 1816 had scant financial resources, they clustered where they landed, living in slums called shantytowns in the eastern cities. Even John Hughes admitted their destitute condition:

> The better class of emigrants . . . those who have some means, those who have industrious habits, robust health, superior intelligence, naturally pass through this city [New York] and push onwards . . . On the other hand, the destitute, the disabled, the broken down, the very aged and the very young, and I had almost added the depraved of all nations, having reached New York, usually settle down here, for want of means, or through want of inclination to go farther.[11]

Thus, the Irish, in particular the famine Irish, were a highly visible, undesirable element situated in the nation's most populous areas. They became a natural target for nativist opposition to further immigration.

In the eastern cities, the famine Irish immigrants utilized a disproportionate share of public funds in alms houses, poor houses, prisons, and reform schools. Yet in the inland areas, where they formed a smaller portion of the total population, their conditions, though still impoverished, were not as destitute as in the large metropolitan areas where they comprised a large portion of the populace. A comparison of Buffalo and New York City bears this out.

In 1870 New York City had 202,000 Irish immigrants in a population of 942,292 or 21.4 percent, while neighboring Brooklyn, the state's second largest city, had 73,985 Irish representing 19.6 percent of its population. By and large these were famine Irish, the earlier waves having moved on as their economic status improved. Buffalo, the state's third largest city, had only 11,264 Irish in a population of 117,714 or

9.5 percent of its total, most of whom were prefamine and generally not destitute. While the Irish greatly outnumbered Germans in both New York and Brooklyn, Buffalo's German population of 22,249 was double that of the Irish.[12] In fact, Irish imigration to Buffalo had steadily lagged behind that of the Germans. In 1850 the city had 6,307 Irish-born and 6,803 German-born residents. By 1865 there were 9,689 Irish and 19,631 Germans in a population of 94,210. By 1875 10,705 Irish-born and 27,018 German-born persons lived in the city of 134,557, an absolute decline in Irish numbers since the 1870 census.[13]

Small though the Irish were in numbers, they occupied a disproportionate share of the inhabitants of Buffalo's poor house. In 1855, of 252 inmates, 138 or 54.7 percent were Irish, 56 or 22.2 percent were German, and the remainder were native born.[14] Still, Buffalo's Irish were much better off than those of New York City. First, they did not form a huge ethnic bloc and so were not targeted as unassimilable aliens. There were no anti-Irish nativists or Know Nothing riots in Buffalo. Then, too, Buffalo's ethnic mixture was, by and large, complementary. The native-born dominated the entrepreneurial, legal, political, and professional classes. Germans predominated in skilled and semi-skilled labor, as artisans and small shopkeepers. The Irish provided unskilled and semi-skilled labor as construction, canal, railroad, and dock workers. Since Buffalo was a relatively young city, experiencing explosive growth only since 1825, almost all residents were immigrants. An analysis of the city census for 1855 shows a remarkably small spread in persistency among the groups. The average native-born person had been residing in Buffalo for 12.5 years, the average German for eight years, and the Irishman for seven years, respectively. Though there was an established native aristocracy which had been present for twenty years or longer, it comprised only 25 percent of the native-born, while only 8.5 percent of the Germans and 4.9 percent of the Irish had such residential longevity.[15] Unlike New York, then, there was little or no entrenched native-born class to feel threatened by the Irish. Also, unlike New York, the Irish never exercised direct political power in Buffalo. Few police were Irish and no Irish-Catholic mayor was elected until the second half of the twentieth century. Again Buffalo's native-born felt no political threat from the Irish as did New York's, where the Irish quickly moved into the police force and urban administration through sheer force of numbers. Moreover, because Buffalo was and always has been a city of single and multifamily homes, it never developed the tenements into which New York's Irish were crowded. Census data from 1875 show Buffalo with an average of six residents per dwelling unit, while New York had an average of sixteen. To be sure, few Buffalo Irish owned

their homes, renting instead from native-born landlords, and they sub-
divided them to share with other Irish families or took in boarders.
But Irish living conditions were probably less congested in Buffalo than
in New York. Shantytowns were all but nonexistent in Buffalo.

What was true of Buffalo was also the case in other inland cities
where the Irish formed a small percentage of the population. In such
settings, they were more tolerated, better housed, had greater employment opportunities, and were more likely to assimilate. All this caused
John Timon to back colonization as the solution to the Irish "problem."

This "problem" was recognized and feared by native-born Catholics.
Quite simply, they understood the anti-Catholicism of nativists and
Know Nothings as essentially an anti-Irish reaction and were dismayed
that the Catholic church as a whole was being identified as Gaelic and,
hence, foreign.

Part of the reason for this was the great influx of Irish priests who
followed flocks to whom they were natural leaders. Often they were
no better educated than those they led and, like them, were seen as
given to drink, championing Irish nationalism, resisting assimilation,
and refusing obedience to any bishop who was not himself Irish born.
Even more worrisome was that Rome was appointing more and more
Irishmen to American sees, further strengthening the perception of
the American church as Irish. As native-born Samuel Eccleston, archbishop of Baltimore, complained:

> I am sorry that any more Irish bishops are added to our hierarchy, as
> I fear that their increase in numbers will have power to have others of
> their countrymen nominated thereafter and bring over to this country
> a great number of Irish priests, whilst I wish, with a few exceptions,
> they would all stay at home.[16]

The Catholic journalist, Orestes Brownson, himself native-born and
a convert, bemoaned the fact that the Irish were over-drunk, over-
belligerent, and over here. In a letter to a fellow convert, the Reverend
Isaac Hecker, he denounced their clergy as "either bent upon making
money, or else they are Irishmen before they are Catholics."[17] Their
Americanism was to him suspect, for he felt the Irish-born clergy were
overly interested in setting up a national Gaelic church that would ig-
nore missionary work among Americans and render Catholicism a
foreign and hence irrelevant force in America.[18] Bluntly, he warned
that "The Church here has hitherto been and is even now to a great
[e]xtent the Church of a foreign colony, with a foreign or quasi-foreign
clergy, with slender acquaintance with the real American character

and less sympathy with it."[19] Brownson's solution was simple. Only native-born priests and prelates should govern the Church or Americans would never accept it. John Dubois, a French-born bishop of New York, who suffered great persecution at the hands of his largely Irish flock and clergy, agreed. As he confided to Bishop John Purcell of Cincinnati in 1835: "Moderate Protestants tell me that their opposition to our church is as Irish not as Catholic."[20]

To such critics of the "Irish" church in America the obvious solution to the Irish problem was colonization. This would accomplish several goals. In the first place, by scattering the large, unassimilable Irish, populations of the seaboard cities across the country, it would remove an easily focused target for nativist wrath. Further, by surrounding the Irish with the native-born it would break their clannishness and hasten assimilation. Given a chance to earn a livelihood in midwestern cities or farms, relocated Irish would secure employment and better their condition. Then too, the dispersal of large groups of Irishmen would frustrate the ability of Irish clergy, prelates, and revolutionaries to use them for their own ends, be it the exercise of political power, support for rebellion against Britain, or preservation of Irish ethnicity. There had been several efforts at colonization prior to 1856. Some achieved modest success. Most were failures.

There were many reasons for this. In the first place, leaders of colonization schemes based their plans on the assumption that the Irish were historically an agrarian people whose residence in urban seaboard areas was an accident of their penurious state on arrival from Ireland. Once settled in the cities, they were afflicted with poverty, unemployment, intemperance, ill health, and inadequate housing. Reversion to their natural status as farmers would restore traditional Irish virtues of sobriety, discipline, and hard work. Unfortunately, this basic premise of the colonizers was false. To be sure, the early prefamine emigrants did include large numbers of farmers who had been forced off their lands by the British. These men could, and many did, ultimately establish their own farms in America. The later prefamine and famine emigrants, however, were not at all an agrarian people. For the most part, they were unemployed town laborers and displaced agricultural laborers who lacked both the means and the knowledge to own and manage a farm. For many the farm in Ireland was an English estate, not a homestead.

Because colonization leaders, by and large, were earlier emigrants who had already achieved material success in the New World or were native-born descendants of Irish immigrants, they were operating on a model of conditions which existed in eighteenth-century America when Maryland and Kentucky Irish, who possessed agrarian skills, had been able to settle farmlands during an era when such lands were cheap, fertile, and close to population centers. Such conditions no longer existed in the 1840s and 1850s when organized colonization efforts peaked. Most available and affordable lands then were in the prairie region, of marginal fertility, distant from markets, and could only be made productive by new and expensive farming methods.

Second, the impetus for colonization, though expressed positively as an effort to improve the material status of impoverished urban Irish, was, in fact, negative. It marked a reaction by naturalized and native-born Irish-Americans to nativist attacks on the American Catholic church. A series of depressions beginning in 1837 had caused the native-born to fear economic competition for scarce jobs from hordes of Irish pouring into the country. Because immigrants willing to work for sub-standard wages were Catholic, hostility to them was transferred to the Church as a whole. In attempting to disperse the urban Irish and as-similate them into rural America where they would be less of a threat to and target of nativists, the colonizers were attempting to protect their own status and acceptance in America. In fact, they agreed with the nativists that the new Irish immigrants did possess undesirable traits, a view that did not endear them to the urban Irish and their clerical leaders.

The first organized Irish colonization movement was the creation of one man, Demetrius Augustus Gallitzen, the son of a Russian nobleman who was ambassador to the Netherlands. A convert to Ca-tholicism, Gallitzen migrated to the United States in 1792, attended St. Mary's Seminary in Baltimore, and in 1795 was ordained, the first priest educated and ordained in America. After working for a time in Conewago, Pennsylvania, he conceived the idea of a Catholic colony in central Pennsylvania for both German and Irish immigrants. With the backing of Bishop John Carroll, who gave him 400 acres of land he had received as a gift, Gallitzen purchased additional land with his own funds and sold it on reasonable terms to settlers, many of them Irish. In time his colony thrived, becoming the town of Loretto which provided light industry and grist mills to service surrounding farms.[21]

The next phase of colonization was piecemeal migration by individual immigrants. During the 1820s America experienced a canal-building boom, particularly the Erie Canal in New York State. Much of the construction was done by Irish laborers who, when the project was com-pleted, settled in the canal towns which sprang up along its route or on outlying farm land. During the 1830s railroad construction boomed, again built by Irish labor, and again resulting in Irish settlements along the right-of-way particularly in southern New York State and north-west Pennsylvania along the route of the Erie and Lackawanna.[22]

By 1840 economic dislocation had terminated this initial transportation boom. During these depressed times the famine Irish began to enter the country in large numbers, without funds. The seaboard Irish population grew, and organized Irish colonization schemes were revived.

With the nation mired in hard times following the panic of 1837, nativist hostility erupted against Irish immigrants. In reaction to this, Irish Emigrant Associations sprang up in New York, Philadelphia, Baltimore, and St. Louis whose original purpose was to seek grants of public lands from Congress, particularly in Illinois, upon which they could relocate immigrants. Led by the elite of the Americanized Irish as well as prominent Protestant laymen, they at first had the backing of the Church. In New York both Bishop John Hughes and his vicar general, Reverend John Power, supported them, as did the diocesan paper, *The Freeman's Journal*. In short order the various groups merged to form the Irish Emigration Society, which was forced to adopt new tactics when the hoped-for federal land grants failed to materialize. Unfortunately, these tactics lacked focus and the society turned into a welfare agency aiding indigent immigrants and a clearing house for immigration information. It posted agents in Irish and English ports of embarkation to warn of the dangers of indiscriminate emigration and to dispel the notion that America was a land flowing with milk and honey. In an 1843 address to the people of Ireland, the Sciety noted that:

> Multitudes flocked into this city [New York], and into other cities on our Atlantic border, to encounter only want and wretchedness to an extent that baffled our means of alleviation: friendless, moneyless, unable to procure employment, crushed in spirit and emaciated in body, many sought refuge in the alms-houses; thousands contrived to return to the land they had left and nearly all bitterly bewailed their own imprudence.[23]

It further warned that clerks and day laborers should avoid emigration, for the depression in America had dried up employment opportunities in these areas. Work was available for mechanics, and farmlands could be had by those with investment funds. The Society provided information on the availability, location, and cost of public lands but could offer no help either in transportation or financing.[24] For the most part, however, the Society confined itself to providing social services to New York Irish. It helped them secure decent lodging, ran an em-

ployment agency, investigated complaints of unfair treatment by landlords or employers, and helped establish an Emigrant Industrial Savings
Bank to manage Irish savings. In fact, it was not a colonization society.

In 1843, impetus for organized Irish colonization shifted to Ireland
itself. Daniel O'Connell, the nationalist, with the support of both Catholic and Anglican Irish prelates, created the Catholic Emigration Society of Ireland. It planned to purchase public lands in Wisconsin and
Illinois, then send impoverished Irishmen to work them as indentured
servants for three years. This would reimburse the society for the cost
of transportation and land acquisition while guaranteeing each emigrant a small freehold of ten acres at the completion of the indenture.
Contracts would be made with Irish priests. Once in America, the immigrants would be met by other priests who would accompany them
to the settlements and function as managers as well as spiritual guides.[25]

At first Bishop Hughes endorsed the scheme, probably because of
his respect for O'Connell and confidence that his leadership would as-
sure success. He applauded it as "an undertaking from motives of pure
philanthropy" and backed it from "motives of Irish patriotism . . . or
at least a love of my country."[26] Hughes, however, quickly changed his
mind. As he explained, "when I spoke of it to gentlemen of means and
intelligence, they said it was all nonsense." The *Freeman's Journal* con-
curred, doubting such contracts could be enforced and speculating that
most immigrants would disavow the contract once landed in America.
O'Connell's plan, then, died still-born, and the whole experience seems
to have permanently soured Hughes on colonization.[27]

In 1853 yet another colonization plan surfaced. This one was the
brainchild of Bishop Jean Mathias Pierre Loras, a French priest who
had emigrated to America, served as president of Spring Hill College
in Alabama, and, in 1837, was named to head the newly created Diocese of Dubuque. Impressed by Iowa's fertile farm lands, Loras was
determined to attract both German and Irish Catholic immigrants to
settle there in carefully planned colonies. To this end, he began to ad-
vertise the attractions of the region in eastern Catholic newspapers.
As his agent in the scheme he appointed one of his diocesan priests,
the Reverend Jeremiah Trecy, who had emigrated from Ireland as a
child. His job was two-fold: to tour eastern dioceses delivering lectures
on the benefits of colonization in order to lure settlers, and to secure
land for the planned colonies.

The final colonization plan was the idea of yet another Irish immigrant, James Shields, who had served in the Mexican War as a brig-
adier general in the United States Army and had been for a time
Governor of Oregon Territory, then Senator from Illinois. By 1855 Shields

lived in Minnesota where he owned large land tracts awarded him by
the government for his war service. This land, he realized, would be
ideal for Irish colonization in small farm communities. Filled with en-
thusiasm, he traveled to New York to present his plan to a thoroughly
unsympathetic John Hughes, who refused any cooperation. The archbishop, it appeared, objected to the lack of priests and churches in the
Minnesota wilderness. As Shields recalled, he berated Hughes for his
shortsightedness and insisted the clergy would follow the people if
Hughes encouraged them. Moreover, the colonists:

> would not only benefit themselves, but would prove benefactors to your
> poorly paid and apparently half-fed curates, one of whom they would
> invite to come and dwell in their midst as their honored parish priest.[28]

Hughes' response is not known, but he remained unmoved. Despite
his opposition both Loras and Shields, especially the former, continued
their efforts with enthusiastic support from at least two Catholic papers,
the Boston *Pilot* and the *American Celt*. These efforts eventually culminated in the Buffalo Colonization Convention of 1856.

The most logical explanation for the sudden renewal of organized
colonization activities in the 1850s was as a reaction to a new nativist
uprising under the guise of the Know Nothing party. Know Nothingism was a complex movement that transcended simple anti-Catholicism.
To a great degree it began as a protest movement against the influx
of cheap, unskilled foreign labor, mainly famine Irish, who competed
with the native born for scarce jobs. It evolved, however, into a political movement that resulted from the disintegration of the Whig party
over the slavery issue. New York State provides a clear example of this.
There Know Nothingism originated among anti-Catholics and anti-
Foreigners but was soon seized upon by the Silver Grey faction of the
state Whig party, which backed Millard Fillmore in his fierce power
struggle with William H. Seward and Thurlow Weed. Seward and
Fillmore differed strongly on slavery, the latter urging compromise and
toleration of the "peculiar institution" while the former appealed to
a "higher law" than the Constitution which made abolition a moral
imperative. Under the smoke-screen of anti-Catholic rhetoric which
would appeal to nativist voters, the Know Nothing movement in New
York and elsewhere was actually a phase in the continuing debate over
slavery.

Still, Know Nothing rhetoric, though uttered for political purposes,
did inflame passions directed at the Catholic church and the most viable
symbol of its foreignness, the urban famine Irish. This is evidenced

in an editorial in Fillmore's organ, the Buffalo *Commercial Advertiser*, which sought to justify its nativism by quoting anti-Irish utterances of Orestes Brownson, the Catholic journalist. One example is worth citation at length because it indicates the common ground shared by the native born, both Protestant and Catholic, and gives a clue to the real target of Know Nothings.

> In the parts of the country where the prejudices against Catholicity are the strongest, it has seemed to be *Celtic rather than Catholic*; and Americans have felt, that to become Catholics, *they must become Celts*, and make common cause with every class of Irish agitators, who treat Catholic America *as if it were a province of Ireland*. A considerable portion of our Catholic population have brought with them their old prejudices of race, national animosities, and bitter passions, and *makes our country the arena for fighting out their old hereditary feuds*. Our so-called Catholic journals are little else than Irish newspapers, and appeal rather to Irish than Catholic interests and sympathies. Some of them *teem with abuse of Americans, and are filled with diatribes* against the race from which the majority of non-Catholic Americans claim to have sprung. Their tone and temper are foreign; and their whole tendency is to make an American feel that, practically the Church *in this country is the church of a foreign colony, and by no means Catholic*. All this may be very natural and very easily explained to the Catholic, who is willing to pardon almost anything to a people that has stood firm by the faith during three centuries of martyrdom, but everyone must see that it is far better fitted to repel Americans from the Church, than to attract them to it; especially when they find the *foreignism which offends them defended by a portion of the clergy*, and apparently opposed by none; and carried even into politics, *and made or attempted to be made, the turning point in our elections*.[29]

There is little doubt that Brownson was referring to New York City's Irish Catholics and their bellicose, intensely Irish leader John Hughes. The two men had fought bitterly before over the Americanization of the Church, with Hughes condemning Brownson while Timon defended him. Then, too, Hughes was in open alliance with Seward and thus an apt target for Fillmore's paper. It is also evident from the emphasis the *Commercial Advertiser* added to Brownson's words that its opposition was not to Catholicism, but to Irish Catholicism as espoused by the urban famine Irish. It was to rid the urban areas of these objectionable Celtic poor that a grand colonization convention was called after years of agitation by one Thomas D'Arcy McGee.

McGee, born in Ireland in 1825, had emigrated to America in 1842 to work on the Boston *Pilot*, eventually becoming its associate editor. In 1845 he returned to Ireland to join the radical "Young Ireland" movement which advocated a violent overthrow of British rule. His propaganda in its cause was so effective that he persuaded Bishop Hughes to endorse its goals during the course of a speech he delivered in New York on August 14, 1848. Hughes declared that "in my conscience I have no scruples in aiding the cause in every way worthy [of] a patriot and a Christian."[30] Going beyond mere verbal approval, Hughes donated five hundred dollars to the cause.

Evidently, McGee had convinced Hughes that Irishmen solidly backed the rebels and, given the heady revolutionary atmosphere sweeping Europe in 1848, that the rebellion's success was assured. Unfortunately, when the rebels struck, popular support failed to materialize, in large part because Ireland's Catholic bishops opposed them. As a result, the British easily crushed the rebellion, while McGee fled to New York with a price on his head to start another paper, *The Nation*, to continue the struggle. He had, however, been the man most responsible for making Hughes look ridiculous and for bringing on the bishop's head the wrath of Ireland's prelates for his meddling in Irish politics. McGee's reward was Hughes' undying enmity, no light matter in the case of a bishop who never forgot nor forgave.

McGee made matters worse by blaming clerical opposition for the failure of the uprising, a reason as true as any, but which Hughes denounced as "insidious poison."[31] In retaliation Hughes forbade any Catholic in his diocese to purchase or read *The Nation*, thus killing it. McGee then began publication of the *American Celt*, but continued to be dogged by Hughes' disfavor, which caused him to move its publication first to Buffalo, then to Boston. Nor did McGee improve his standing with New York's bishop by denouncing urban American Irish as "a horde of hardy, vulgar ruffians, unmatched in any former state of society."[32] As Richard Shaw has noted: "It was no way to win over either the members of the horde or their spirited leader [Hughes] who had spent his adult life telling Americans that the Irish were not 'a horde of hardy, vulgar ruffians'."[33]

With McGee's support, preparations for a grand colonization convention that would unite into one organization all colonization plans proceeded apace. On November 10, 1855, the Reverend Dean Kirwin, vicar general of the Diocese of Kingston, Ontario, announced in the pages of the *American Celt* the formation of the Irish Immigrant Aid Society. It would hold its first convention in Buffalo on February 12, 1856. Buffalo had been chosen because of its central location and the fact that its bishop, who favored colonization, had issued an invitation. Kirwin's letter, however, stirred up considerable controversy even among supporters of colonization because he advocated the creation of purely Irish farming villages only in the American and Canadian West. He justified this by arguing that not only was there cheap public land available but that creating compact settlements solely inhabited by Irishmen would give them political clout. In his view this was the secret to the special status accorded French Canadians by British-ruled Canada:

> They are settled on the soil, form a compact and united body, having schools, colleges, and universities, a clergy to instruct them, and, therefore, have a national existence.[34]

Kirwin's ideas were supported by McGee, Bishop Loras, and General Shields. They did, however, enrage Protestants in western Ontario and the American Midwest who viewed them as evidence of a papist plot to establish an inland Catholic empire. Also aroused were the three eastern bishops who supported colonization, John Timon of Buffalo, Michael O'Connor of Pittsburgh and Richard Whelan of Wheeling. They wished any settlements to be in what they termed the "near west," by which they meant the southern tier of New York, western Pennsylvania, and western Virginia. Nor were they in favor of exclusively Irish settlements, preferring instead to have the colonists distributed among Yankee neighbors. In the face of their opposition, Kirwin and his backers agreed that colonies would be established in all sections of both countries.

The Irish Immigrant Aid Convention opened in Dudley Hall in Buffalo on February 12, 1856, with 72 delegates, elected by local organizations, in attendance. Among them were 32 clergymen from dioceses in both Canada and the United States, including the vicars general of Buffalo, Chicago, Pittsburgh, Wheeling, Kingston, Toronto, and Bytown (Ottawa). As expected, the Buffalo contingent of fifteen (ten of them clergymen) was the largest, followed by the delegation from the neighboring diocese of Hamilton, Ontario. Clergymen also attended from the dioceses of Cleveland, St. Louis, Dubuque, Newark, Albany, and Hartford in the United States. Conspicuous by their absence were any delegates from the archdiocese of New York, save for D'Arcy McGee, who had recently moved his paper back into Archbishop Hughes bailiwick.[35]

The Convention decided to hold its meetings in secret and to present a summary of its proceedings to the press only at its conclusion. This,

it was hoped, would give the impression that harmony and unanimity
had reigned. Dean Kirwin, elected president of the convention, delivered the opening address in which he defined its purpose as:

> devising the means of protecting the emigrant and placing him in a po-
> sition in which he can safely enjoy the rights and privileges of a citizen,
> under the broad shelter of our respective governments.[36]

He deplored the miserable state of immigrants in the seaboard and
canal cities, lacking skills and dependent on a precarious daily wage
to support their families. The helpless state of these new arrivals could
be blamed on Irish and Scottish landlords who had held them in me-
dieval serfdom. Colonization was the best means available of delivering
them from destitution. He urged settlement on farms, for, he argued,
Irishmen were historically agrarian, and thus had the requisite skills.[37]
He further urged the Convention to consider ways of supplying the
proposed Irish villages with schools, churches, and clergy. Thus, Kirwin
was once again pushing his original concept of isolated and segregated
rural settlements.

Delegates were divided into various committees which, after deliber-
ation, presented reports on the final day. Prefacing the written reports
was an address to the intended beneficiaries of the Convention's lar-
gesse. It articulated some assumptions also championed by the nativists
in stating that:

> the social condition of many of the Irish, landed in America, in our
> time, is somewhat beneath that of emigrants from other countries of
> equal opportunity, and much below that of nations of no greater in-
> dustry and intelligence.[38]

The convention delegates also appeared to view the urban famine Irish
as a potentially revolutionary force when they declared that:

> the social fabric is menaced by the existence of a large and steadily in-
> creasing class, to whom the acquisition of land is absolutely impossible,
> and who have no hopes of permanently improving the condition of them-
> selves or their posterity.[39]

Rural relocation would solve the "Irish problem" to the betterment
of the state, the Church, and the immigrant. The state would benefit,
for it would be rid of a pauper population which might create civil
unrest. The Church would benefit, for the removal of these Irish from

an urban environment which threatened their faith would secure them for Catholicism. Finally, the immigrants would gain a decent home, a steady income, and congenial social life. The address concluded by begging the cooperation of pauper immigrants in accepting resettlement and the financial backing of wealthy Irishmen in providing the means to this end.

The report of the Committee on Finance detailed how these means could be secured. A survey estimated Irish deposits in savings banks, credit unions, loan funds, and building associations at more than fifty million dollars. In addition about seven million dollars was annually sent home to families in Ireland by American Irish. Noting that with but a single exception Yankees controlled these financial institutions, they suggested these funds be diverted instead into colonization. They further estimated that about 200,000 Irish males crowded into the cities were willing but lacked finances needed to relocate. The Convention would direct its aid to this class, though only to the virtuous and sober among them whose poverty was not self-inflicted. To finance colonization, delegates urged the creation of joint stock companies. Wealthy Irish Americans would purchase this stock. The companies would then use the funds raised to purchase tracts of western lands, lay out townships, and sell farm lands, on credit, to immigrants at seven percent interest for five, seven, or ten years. Each township would set aside forty acres for a church, school, and rectory to be deeded in the bishop's name. The price of land per acre would not exceed ten percent of the cost of acquisition by the company. This ten percent profit would cover administrative costs. The Convention finally recommended that collections be taken up in the nation's churches to aid the work.[40]

The Committee on Lands reported the availability of government lands in the western states at prices ranging from twenty-five cents to one dollar and twenty-five cents per acre. Though New York and Pennsylvania lacked government lands, farms were available there at two to ten dollars an acre. Michigan, Wisconsin, and Illinois appeared to have the cheapest, most fertile land available. The Canadian committee reported large government tracts for sale along the Ottawa and St. Maurice rivers at sixty cents per acre.[41]

The final report, issued by the Committee on Organization, recommended the creation of paid agencies in Boston, New York, Pittsburgh, Buffalo, Chicago, and St. Louis, as well as in Canada, to deliver colonization information to immigrants. In addition, each agency should be headed by an appointed executive agent, serving without pay, to superintend the work of the salaried agents. There would also be a Supreme Director of five men in both countries to direct the joint stock companies and oversee finances.[42] With its work completed, the Convention adjourned on Friday, February 15, 1856.

Almost immediately the Catholic press began to choose up sides on the Convention. The Boston *Pilot* praised it unreservedly as "the first practical movement for the benefit of our race on this side of the Atlantic."[43] Buffalo's *Catholic Sentinel* also lauded its *"fervent desire to serve the temporal and spiritual interest of our people to the utmost."*[44]

The most important voice of all, however, had yet to be heard. While the archbishop of New York kept his silence, he did unleash his journalistic mouthpiece, the *Freeman's Journal*, in a savage attack on the Convention. An editorial of March 1, 1856, entitled "The Irish in America— Their Position and Destiny—Their Duty to the Church and to the Country," made clear the duty of Irishmen to remain in New York City, not to go off pioneering in Wisconsin. Denouncing the convention for preaching "a Know Nothingism which calls itself Irish and assumes to be Catholic," it urged its readers to adhere to the words of Archbishop Hughes:

> I do not wish you to understand, dearly beloved Brethren, that you should degrade yourselves one iota below the highest grade of American citizenship.[45]

These enigmatic lines appeared to mean that admission of Irish inability to succeed in urban America, where others had, was to accept their inferiority as a race. The paper continued:

> to preach a general stampede from our cities is merely Quixotic and can result in nothing more serious than calling forth the jeers of the country.[46]

Future issues added the charge that the Convention was a plot to lure the Irish to Canada where they would be made "catspaws of the British."[47]

The colonization scheme was in trouble from the start, and not just because of the attacks of its enemies. Its supporters remained deeply divided over the location and nature of the settlements. The majority, led by Kirwin and Loras, continued to push for segregated western villages much to the displeasure of the eastern bishops led by John Timon. Timon voiced his displeasure in his diocesan paper:

> There are still some who, looking at but one side of the question, urge to the utmost all that has ever been said or written about an *exclusive Irish Colony*; and who see in the dreams of their own imagination but

one bright land of promise. The prayer of every lover of the Irish race
would be, that men of that class [those who urged segregated western
settlements], however estimable in other respects, should not be appointed
to the office of District Executive.[48]

Timon reiterated his position that Irish colonists be directed to the
near West and that they be interspersed among the Yankee population. Timon's reason was his desire for assimilation. For the benefit
of the Irish, however, he sugar-coated his plan by arguing that God
had set them aside as a special people to be missionaries of the Church.
"Hence the plan once advocated of crowding them into exclusive colonies of their own race and creed, is an attempt to frustrate those de-
signs of Providence."[49] The advantages he saw from intermingling Irish
and Yankee tip his real reason, for he said the Irishman could "learn
with profit from his Yankee neighbor" about "improvements in Agriculture, in Implements, in Mechanics, &c . . . and through his greater
powers of endurance, or native shrewdness, soon perhaps becomes able
to teach his teachers."[50]

Every Irishman should be aided to get a homestead, Timon argued,
but not necessarily on a farm. Some were better suited for urban life
and should be helped to purchase a home in the city. As for the Far
West, Timon knew it well from his travels. Though fertile, it was difficult
to settle, presented health problems, and lacked schools and churches.
Immigrants would be better off settling in the southern tier within his
diocese, whose future growth he thought promising, or in Pennsylvania. Land was available in southern New York at fifteen dollars an
acre. While more expensive than public western lands, their value would
more than double in ten years and so would be a good investment.
Only the shiftless poor "that do not even aspire to obtain a homestead"
should be candidates for far western segregated villages. They did not
have the ambition to succeed in the near west and anything would be
better than "their miserable cellars, and garrets, or their frail shanties."[51]

McGee, in turn, denounced Timon's plan as impractical. Land costs
in Pennsylvania and New York were simply too high for Irish immigrants
to afford.[52] Again he insisted on settlement in the Far West. This explains why, though auxiliary Societies for the Promotion of Actual Settlements were established in Dubuque, Boston, New Haven, Jersey
City, and Oswego, none were formed in Buffalo, Pittsburgh, or
Wheeling, all of whose bishops opposed McGee's plan.

Timon returned to the attack on May 31, 1856, decrying the misplaced emphasis on western colonization which he considered a
deliberate perversion of the Convention's will.[53] Instead of locating the

indigent in that area, as he recommended, district agents were luring west "the thrifty who had already a home, or who, having saved enough, are just about to buy one."[54] As for the ambitious poor, they too were being ignored. Timon painted a pathetic picture of Irish families who had left western New York to seek a better life in the West only to return penniless and diseased after a futile effort to eke out a living on wild lands they lacked the ability to tame.[55] McGee struck back by accusing Timon, O'Connor, and Whelan of opposing western colonization because they feared their churches would empty, lessening their power and influence. This blast completely alienated Timon, whose support was badly needed to offset the opposition of Archbishop Hughes. As for Hughes, it finally goaded him to attack the Convention publicly.

In the December 1856 issue of *The Metropolitan* magazine, Hughes contributed an article entitled "Reflections and Suggestions on what is called the Catholic Press in the United States." Straying from his subject, he paused to attack the Buffalo Convention in general and McGee's *American Celt* in particular. Using twisted logic, Hughes claimed they were preaching a form of racism, for by ridding themselves of Irish immigrants eastern bishops amd clergy would "have ample time to address their ministry to those who are to the 'manor born'."[56] Besides, Hughes noted, the picture painted by McGee of the wretched living conditions of the Irish in New York was exaggerated. But even if McGee were correct, the Irish were still better off in New York City "surrounded by appointments of civilization, and even the comparative comforts of a temporary home," than they had been in Ireland or would be on the waste land of an Illinois prairie.[57]

Hughes' next outburst against colonization was more dramatic. In late March 1857, Reverend Jeremiah Trecy, the representative of Bishop Loras at the Buffalo Convention who had recently founded a colony in Nebraska, arrived in New York to deliver an address promoting the settlement. As was required, he stopped by the archbishop's residence to receive faculties to say Mass while in the New York archdiocese. He failed, however, to inform Hughes about the impending talk. After he had granted Trecy the needed permissions, Hughes received a visit from Bishop James Roosevelt Bayley of Newark who informed him of the proposed speech. Bayley also mentioned that it was rumored that Hughes favored the colonization scheme, presumably because Trecy was promoting it in his archdiocese. Hughes was outraged. His first impulse was to write an open letter to Bishop Bayley scotching the rumor and opposing colonization. In fact he did write out his ideas in long-hand on six legal-size sheets of paper. But he never sent the letter. In the document Hughes accused the Buffalo Convention of producing no new ideas but merely reiterating what was general knowledge "that there is a great deal of waste land, fertile withal, in the Eastern and Western provinces of Canada and on the Western boundaries of the present United States."[58] Zeroing in on McGee, he noted that he could hardly take seriously a movement in which a leading role was played by a man who could not manage his own affairs, yet felt free to give unsolicited advice to others. Hughes excoriated the clergy who had attended the Convention for urging the Irish immigrant to brave the hardships of the West while they remained secure in the East, a strange charge in light of the large number of western missionaries who attended the meeting and the experience of its sponsor, Bishop Timon, who had spent much of his priestly life laboring there. Hughes denied that he opposed colonization as such, but insisted that it take place naturally, by individual immigrants who had acquired the means and knowledge to survive in the wilderness. Colonizers' propaganda lauding cheap land to be had for the taking was misleading. In reality the area bred disease and lacked the necessities of civilization such as schools, churches, mail service, doctors, and even neighbors. Besides, as the Convention had not been able to raise funds to relocate immigrants it was dishonest to encourage migration. In addition, he believed that the urban Irish were totally unfit for a pioneer life.[59] Hughes even attacked the Convention's survey of Irish bank funds claiming this should not have been done without the owner's permission. Furthermore, the Convention had no right to finance its schemes with other people's money.

Hughes never sent this powerful letter. He conceived a better idea; he would deliver the message in person by showing up incognito at Trecy's lecture and disrupting it, an incident reported in detail by the *New York Times*.

Trecy spoke about the advantages of his Nebraska colony with D'Arcy McGee seated on the platform. In denying that eastern bishops opposed the project, he alluded to Archbishop Hughes' past, though brief, support of Wisconsin colonization. When Trecy had finished, Hughes stood up in the galley wrapped in a heavy overcoat and muffler and began to speak. Only gradually did the stunned audience recognize His Grace. The archbishop accused Trecy of deception in not informing him of his speech and blasted him for betraying the priesthood by "turning himself into a recruiting sergeant."[60] He repeated most of the arguments he had made in his draft letter but added a few choice ones as well. The clamor for western colonization, he claimed, was drummed up by McGee "who, perhaps, had nothing else to write about," and the whole concept "grew out of a joke."[61] Though he admitted there were good men of upright intentions at the Buffalo Convention, he asserted that it was also attended by land speculators who wanted to unload their worthless property on unsuspecting Irishmen. Exclusively Irish settlements, Hughes fumed, would cut the Irish off from the mainstream of American life as effectively as the Mormons. Individual colonists who migrated on their own initiative would go with his blessings, but he would oppose to the end any organized colonization movement. Finally, he lashed out at Catholic priests and newspapers who had supported the Convention, suggesting they had acted improperly as flacks for land speculators instead of maintaining the dignity of the Church.

When the archbishop had completed his tirade, Trecy rose to deny the charges. Hughes cut short this effort by another diatribe, the main point of which was that Trecy was a liar. As the *Times* noted "the awestruck audience then retired in profound silence."[62]

Hughes' personal attack spelled the end of the colonization movement. A second convention, which was supposed to be held in Chicago in 1857, never met and the organization's structure was dismantled. Besides raising a few thousand dollars, the movement accomplished little. No land was ever purchased or colonized.

The reasons for colonization's failure are varied. In the first place, the participants at the Buffalo Convention never reached a unified vision of what they were trying to accomplish and why. Moreover, their motives differed. Those who supported segregated, western agrarian Irish settlements (e.g. such men as Kirwin, Loras, and McGee) advocated a policy proven futile by previous colonization efforts. Even had funds been raised to finance such an undertaking, its rationale was based on the erroneous assumption that the famine Irish were skilled farmers rather than unskilled farm laborers. They would have been incapable of farming in the West which required specialized knowledge and adequate funding. All these men would have accomplished would have been to relocate the Irish from urban to rural ghettoes. In McGee's case, his motivation was based on a romantic, and unrealistic, effort to recapture the glories of Ireland's past by returning to an agrarian lifestyle. He had no interest in the process of Americanization.

John Timon's plan of resettling seaboard Irish piecemeal among the Yankees of western New York and Pennsylvania, in both rural and urban areas, offered the greatest hope of success. It would have avoided Irish ghettoization, encouraged assimilation, and, most importantly, ended the foreignness of the American Catholic church. He based his vision on the ethnic mix in Buffalo which worked to the advantage of each ethnic group and prevented mutual hostility and misunderstanding. American-born himself, Timon opposed the preservation of Irish ethnicity, be it urban or rural. Hence his resistance to both McGee and Hughes. He was neither blind to Irish faults nor deaf to nativist complaints. Indeed, he shared many of the nativists' fears and sought to alleviate them by Americanizing the Irish.

The motivations behind John Hughes' actions in this affair are complex. In part, he acted from personal animosity toward McGee. He was bound to oppose any plan put forward by an enemy, regardless of its merits. Then, too, Hughes was an ethnic Irishman himself, and proud of his heritage. He recalled bitterly the humiliations he had faced in Ireland and in his early life in America and would never countenance a movement that suggested that American Irish culture and lifestyle left something to be desired. This is evidenced by his denunciation of colonizers as Catholic nativists. The archbishop of New York was no Americanizer. As Andrew Greeley put it: "Hughes viewed the culture outside the Church as dangerous to its very existence. There was only one way to handle American society, and that was ultimately to convert it. And to convert it not on its own terms, but on his."[63] Finally, personal considerations played a part in determining Hughes' actions. He reveled in his role as the preeminent ecclesiastic in the United States, with all the public acclaim and political clout it brought him. Governors and presidents sought his advice, surely a heady experience for the son of an impoverished Irish immigrant, and an immigrant himself. But Hughes' power was based on his position as head of the largest diocese in the nation, largely populated by Irishmen whom he could manipulate. It is not coincidental that he ceased to favor colonization after he discovered that he could use Irish votes in a political struggle to attain his goals. Because colonization would, in fact, remove this power base, Hughes was bound to oppose it.

Extraneous factors also doomed the movement. The utter rout of the Know Nothings in the election of 1856 and the subsequent rapid disintegration of the party obviated the need to remove those who had occasioned nativist attacks. Then too, the government's withdrawal from sale of public lands in 1857 and the initiation instead of large grants to railroads to finance construction dried up the source of cheap land on which colonization depended.

In the final analysis, colonization involved much more than the mere relocation of Irishmen. It was rather a means to an end, the Americanization of the Catholic church and the assimilation of the Irish into the nation's mainstream. The Buffalo Convention represented a clash of two visions, that of John Timon's Americanized Catholicism and that of Hughes' Irish-dominated, ghettoized church. Unfortunately the vision of Hughes triumphed. In Greeley's words: "At precisely the time when the crises of the immigration experience were most severe, Hughes' influence can only be considered a major disaster."[64] John Timon was the last great spokesman for the old native American Church. From the time of his death, power within the Church fell almost exclusively to Irish prelates, spiritual children of the archbishop of New York. As a result, the Catholic church withdrew from American life and remained irrelevant to it for nearly a hundred years. This was the lasting legacy of John Hughes.[65]

Notes

1. Kerby A. Miller, *Emigrants and Exiles: Ireland and the Irish Exodus to North America* (New York, 1985).
2. *Ibid.*, 170–171.
3. Charles G. Deuther, *The Life and Times of the Rt. Rev. John Timon, D.D., First Roman Catholic Bishop of the Diocese of Buffalo* (Buffalo, 1870), 22–23. This is the source for unattributed biographical information early in this article.
4. Richard Shaw, *Dagger John: The Unquiet Life and Times of Archbishop John Hughes of New York* (New York, 1977), 14. This is the source for unattributed biographical information early in the paper.
5. *Ibid.*
6. Miller, *Emigrants and Exiles*, 194.
7. Shaw, *Dagger John*, 3–4.
8. Andrew M. Greeley, *The Catholic Experience: An Interpretation of the History of American Catholicism* (Garden City, N.Y., 1967), 115–119.
9. Shaw, *Dagger John*, 256.
10. Quoted in Greeley, *The Catholic Experience*, 108, which is the source for the next several paragraphs.
11. *Ibid.*, 222.
12. Leonard Dinnerstein and David M. Reimers, *Ethnic Americans: A History of Immigration and Assimilation* (New York, 1975), 29.
13. Mary Catherine Mattis, "The Irish Family in Buffalo, New York, 1855–1875: A Socio-Historical Analysis" (Ph.D. dissertation, Washington University, 1975), 95.
14. *Ibid.*, 147.
15. Laurence A. Glasco, "Ethnicity and Social Structure: Irish, Germans and Native-Born of Buffalo, New York, 1850–1860" (Ph.D. dissertation, State University of New York at Buffalo, 1973), 41.
16. Samuel Eccleston to Rev. Nicholas Wiseman, June 6, 1833, cited in Thomas T. McAvoy, *A History of the Catholic Church in the United States* (Notre Dame, 1969), 131.
17. Brownson to Hecker, June 25, 1845, in Joseph F. Gower and Richard M. Leliaert, eds., *The Brownson-Hecker Correspondence* (Notre Dame, 1979), 124.
18. Brownson to Hecker, June 1, 1855, in *ibid.*, 182–183.
19. Brownson to Hecker, August 5, 1857, in *ibid.*, 194–195.
20. John Dubois to John Purcell, July 2, 1835, (Purcell Papers, Archives of the University of Notre Dame; hereafter AUND).
21. John O'Grady, "Irish Colonization in the United States," *Studies: An Irish Quarterly Review of Letters, Philosophy and Science*, 19 (1930) 397.
22. *Ibid.*, 389.

23. Cited in Richard J. Purcell, "The Irish Emigrant Society of New York," *Studies: An Irish Quarterly Review of Letters, Philosophy, and Science*, 27 (1938), 591.
24. *Ibid.*
25. *Ibid.*, 592.
26. Cited in Henry J. Brown, "Archbishop Hughes and Western Colonization," *The Catholic Historical Review*, 36 (October 1950), 262.
27. *Ibid.*, 263.
28. Shaw, *Dagger John*, 309.
29. Buffalo *Commercial Advertiser*, July 15, 1856.
30. Cited in Shaw, *Dagger John*, 234.
31. *Ibid.*, 235.
32. *Ibid.*, 309.
33. *Ibid.*
34. Quoted in Mary Gilbert Kelly, *Catholic Immigrant Colonization Projects in the United States, 1815-1860* (New York, 1939), 286.
35. A list of delegates appears in the Buffalo *Catholic Sentinel*, February 23, 1856.
36. "Remarks of the President," Buffalo *Catholic Sentinel*, February 23, 1856.
37. *Ibid.*
38. *Ibid.*
39. *Ibid.*
40. *Ibid.*
41. *Ibid.*
42. *Ibid.*
43. Boston *Pilot*, February 23, 1856, quoted in Brown, "Archbishop Hughes and Western Colonization," 266.
44. Buffalo *Catholic Sentinel*, February 23, 1856. Emphasis in original.
45. New York *Freeman's Journal*, March 1, 1856, cited in Kelly, *Catholic Immigrant Colonization Projects*, 242-243.
46. *Ibid.*, cited in Brown, "Archbishop Hughes and Western Colonization," 266.
47. *Ibid.*
48. Buffalo *Catholic Sentinel*, March 22, 1856.
49. *Ibid.*
50. *Ibid.*
51. *Ibid.*
52. *American Celt*, April 5, 1856, in Kelly, *Catholic Immigrant Colonization Projects*, 246.
53. Buffalo *Catholic Sentinel*, May 31, 1856.
54. *Ibid.*
55. *Ibid.*
56. Cited in Brown, "Archbishop Hughes and Western Colonization," 268.
57. *Ibid.*
58. Quoted, *ibid.*, 270.
59. *Ibid.*, 272.
60. New York *Times*, March 27, 1857, reprinted in the Buffalo *Catholic Sentinel*, April 4, 1857.
61. *Ibid.*
62. *Ibid.*
63. Greeley, *The Catholic Experience*, 107
64. *Ibid.*, 103.
65. Little primary source material exists for Archbishop Hughes, Bishop Loras, and, in part, Bishop Timon. Bishop Loras' correspondence was not preserved. The Timon-Hughes correspondence has not survived. When the author visited the archives of the archdiocese of New York, he was told that Hughes' correspondence was not extant and that the archives possessed few letters from Bishop Timon to Archbishop Hughes, none of them dealing with colonization or the Buffalo Convention. Hence the need to rely on secondary material and newspaper accounts.

3

From the Barricades of Paris to the Sidewalks of New York: German Artisans and the European Roots of American Labor Radicalism

In recent years several scholars have produced very significant discussions of the developing politics of nineteenth-century working Americans.[1] They have focused on the process by which these workers, particularly artisans, appropriated republican ideological forms and transformed them to serve their own interests. Sean Wilentz's *Chants Democratic*, one of the best of these studies, developed and effectively applied these concepts to the history of artisanal politics in New York City. In doing so, however, Wilentz posited a continuity in the evolution of workers' politics in New York from the end of the eighteenth century to a climax in the labor upsurge of 1850. While convincing in tracing the development of artisan republicanism among New York's native-born workers, Wilentz's analysis, like most other studies of mid-nineteenth-century New York (and other American cities) makes insufficient allowance for the severe discontinuity which massive im-

56

migration introduced into the labor movement in the late 1840s. By 1850, only a few New York workers had experienced the full sequence of developments which Wilentz depicts as reaching a climax that year. Most of them had not undergone these developments because they had only recently arrived in the city. During the late 1840s, New York City's labor force had been almost totally transformed by a process which would continue to remake the social map of America for a century.

Early in the 1840s, New York City was what it had been for generations, an American city with an American-born labor force of mostly British descent. That was no longer true by the end of the decade. By 1850, native-born Americans constituted only 36 percent of *adult* New Yorkers.[2] Not only were two-thirds of the city's adults foreign-born, but these immigrants formed an overwhelming majority of the manual labor force. Indeed, five years later there were only about 24,000 native-born whites engaged in manual labor in the entire city out of a manual labor force of nearly 147,000.[3] Native-born whites were thus less than 17 percent of the city's manual labor force by 1855. The native born workers were concentrated in the artisan trades, to be sure, but only in the building and printing trades did they still constitute a significant proportion. The continuing influence of New York's artisanal traditions was, therefore, necessarily limited by the virtual elimination of its carriers from many sectors of the city's labor force.

These traditions were not irrelevant to the working-class politics in New York after the 1840s. But they had become only one of many sources of political ideas for a radically transformed labor force. European-born workers, who came to dominate the new labor force, brought other traditions. They tapped other sources of political ideas which often had only the most tenuous connections with American experience. This paper explores the development of a new labor and radical politics by one such group of immigrants, the German-American workers who came to dominate an increasing number of New York's artisan and skilled trades after 1845. These immigrants were, in a sense, the successors of Wilentz's artisan republicans. By 1855, Germans were already a majority of tailors, shoemakers, cabinetmakers and upholsterers, bakers, brewers, cigarmakers, locksmiths, paperboxmakers, potters, textile workers, gilders, turners, and carvers. Over the next two decades they came to dominate most other skilled trades as well.[4]

German artisans came to New York with high levels of skills and brought their own artisanal traditions with them. Some of these skills and traditions were rooted in the ancient crafts of Europe where guilds and journeymen's associations had defined the artisan's world. Even in Germany, however, the guilds were a fading memory by mid-century and German artisanal traditions were in ferment. The French Revolution had led to the abolition of guilds in western Germany and revolutionary French ideas made a strong impression on many Germans. German artisans developed their responses to the new capitalist order of the nineteenth century from both their own experiences and those of the French labor movement.

The French artisan experience was not foreign to German artisans. By the second quarter of the nineteenth century Paris was a standard stopping place for German artisans of many trades. Not only were fashions set in Paris, but French artisanal techniques were reputed to be the finest in the world.[5] Thus, German artisans who wished to achieve true mastery of their trades went to Paris. By the 1840s, as many as 80,000 German journeymen may have worked in Paris at any one time.[6] Tailoring, shoemaking, and furniture making were the most common trades for Germans in Paris, but others worked in a large proportion of the city's most skilled trades. As the average journeyman stayed in Paris for only a limited period, perfecting his trade and then moving on, we have to assume that somewhere between a hundred thousand and a half million veterans of the Paris workshops had returned to Germany before the end of the decade.

In France, German journeymen learned far more than just refinements of their craft. They also learned the language and skills of social revolution. The tailors of Paris had been known for their commitment to republican and secularist organizations ever since the days of the *sans-culottes*,[7] and German tailors comprised the largest contingent of German journeymen in the Paris workshops. The famous utopian communist Wilhelm Weitling formulated his ideas while working as a tailor in Paris.[8] The other Paris crafts most affected by an increasing division of labor and class conflict were the shoemaking and furniture trades, and these too were among the largest of the German trades in Paris.[9] Even the elite makers of musical instruments were swept up in the Parisian social ferment. In later years, the German piano makers of New York boasted that they still possessed a flag which the journeymen piano makers of Paris had carried "upon the barricades during the stormy days of the French Revolution."[10]

Furthermore, the radicalism which tramping German artisans learned from the Parisian workers was not simply the traditional republicanism of the Jacobins and *sans-culottes*. Responding to Saint-Simonian ideas, French artisans began to develop a more radical version of republicanism in the 1830s. The new social republicanism demanded a fundamental reorganization of society to end the treatment of labor as a commodity—a condition social republicans had come to see as a barrier to true republican equality and fraternity. They proclaimed that "our industry [labor], which you have exploited for so long, belongs to us alone."[11] This was not merely rhetoric. In Paris in 1833, striking tailors, casemakers, shoemakers, and cabinetmakers set up producers' cooperatives to break the employers' stranglehold on their trades. (Again these were the very trades which employed the greatest numbers of German journeymen.) The tailors, at least, saw their cooperative as a permanent institution of broad social significance and termed it a "national workshop."

While the organized trades were attempting to create new forms of property relations, Efrahem, the radical shoemaker and leader of the Partisan Society of the Rights of Man, called for a class wide "Association of Workers of All Trades" to unite all artisans into one corporate association. Another leader of the Society, the tailor Gringnon, wrote that the workers were "the most numerous and most useful class of Society." These claims echoed and transformed the classic assertion of the primacy of the Third Estate from the French Revolution: the workers (rather than the broader Third Estate of the classic formulation) were synonymous with the sovereign people—the rightful rulers of a republic.[12]

While these radical notions were the preserve of Parisian worker-intellectuals in the 1830s, they had become the basis of a widely shared discourse by the early 1840s. Etienne Cabet, Louis Blanc, and Pierre-Joseph Proudhon picked up on these radical social ideas and systematized them in ways which caught the popular imagination. Cabet's Icarian communism especially appealed to a popular artisan following, and again it was the trades which included the most Germans that took the lead. As Christopher Johnson has noted, "Everywhere in France, but especially in Paris, tailors, shoemakers and cabinetmakers flocked to the Icarian cause."[13] A leading historian of the French labor movement writes:

> From 1840 on, socialist ideas were discussed . . . in workshops and working-class cabarets . . . and journalistic and literary writings of all kinds. From the beginning, manual workers played a significant role in this discourse, writing articles for workers' newspapers, publishing tracts and manifestos, and intervening by means of letters in the bourgeois press. . . . In the course of the 1840s, ideas about cooperation, about the reorganization of labor, about joint ownership of the means of production, were discussed, debated, and assimilated by thousands of French workers.[14]

These ideas were assimilated by thousands of the German journeyman who passed through Paris. Early in 1832 a *Deutsche Volksverein*
was organized in Paris which combined republicanism and German
nationalism with the discussion of the social question.[15] Two years later,
a revolutionary League of Exiles was established in Paris to promote
a German revolution. Its heroes were those of the French revolutionary
left (Robespierre, Babeuf, and Lamennais) and the vast majority of
its members were journeymen. Its slogan was that of the 1831 Lyons
silkworkers' rebellion, "Live Working or Die Fighting"[16] A German
tailor who belonged to a Swiss branch of the League recalled its ideology
in terms of "[s]trivings for German unity and freedom, for the republic
and the brotherhood of peoples, for free thought, primitive Christianity
and communism—all these ideas ran together there."[17] In 1836, the
League of Exiles broke apart over the social question. Artisans increasingly influenced by their French co-workers' socialism broke with the
League's leadership and established a new group, the League of the
Just, to agitate for socialism. The new League promoted the socialist
ideas of Saint-Simon and Fourier, and was closely associated with August Blanqui's Society of the Seasons. In keeping with the League's
artisanal character, a journeyman shoemaker, Henrich Bauer, and a
journeyman watchmaker, Karl Joseph Moll, were members of its central committee. Journeyman tailor Wilhelm Weitling, the premier ideologue of German socialism before 1848, soon joined them.

Weitling, who later played an important role in New York, combined the socialism of the French utopians with a call for revolutionary
mass action by the workers. Like later communists, he had few illu-
sions about the possibility of a peaceful social revolution in Europe.
He wrote about a "bloody battlefield in the streets" and the "guerilla-
warfare" which would be necessary to create socialism.[18] Towards the
end of the decade, the League of the Just was renamed the Communist
League and Weitling was displaced as its chief ideologue. The author
of the renamed League's new *Communist Manifesto* was Karl Marx.

This legacy of revolutionary Europe—from the *sans-culottes* to the
national workshops and workers' barricades of 1848, from Robespierre
and Babeuf to Louis Blanc and Karl Marx—formed the tradition that
many German immigrants would bring to New York.

This legacy of revolutionary Europe was apparent even in some of
the more conservative and "respectable" sectors of German New York.
The city's leading German-language newspaper, the pro-Democratic
New Yorker Staats-Zeitung, was published by a political refugee of firmly
republican bent named Jacob Uhl. Son of a Bavarian army officer, Uhl
had learned the printers' trade before getting arrested for revolutionary

activities in 1833.[19] He emigrated to New York in 1835, and soon identified his republican ideals with the Democratic Party. Nonetheless, he continued to follow more radical currents in Europe and introduced them to any German New Yorkers who had missed them in Europe. Early in 1846, for example, the *Staats-Zeitung* carried a review of Friedrich Engles' *Condition of the Working Class in England*, while Uhl also published a German translation of the French socialist novelist Eugène Sue's *Mystères de Paris*.[20] Nor was Uhl the only purveyor of radical European writings to German New Yorkers. While Uhl sponsored the translation of one of Sue's works, a competitor advertised that he had imported a German translation of another novel by the same author from Leipzig.[21] Judging from the booksellers' advertisements which appeared in the German papers in the mid-1840s, German artisans in New York had access to a fair range of Europe's most radical ideas.

In the mid-1840s German New York also experienced a brief prefiguring of the German-American labor movement which would make its first real mark in 1850. Late in 1845, Hermann Kriege, a republican propagandist and member of the League of the Just, arrived in New York City and sought to promote its doctrines. He immediately established a small and secret German-American branch of the League.[22] Early the next year, Kriege and his associates set up a *Sozialreformassoziation* (Social Reform Association) as the public arm of their secret organization (thus establishing the first "communist front" in American history). The Sozialreformassoziation was intended to be a workers' political association which would draw in large numbers of German workers and encourage them to engage in independent political action of a communist nature. To attract members, and perhaps harking back to the *Deutsche Volksverein* of Paris, the Sozialreformassoziation sponsored a large variety of social activities which were extraordinarily successful. Soon the Sozialreformers numbered nearly a thousand and had become the leading voluntary association in German New York.[23]

Kriege came out of an international movement for social reform and he rapidly sought out like-minded reformers among English speaking New Yorkers. He found them among New York's "subterranean radicals," and affiliated with the National Reform Association of George Henry Evans.[24] In keeping with its American affiliation, and a measure of the Anglo-American reformers' influence on the Germans, the Sozialreformassoziation concentrated its political efforts on agitation for a Homestead Law, then known as "land reform." Kriege's overblown sentimental appeals and the Sozialreformassoziation's concentration upon "land reform" rather than communism soon led to Kriege's expulsion from the League of the Just.[25]

With many of their members poorly educated and attracted by social activities, the Sozialreformers were politically very unstable. Early
in 1846, the Sozialreformassoziation set up its own newspaper, the *Volks-
Tribun*, with the slogan "Up with Labor! Down with Capital!" displayed
prominently on the masthead. Named after the French revolutionary
Babeuf's *Tribun du peuple* and edited by Kriege, the paper advocated
a "communism" which would protect producers from capitalist exploitation.[26] Hardly had the *Volks-Tribun* appeared, than the *Staats-Zeitung*
attacked it for distorting reality by falsely depicting American workers
as poverty stricken and living in a society divided by hard and fast
class lines.[27] This attack was followed by many more, including a very
effective polemic that ridiculed the utopianism of the communists. The
radicalism of the Social Reformers waned rapidly under this barrage.
Realizing the partisan considerations behind the Democratic *Staats-
Zeitung* yet noting fellow land reform advocate Mike Walsh's success
within the New York Democracy, Kriege sought to adapt the Sozialreformassoziation to New York partisan politics. In May of 1846, he
called upon the Sozialreformassoziation to establish itself as the "left
wing of Tammany Hall." On July 4th, the *Volks-Tribun* dropped the slogan
"Up with Labor! Down with Capital!" from its masthead and declared
that the Sozialreformassoziation was no longer communist.[28] Stating
that America was "the asylum of the oppressed, land of the workers
and free farmers," the Sozialreformers became intensely patriotic. They
even sent fifty of their members to fight against Mexico in a war condemned by both the European left and the American National Reform Association.[29]

While the Sozialreformers and the *Volks-Tribun* quickly abandoned
their advocacy of class struggle and communism, some New York
German workers began to experiment with unions. Just as the *Volks-
Tribun* first appeared, the German handweavers met to protest the reduc-
tion of their wages from $4.00 to $2.50 a week over the preceding year.[30]
By the end of the summer they had organized a carpet weavers' union
(along with their English speaking co-workers) which had over 1,000
members in thirty-one factories. The union declared it would use strikes
if necessary to resist any further wage cuts.[31] Nothing more was heard
from this union, the only German union of the 1840s. Nonetheless,
with the Sozialreformassoziation and the *Volks-Tribun*, it marked the
beginnings of a German-American labor movement in New York City.

Wilhelm Weitling, the famous German utopian communist and Hermann Kriege's mentor, had been invited to come to America by the
Sozialreformassoziation when it began its agitation in the spring of
1846. By the time he arrived at the beginning of 1847, the union move-

ment had ended, the Social Reformers had abandoned communism, and the *Volks-Tribun* was bankrupt. Little daunted, Weitling soon hit upon the idea of setting up a communist fraternal order, the *Befreiungs-bund* or Liberation League. Weitling's new League had little impact on German New York, though one leading member was Eugen Lievre, owner of the Shakespeare Hotel which afterwards hosted a generation of radical activities. What ended Weitling's agitation (and Kriege's) was the news of the outbreak of the German Revolutions of 1848. The New York Lodge of the Befreiungsbund, turning its attention to a real revolution, sent Weitling to Berlin to organize the workers of Germany for the League. Kriege too returned to Germany.[32]

Weitling's and Kriege's departures did not leave German New York entirely bereft of radical activists. A German saloonkeeper named Erhard Richter tried to keep the pot simmering. Richter, who was active in a broad range of radical causes over the next decade, took a leading role in a little-known *Deutscher Arbeiter Verein* (German Workers Union) in 1848. The organization first attracted notice in May of 1848, when it marched in German New York's grand parade celebrating the outbreak of revolution in Germany.[33] In June, Richter published a piece in the *Staats-Zeitung* which claimed that the Workers Union was the only real representative of the working class. More interesting than this grandiose claim was the rhetoric he used in presenting it. Echoing the tailor Gringnon and other French socialists, Richter used their characteristic phraseology in referring to the workers as "the most numerous and most powerful class in society." He went on to talk of a new society in which workers would elect the heads of their work-shops.[34] If there was any connection between the Workers union and Weitling's Befreiungsbund no record remains, but there can be no doubt about the Arbeiter Verein's debt to the Paris socialists.

The German Revolutions dominated the politics of German New York for the remainder of the decade. Revolutionary organizations, fraternal orders, singing societies, newspapers, and the vast majority of German New Yorkers seem to have thrown all their organized activity into celebration of, or support for, revolutionary activities in the homeland. Political thought focused on Berlin, Vienna, and Frankfurt — a German constitution and German politics — rather than on New York and American conditions. This revolutionary agitation continued well into the 1850s, especially in the social circles of the post-revolution refugees — the real "forty-eighters." It totally dominated the political life of German New York, however, only as long as the revolutions themselves appeared to have serious prospects for success.

The labor movement which had appeared so briefly in 1846 returned to German New York as a serious force in 1850. Industry was booming and the expected influx of gold from the California gold fields was contributing to a rapid increase in prices. While prices were rising, employers continued to cut wages as they had become accustomed during the deflationary 1840s. Workers called meetings to protest wage cuts or to demand higher wages, leading to strike calls and the formation of trade unions. The German workers were conspicuous in their participation. The first workers to go out on strike, at the end of February, were the cabinetmakers resisting a wage cut. It was reported that a large number, representing all the nationalities in the trade, were participating.

While all nationalities were represented among the strikers, the cabinetmakers' union was German-led. Union President Steffens came from Hamburg, the German furniture manufacturing center known for its advanced politics (they were said to be years ahead of southern Germany and only weeks behind Paris). Steffens took the lead in exhorting the strikers to maintain their solidarity and to keep up their courage, but his speeches went beyond the issues and tactics of the strike. He also addressed the strikers' long-term problems and advocated socialist solutions. Like the French artisan socialists of Paris, he proposed establishing cooperative workshops both as a strike tactic and as a longer term solution to the increasing subordination of the artisan crafts to capitalist control. Beyond the adoption of producers' cooperatives, Steffens urged the creation of a Trade-Exchange Bank to destroy capitalist relations of production and exchange. The Trade-Exchange Bank was the key to Wilhelm Weitling's version of communist ideology.[35]

Weitling himself had returned to New York at the end of 1849, having fled from his latest revolutionary agitation in Hamburg only hours before the police moved in to arrest him.[36] He lost no time in reviving his New York contacts and was able to get out the first issue of his new newspaper, *Die Republik der Arbeiter* (The Worker's Republic), in January 1850. He was again preaching his distinctive form of utopian communism to the German workers of America. Unlike the multi-class appeal of the utopianism of Owen, Fourier, and Proudhon, Weitling appealed primarily to the workers to make their own revolution, although he did include petty employers who had "once been workers themselves" in his scheme for social reorganization. He supported unions and strikes to organize workers, but saw their potential for raising wages as limited. Real success, he argued, could only lead to an inflationary spiral which would then eat up the gains.[37] Producers' cooperatives were an important element in his scheme, but only when organized into his master conception, the *Gewerbetauschbank* or Trade-Exchange Bank. He described the bank in the first issue of his paper.

> The founding of a Trade-Exchange Bank, if it is to serve its intended purpose, requires the issuing of a new worker's paper money and the opening of stores and warehouses. In these warehouses (or to their agents) workers, employers and farmers can sell their products at any time for worker's paper money. With this paper money they can buy whatever they need in return, so that with the founding of this Exchange Bank, each member always has work and can always sell and buy his products without appealing to the capitalists and middlemen and submitting to their swindling. Everyone will always, by the exchange rules of this Trade-Exchange Bank, receive the full value of his expenses and labor.

Weitling went on to explain how the Bank would produce massive profits, to finance cooperative factories and utopian colonies.[38]

Part of the idiosyncratic flavor of Weitling's communism lay in his appeal to Christian principles even though most of his fellow German radicals were flaming atheists. In this respect, Weitling was much more in the French tradition of Lamennais, Cabet, Proudhon, and the other Christian socialists, a tradition despised by German heirs of the Enlightenment like Karl Marx.[39] Weitling wrote his *Evangelium der armen Sünder* (*Testament of a Poor Sinner*) while he was still in Europe. He referred to Lamennais as an inspiration for his own work.[40] An especially fine example of Weitling's religiosity was a poem he wrote for young communists sometimes recited at their gatherings:

Ich bin ein kleiner Kommunist	I am a little communist
Und frage nicht nach Geld,	and do no ask for cash,
Da unser Meister Jesus Christ	because our master Jesus Christ
Davon ja auch nichts hält.	has no regard for wealth.

Ich bin ein kleiner Kommunist	I am a little communist
Und bins mit Lieb and Treu,	and am with love and faith,
Und trete einst als treuer Christ	and as a faithful Christian, I
Dem Arbeitsbunde bei.[41]	support the Workers' League.

Back in 1846, *Staats-Zeitung* owner/editor Jacob Uhl had ridiculed Weitling's followers for suggesting "utopian" schemes. By 1850 Weitling was a (minor) hero of the German Revolution and deserved respect. The *Staats-Zeitung* thus expressed sympathy with Weitling's goals, but

gently suggested that the Trade-Exchange Bank was thoroughly impractical. Uhl demonstrated his familiarity with European socialist
thought when he pointed out that without the bank's profits, producers'
cooperatives were possible only for elite workers who had the money
needed to finance them. Cooperatives would therefore be of no use
to the majority of workers unless they received state support, as suggested by the state-sponsored socialism of Louis Blanc and the Paris
workers in 1848.[42] Having verged on socialism, Uhl then retreated to
a more traditional republican position and concluded by stressing the
possibilities for promoting the workers' interests through democratic
electoral politics. Referring to a "Socialistischer Revolutionsfier" where
Weitling was a star speaker, the *Staats-Zeitung* noted with regret that
all the socialist heroes whose portraits decorated the hall were Europeans (Babeuf, Lamennais, Buonarrotti, Kinkel, Cabet, Owen, and
Proudhon). The *Staats-Zeitung* had no objection to any of these, but
asked that some republican Americans be added — such as Paine,
Washington, Franklin, and Jefferson. The *Staats-Zeitung's* bracketing
of Washington and Franklin between Paine and Jefferson is itself an
indication of Uhl's left republicanism and deism (Uhl was apparently
a supporter of Paine's ideas and he published an anti-religious magazine, *die Asträa*, as well as the *Staats-Zeitung*). This more noticeably left-
wing orientation of the *Staats-Zeitung* did not last long, but it might
have been expected in the newspaper that had just become the New
York agent for the *Neue Rheinische Zeitung* of "Carl" Marx.[43]

   With Weitling and even the *Staats-Zeitung* urging them on, the German
workers organized rapidly. The cabinetmakers were only the first. The
house carpenters immediately followed their example. Even as they
prepared to strike, the German carpenters met with the cabinetmakers
and with a shoemakers' organizing committee. In mid-March, 1850
they agreed to unite their organizations on a "social basis" and lead
their joint membership of over one thousand in an attempt to implement Weitling's ideas.[44] The next day the German shoemakers held
a mass meeting at the Shakespeare Hotel to organize an association
based on Weitling's program.[45]

   Upholsterers, carvers, paper-hangers, shade painters, varnishers,
polishers, clockmakers, cigarmakers, and bakers also formed German
unions, German workers' associations, and German sections of mul-
tilingual unions.[46] Weitling took credit for all this activity. He claimed
that his agitation had led to strikes in twenty trades, which achieved
wage increases averaging 25 percent. The communist tailor was especially proud of New York's German tailors, who he reported signed
up 2,000 members in one day in March. He also claimed that the

German example provided the impetus for the organization in New York of English speaking unions with 60,000–80,000 members.[47]

Weitling immediately proposed a central labor body for the unions. His fellow tailors selected him to represent their union in organizing one. At the end of April they succeeded in organizing a Central Commission of the United Trades for the organized German workers in fifteen trades. Weitling then represented the Central Commission in the Industrial Congress set up by the English-speaking workers the next month.[48] The United Trades had about 2,400 members, most of them from the unions, though it also had representatives from the Sozialreformers and an "Economic Exchange-Association."[49]

Weitling's influence soon waned, however. It became clear that his program focused on the Exchange-Bank, and that he really failed to support either trade unions or cooperatives for their own sakes. That Weitling demanded complete deference to his leadership also generated conflict, and he resigned from the Central Commission in October. He concluded his resignation by saying: "Under the existing circumstances it would be more damaging than useful to the movement which I lead in spirit, should I continue to let my feelings be abused at your meetings." The United Trades replied, "that we feel strong enough to guide the movement of our brothers and . . . we need no spiritual leader which Weitling pretends to be."[50]

The most dramatic events of 1850 were precipitated by the Irish tailors calling a strike in July. The German tailors also walked out with the support of most of German New Yorkers including the conservative *Staats-Zeitung*. The *Staats-Zeitung* particularly attacked the exploitative putting-out system which predominated in the ready-to-wear clothing trade. In this trade, clothing merchants drove down wages by cutting cloth in their factories and then distributing the pre-cut cloth to sewers who stitched the seams at home. This system put skilled tailors into competition with semi-skilled women sewers and drove the tailors' wages down sharply.

Although most of German New York supported the strikers, the Redemptionist Priest, Father Müller of Most Holy Redeemer Church attacked the strike as anti-religious. He even called the police to arrest a tailors' committee which came to remonstrate with him. The *Staats-Zeitung* was outraged at the arrests, but the nativistic New York *Herald* was delighted and claimed that the workers had gone to burn the church down. A few days later a group of sixty to eighty tailors, "apparently all Germans," tried to picket the uptown home of an employer. Again the German and English papers reported the events very differently. The *Staats-Zeitung* reported that the tailors were attacked by the police

and an armed mob of "loafers and niggers," leading to many injuries
and arrests. The English papers reported that the tailors rioted, breaking
windows and fighting the police, leading to about forty arrests. The
police denied reports that three tailors had died of their wounds. In
the end, thirty-nine tailors were convicted of rioting and served prison
sentences.[51] The *Staats-Zeitung* concluded that it was proud of the leading
role the Germans had played, but perhaps a workers' cooperative might
have fared better than a strike.[52]

The tailors and many of the other German unionists seem to have
agreed with the *Staats-Zeitung*. The majority of the workers who had
won their strikes soon drifted out of the unions because they saw no
further need for the organizations (a common weakness of early trade
unions). The majority of those who remained turned enthusiastically
to the creation of cooperative workshops. These projects then absorbed
the energies of both the unions and the Central Commission for the
remainder of their existence. That existence was brief, however, as
the Central Commission and many of the unions soon collapsed from
the recriminations and disillusionment which followed the failure of
the undercapitalized and inexperienced cooperatives.

The Germans' preference for forming cooperatives was predictable.
Cooperatives were generally the rage in labor circles, including Horace
Greeley's *New York Tribune*. They also had a natural appeal for proletarianized artisans — a fair description of most of New York's organized
German workers. These artisans had no objections to a petty producer
capitalism where workers had a reasonable prospect of becoming their
own masters. What they resented was the prospect of indefinite em-
ployee status. Cooperative workshops offered them the renewed prospect of becoming their own masters through an appeal to the familiar
artisan ethic of cooperation, rather than the alien notions of competition and conflict. Because cooperative workshops seemed such an obvious solution to artisan proletarianization, the ideal survived the failure
of the 1850 cooperatives and was resuscitated nearly every time there
was a labor movement revival in small-scale industries.

Weitling himself continued his agitation for another four years. He
organized his followers into the *Arbeiterbund* (Workers' League) and
promoted its activities in his *Republik der Arbeiter*.[53] For a while, the
New York Society of the Arbeiterbund had several hundred members
who continued to look to him for leadership. Weitling promoted his
vision of cooperatives, the Trade-Exchange Bank, and a utopian colony
at Communia, Iowa. Indeed, the New York local of the League was
prosperous enough in October 1852, to open a Workers' Hall which
provided the usual range of German social activities — theater, singing,

dancing, bowling, and beer. But the League began to fade in New York with the creation of a Marxist rival in the spring of 1853 (see below) and finally collapsed in 1854 as charges flew concerning the causes of the bankruptcy of the utopian colony at Communia. Fighting charges of dishonesty, Weitling tried to keep the League alive and continued publishing his newspaper until July 1855. It was a bitter end. In later years, Adolf Sorge (the Marxist leader of the First International and Weitling's friend) continued to defend Weitling's honesty as "above suspicion" and honored him as a founder of the German-American labor movement.[54]

While the Sozialreformassoziation and the Arbeiterbund constituted two major early incarnations of German-American radicalism, possibly the most important incarnation in the 1850s was the *Turnverein*. The *Turnverein*, or Gymnastics Union, had its roots in a nationalistic physical culture movement which arose in Napoleonic Germany. By mid-century this German movement, which had added republicanism and free thought to its ideology, was largely a working-class movement and had strong links to the German artisan colony in Paris.[55] When the Revolution of 1848–1850 broke out in Germany, thousands of Turners (as they were called) played an active and leading role in the fighting, particularly in Baden. Some of the activist Turners had been recruited from revolutionary Paris, where hundreds of German journeymen enrolled in an armed force known as Herwegh's Legion. The Legion was organized to carry social republicanism back to Germany on the points of French revolutionary bayonets, and was subsidized by a French Provisional Government anxious to be rid of the turbulent German radicals.[56] When the revolutions in Germany failed, many of the Turner veterans of the Baden Legion, Herwegh's Legion, and other revolutionary forces joined comarades who had previously emigrated to the United States. Together they formed the German-American Turner movement.[57]

The first move towards establishing a Turner movement in New York had come in 1846, when the *Staats-Zeitung* ran a long story on the founder of the German movement, "Father Jahn."[58] It was another two years, however, before the Turners in New York set up a small *Turngemeinde*, or Gymnastics Society.[59] The Turngemeinde members practiced their gymnastics and occupied a minor place in the social life of German New York for two years. Then the Society was disrupted by an influx of more revolutionary Turners who had recently fled from Germany. These radicals pushed for greater political activity. When their proposals were not accepted, they withdrew to form their own organization — the New Yorker *Socialistischen* [Socialist] *Turnverein*.[60]

The socialism of the Socialistischen Turnverein ran the full gamut from a social republicanism which was more republican and atheist than social to a proletarian communism expounded by followers of Karl Marx. The editor of the *Turn-Zeitung* proclaimed that "the communist visionary, with a hatred of all Capital and dreaming of revolution, is as well represented in our association as the prudent reformer who would be satisfied with a fair compromise between Labor and Capital created by government regulation of wages." He announced that the pages of the *Turn-Zeitung* would be open to both.[61] The common denominator, disclosed in an article on Turners and socialism in the second issue, was a mixture of classic formulations of the French Revolution ("the socialist is an opponent of all monarchical or aristocratic state formations; he is an opponent of all hierarchical or religious power . . . privilege and monopoly") and the newer social republican formulations of 1848 ("he is an opponent of any system of exploiting workers and is finally an opponent of a society which contains the seeds of future destruction in its neglect for their well being").[62] In the same issue, the *Turn-Zeitung* contained a sophisticated analysis of the transformation of workers from artisans into proletarians.[63]

The *Turn-Zeitung* turned out to be an important element in the introduction and spread of European notions of social radicalism to the United States. It ran regular articles and series on the history and meaning of socialism. One article attributed the origin of socialism to the independent organization of the workers of Paris in 1834, while a series devoted to "The Socialism of the French" devoted its first article to events from the outbreak of the Revolution to the fall of Robespierre.[64] New York's German workers were also introduced to different varieties of socialism through the pages of the *Turn-Zeitung*, with the series on French Socialism extolling Louis Blanc and concluding with a quote from Karl Grün. Other articles promoted a Marxian "Dictatorship of the Proletariat" or condemned French communists for a materialism which "would abolish art and science and make spiritual life a crime."[65]

Even as the *Turn-Zeitung* introduced European ideas to a widening circle of German-American workers, it also introduced the Germans to the radical traditions and history of their new home. In spring 1853 the paper ran a series of articles on American labor history which focused on the New York City labor movement of the 1830s.[66] In this way, part of the historical development which Wilentz' *Chants Democratic* explores was introduced as a minor influence on the developing labor tradition of German New York.

As recent refugees, the Turners naturally threw their first efforts into preparing for a new revolutionary outbreak in Europe, but they also expanded the scope of local Turner activities in ways reminiscent of the *Sozialreformers*. The first addition was (of course) a singing society, followed by a drama society, a German school, a rifle company, and a chess club. Before long it was possible for a resident of German New York to carry on an active *Vereinsleben* without ever leaving the Turnverein. About two hundred German New Yorkers joined the new *Verein* in its first year. It had over five hundred members by 1853.[67]

The republican principles of the Turners carried them into the struggle against slavery. Many followed the antislavery impulse into the Republican Party. Their renown as effective fighters also brought them out of German New York to act as defense squads for antislavery meetings in English-speaking sections of the city.[68] The Turners' main struggle, however, took place within the German community itself. There they had to combat the active proslavery propaganda of the *Staats-Zeitung* and the efforts of the Democratic Party machine, which included the Sozialreformers and some of the fraternal orders.[69] These groups used their own versions of republican ideology and even social republicanism to attack abolitionism and the Republican Party as capitalist conspiracies designed to drive down the cost of labor and thus to intensify the exploitation of immigrant "wage slaves." Whatever success the Turners may have had in generating antislavery sentiment (and they claimed a great deal), it was never translated into a Republican majority in German New York.[70] They were sufficiently successful, however, to lay claim to a fair amount of Republican patronage in later years. Leading Turners filled posts in the County Coroner's office and the New York office of the Internal Revenue, among other places.[71]

While the reform impetus of the Sozialreformers and the Turners lost much of its strength after their first years, these two successful social organizations were tremendously important in establishing and maintaining a generally pro-radical climate of opinion in German New York. It was in this atmosphere that the German-American trade union movement of New York developed and the seeds of a socialist movement began to germinate in American soil.

Full employment and satisfaction with the gains of 1850 had proved the downfall of most of the German unions, whose members appear to have envisioned them as temporary organizations designed to achieve immediate goals. The continuing boom offered little incentive to further organization in 1851 and 1852, but continued inflation began to reduce the value of wages. The rate of inflation began to increase sharply towards the end of 1852. By the beginning of 1854 the newspapers reported that the cost of necessities had increased 30 percent in eight months.[72]

As the situation worsened, first the *Staats-Zeitung* and then the New York *Times* urged employers to raise wages voluntarily in order to not provoke strikes.[73]

Everyone was concerned about the effects of inflation, but most of the "respectable" elements publicly worried more about unions and strikes than about the workers' living conditions. Even Weitling and his *Arbeiterbund* were now saying that communism was the only solution to the workers' plight and had joined the opposition to wage-conscious unions and strikes.[74] There was, however, a new faction in German New York ready to urge militant action.

In November 1851, a close political associate of Karl Marx named Joseph Weydemeyer had arrived in New York. He was determined to create a revolutionary workers' movement by spreading the new ideas of "scientific" socialism to America. A former Prussian army officer converted to socialism, Weydemeyer had had extensive editorial experience during the German Revolution and he plunged into leftist journalism in New York. Only two months off the boat, he took over a small atheist paper, *Luzifer*, and renamed it *die Revolution*. It died after two issues. Weydemeyer had also, however, begun to write for the new *Turn-Zeitung*, and he reached many German workers through its pages. Soon, the Turners were publishing Weydemeyer on "The Dictatorship of the Proletariat" and the meaning of "class consciousness."[75] In these and other writings, Weydemeyer, like all good Marxists, stressed the importance of trade unions and strikes as basic forms of class struggle.

Weydemeyer also moved to generate a revolutionary political organization. He considered trying to take over the *Arbeiterbund*, but Marx had advised him to avoid Weitling, so he joined the *Sozialreformassoziation* instead.[76] In six months he had enough followers to set up a small Marxist club called the *Proletarierbund*, which was influential in Turner circles.[77] He became even better known when he became the leading publicist for the defendants in the notorious Cologne anti-communist trial of 1852–53 and was given access to the pages of the literary newspaper, the *Belletristisches Journal*, for his campaign. By the spring of 1853, therefore, as an influential journalist with a small organized following in the reviving labor movement, he was ready to try to create a new, militant labor organization.

The German trade unionists, who had allowed their unions to lapse into dormancy, or had only maintained them as mutual benefit societies, began to plan a spring organizing campaign during the winter of 1852–53. While the *Arbeiterbund* planned a fund-raising banquet for a renewal of the German Revolution (the *Staats-Zeitung* reported that they "spent more on beer than on revolution"),[78] the Marxists were meeting with the trade union leaders. Even as the first strikes were getting underway they planned to set up a new central body for the German workers. The unions and strikes that followed involved dozens of trades, starting with the German hatmakers' unsuccessful strike for a 12 percent raise. The carpenters and other construction workers were more successful, as were the gilders, typesetters, piano-makers, gold workers, and engravers. The tailors again had the best organization, with shop and district committees in addition to a central office. Even the German waiters organized a union with six or seven hundred members and won a raise from $15 to $18 a month. The German cigar-makers also organized their first real trade union in 1853. At the request of the Marxists (who also wanted to organize English-speaking workers), the cigarmakers set up an English-speaking section of their new union. All of the new and revived unions had a much more clearly trade-union/wage-oriented character than their 1850 predecessors which had stressed cooperatives and mutual benefits.[79]

In the midst of this fervent activity, on March 15, 1853, Weydemeyer and his colleagues put out a call:

> To the Workers of All Trades: For a broad workers' alliance. Not only to win a wage increase in each work place or to forge a pure political union. No, now is the time to create a platform on a modern basis and recommend practical ways to achieve our goals.[80]

Some 800 German American workers responded to this call for a "practical" organization, including a large number of Weitling's followers.[81] They founded the *Amerikanische Arbeiterbund* (American Workers' League) on March 21, in close association with the house-painters', tailors', shoemakers', cabinetmakers', and cigarmakers' unions, the Sozialreformers, and the Turners.[82] Proclaiming the irreconcilability of capital and labor, the "practical" platform focused on a ten-hour day and child-labor laws, a homestead act, the creation of a mechanic's lien law to protect workers, and similar reforms to be implemented by a Labor Party.[83] Weitling did not join, of course, and denounced this platform as reformist, having nothing to do with the "real emancipation of the workers." Even the Marxist historian, Hermann Schlüter, concluded that the new program "poured a goodly portion of petty-bourgeois water into the proletarian wine."[84] Despite the watering of the wine, it seems to have been just what the German proletariat of New York ordered. They flocked to the new Amerikanische Arbeiterbund.

The new League actively encouraged the unions and participated in some of the strikes which followed in the spring and summer of 1853. Despite the influence of the Marxists on the League, however, they were forced to contend with a strong strain of sentimental reformism typical of nineteenth-century Romanticism. Weydemeyer reported to Marx that he had had to smuggle himself into a meeting of the committee drafting the organization's constitution to oppose "as far as possible" the sentimentality of the proposed draft "so that the final product wouldn't be too pitiful [jammerlich]."[85] The sentimental tide was only temporarily stemmed. The Amerikanische Arbeiterbund suffered heavy membership losses about a month later when many of the sentimentalists went over to a newly formed Freethinkers' Society.

German unions, however, continued to form and to affiliate with the League, until both were brought down by the economic crisis of 1854–55. At the time of the crash, late in 1854, Weydemeyer and the Marxists were trying to get the League and the German-speaking unions to merge with their English-speaking equivalents in an attempt to create class-wide organizations. This attempt to implement the slogan "workers of all tongues unite" carried unity too far for most German-American workers. Working-class unity in New York, after all, would have reduced them to a tongue-tied minority in a union dominated by other ethnic groups which the Germans considered culturally backwards at best. Weydemeyer resigned in disgust and soon left New York. But by that time, the economic crisis had wiped out most of the unions. The League was being kept alive only by its mutual benefit and singing societies.[86]

Unlike the labor upsurge of 1850, the labor movement in German New York did not die from lack of interest. It was crushed by mass unemployment on a scale which made survival rather than organization the most pressing concern for New York's German workers. The *Staats-Zeitung* reported over 3,000 unemployed skilled workers in the mostly German 11th Ward alone and called for public works projects.[87]

In January 1855, radical saloonkeeper Erhard Richter (who had led the *Deutscher Arbeiter Verein* of 1848) and two Freethinker leaders, Doctors Schramm and Försch, addressed a large protest meeting of the unemployed in City Hall Park. There, they too called for a broad municipal public works program to alleviate the mass suffering.[88] In the *Republik der Arbeiter*, Weitling waxed eloquent in his protest: "Need pounds with heavy fists on the door of public attention, which has offered only beggars-soup in response. Beggars-soup! Beggars-soup!! In America it has already come to that."[89]

In the mid-1850s, German New York, like the rest of America, was in the throes of economic and social flux. Independent artisans and small factory owners who survived the panic of 1854–55 were faced with another major panic in 1857. Many businesses did not survive and their owners were driven down into the ranks of the wage earners, though many still hoped to rise again. Panics were times of opportunity as well, however, and the more solvent among the German employers expanded their businesses at bargain prices, picking clean the corpses of their failed rivals. By the end of the decade, many of the more successful businessmen from German New York had accumulated substantial fortunes and had risen well above the nebulous line which divides the middle from the upper classes. In the 1860s they would move to assume the social and political prerogatives which they felt were owed them by virtue of their new status.

The short-lived prosperity after 1855 did little to revive the German labor movement, and the slavery question absorbed most of the energies of those who were reform activists. The second panic, in 1857, did stimulate something of a revival in the way of labor reform organizations. In October 1857, Weydemeyer's associate, Albert Komp, gathered some of his friends and fellow radical 'forty-eighters' into a *Kommunisten Klub*, dedicated to free thought and the equality of all mankind. Once again, as in the days of the League of Exiles, they mixed "Strivings for German unity and freedom, for the republic and the brotherhood of peoples, for free thought, primitive Christianity and communism."[90] The thirty members of the new club (including the Freethinker Adolf Sorge, who seems to have moved towards Marxism through this association) joined with the English-speaking labor leader James Maguire in organizing mass demonstrations of the unemployed. On November 5, 1857, 15,000 unemployed English and German-speaking workers marched from Tompkins Square in the heart of German New York to Wall Street, carrying banners reading "Work-Arbeit" and chanting "we want work."[91] With this encouragement, the Kommunisten Klub took the lead in reviving the dormant Amerikanische Arbeiterbund. But the revived League was much more successful in attracting all sorts of reformers (including a contingent of Fourrierist utopian socialists) than it was in appealing to the German workers of New York. Without Weydemeyer's leadership and confronted by prestigious social republican activists like Gustave Struve, the Marxists were unable to dominate the increasingly reformist League. Under Struve's leadership the League took on a Jacobin cast, with members addressing each other as "citizen" in the French revolutionary tradition.[92] The Marxists even had to accept the addition of an anti-communist declaration in the League platform in 1859. By that time the League included both a Republican Club and a Consumer Cooperative Union, but it failed to attract any of the trade unions which had begun to revive once more with the return of prosperity. Marxists later claimed that the League soon died from lack of relevance.[93]

The unions had been slow to revive even after the economy recovered from the 1857 panic. All that was left of the militant cabinetmakers' union, by the spring of 1858, was a small mutual benefit society with forty to forty-five members. The cigarmakers were likewise reduced.[94] This time the old Sozialreformassoziation took the lead and called on workers of all trades to meet in its hall. The piano-makers and furniture-makers were first to heed the call and soon there were German trade unions and associations flourishing in New York once more.[95] Once again an economic boom was followed by a period of widespread unemployment as the country drifted into civil war. The German trade unions of New York again evaporated. This time, however, there were some survivors — the capmakers', cigarpackers', tailors', and shoemakers' organizations.[96]

While only a core of four unions survived the economic crises of the late 1850s, and all the efforts to create a labor movement seemed to have been unsuccessful, thousands of German-American workers had participated in the struggles of the decade. Building on European experience and traditions, they had created a German-American labor movement. Despite its weaknesses, this movement had undergone an important evolution and had laid the foundation for the future.

In political terms, German-American workers had moved from the flaming romanticism of Hermann Kriege, through the utopianism of Wilhelm Weitling, to the marxian socialism of Joseph Weydemeyer with its stress on organizing class-conscious trade unions. Although Weydemeyer gave up on German New York, concluding that in America "the workers are incipient Bourgeois and feel themselves to be such,"[97] his "proletarian propaganda" would be remembered by New York's German workers as class lines hardened over the next few years.

The unions themselves had evolved rapidly from temporary instruments for achieving immediate results into organizations which were intended to be permanent institutions, devised for extended struggle. Even in the economic crises which broke the unions in the winters of 1854–55 and 1857–58, the German labor movement of New York had pioneered in organizing the unemployed — a form of organization which would culminate in the famous Tompkins Square Riot of 1874.

Although this first German-American labor movement failed to keep its organizations alive through the depressions of the 1850s, its veterans later applied its lessons to create New York City's powerful German-American labor and socialist organizations of the 1860s and 1870s.

Samuel Gompers called them the most "virile and resourceful" part of a New York City organization he termed the "cradle of the labor movement." Gompers also attributed both his own labor education and a formative influence on the early American Federation of Labor to New York's German-American labor movement.[98] The veterans of the early German-American labor movement in New York thus provided a crucial link between the late nineteenth-century American labor movement and the radicalism of the European socialists of the 1840s and later. Given the immigrant basis of so much of America's urban and industrial work force after 1850 and the influence of German-Americans on so many other foreign language speaking immigrants, this link was arguably the true taproot of the American labor movement.

Notes

A version of this paper was published in *Labour History* (Winter 1989).

1. Including works by Herbert Gutman, David Montgomery, Alan Dawley, Bruce Laurie, Leon Fink, Nick Salvatore, and many others. Particularly significant here is Sean Wilentz, *Chants Democratic* (New York, 1984).
2. This is a rough estimate based on data from the 1850 census and my own samples from the 1850 census manuscripts. About 42 percent of the city's residents were under twenty years old (*The Seventh Census of the United States: 1850*, 88–89), but only about 20 percent of the city's German-born population was under twenty, see Stanley Nadel, *Little Germany: Ethnicity, Religion, and Class in New York City, 1845–1880* (Urbana, IL, forthcoming). Assuming that the city's Irishborn and other immigrant groups were demographically not too dissimilar from the Germans leads to the conclusion that the city's native-born adults numbered only 107,489 that year while adult immigrants from abroad numbered 188,115.
3. These calculations are drawn from Robert Ernst's retabulation of the 1855 manuscript census: *Immigrant Life in New York City, 1825-1860* (New York, 1949), 214-21. Discrepancies between his retabulation for immigrants and the original tabulation for the entire population make this only an approximation, but it should not be too far off.
4. *Ibid.*
5. William H. Sewell, Jr., *Work and Revolution in France* (Cambridge, New York, and Melbourne, 1980), 153-154.
6. Arnold Ruge, *Zwei Jahre in Paris* (Leipzig, 1846), 53, 431; and Karl Gutzkow, *Parisier Briefe* (Leipzig, 1842), 276.
7. Sewell, *Work and Revolution in France*, 178; Richard M. Andrews, "Social Structures, Political Elites and Ideology in Revolutionary Paris, 1792–94: A Critical Evaluation of Albert Soboul's *Les sans-culottes parisiens en l'an II*," *Journal of Social History* 19 (1985), 71-112.
8. Carl Wittke, *The Utopian Communist* (Baton Rouge, 1950), 11-30.
9. Sewell, *Work and Revolution in France*, 158-159.
10. *National Workman*, October 27, 1866.
11. Sewell, *Work and Revolution in France*, 194-200.
12. *Ibid.*, 210-214.
13. Christopher Johnson, *Utopian Communism in France: Cabet and the Icarians, 1839-1851* (Ithaca, 1974), 153-174.

14. *Ibid.*, 219–220.
15. Werner Kowalski, *Vorgeschichte und Entstehung des Bundes der Gerechten* (E. Berlin, 1962), 178.
16. Ernst Schraepler, *Handwerkerbünde und Arbeitervereine, 1830–1853* (Berlin, 1972), 41–50.
17. *Ibid.*, 31.
18. *Ibid.*, 52–99; Wittke, *The Utopian Communist*, 20–22, 29, 34, 39, 48, 101, 108, 111, 115–116, 122–126, 189; Schraepler, *Handwerkerbünde*, 41–78, 98–103, 117, 122–123, 138–139, 151–163, 181–202, 299–300, 316, 335–336, 384, 432; P. Hartwig Bopp, *Die Entwicklung des deutschen Handwerksgesellentums im 19. Jahrhundert* (Paderborn, 1932), 99–132; and Kowalski, *Vorgeschichte*, 57–81.
19. New Yorker *Staats-Zeitung*, April 28, 1852.
20. *Staats-Zeitung*, January 31 and February 2, 1846.
21. *Staats-Zeitung*, June 27, 1946.
22. *Staats-Zeitung*, January 3, 1851; Philip S. Foner and Brewster Chamberlin, eds., *Friedrich A. Sorge's Labor Movement in the United States* (New York, 1977), 76–77; Herman Schlüter, *Die Anfänge der deutschen Arbeiterbewegung in America* (Stuttgart, 1907) 23–25.
23. Schlüter, *Anfänge*, 24; and Stanley Nadel, *Little Germany*.
24. Wilentz, *Chants Democratic*, 326–362.
25. Foner and Chamberlin, *Friedrich A. Sorge's Labor Movement*, 77; Schlüter, *Anfänge*, 28–40; and Wittke, *Utopian Communist*, 116–119.
26. Schlüter, *Anfänge*, 19–28.
27. *Staats-Zeitung*, January 10, 1846.
28. Schlüter, *Anfänge*, 40–41.
29. *Ibid.*, 44–45.
30. *Ibid.*, 45–47.
31. *Staats-Zeitung*, August 23, 1846.
32. Schlüter, *Anfänge*, 49–56; Wittke, *Utopian Communist*, 120–123.
33. *Staats-Zeitung*, May 13, 1848.
34. *Staats-Zeitung*, June 17, 1848.
35. *Staats-Zeitung*, March 2, 1850; Schlüter, *Anfänge*, 78.
36. Wittke, *Utopian Communist*, 132–133.
37. Schlüter, *Anfänge*, 89.
38. Foner, ed., *Sorge*, 89–91; Schlüter, *Anfänge*, 71–79; Wittke, *Utopian Communist*, 220–225; *Republik der Arbeiter*, January, 1850.
39. Johnson, *Utopian Communism*, 48, 93–95, 100, 142, 173–174, 189, 195, 214–218, 231–235, 254–255; Edward Berenson, *Populist Religion and Left-wing Politics in France, 1830–1852* (Princeton, 1984), especially 37–46; K. Steven Vincent, *Pierre-Joseph Proudhon and the Rise of French Republican Socialism* (Oxford, 1984), 33–118.
40. Schlüter, *Anfänge*, 58–59; *Staats-Zeitung*, March 2, 1850.
41. Schlüter, *Anfänge*, 102.
42. Vincent, *Proudhon*, 138–140; Sewell, *Work and Revolution*, 232–236, 243–255, 265–272.
43. *Staats-Zeitung*, January 26, February 9, March 2, 1850.
44. *Staats-Zeitung*, March 16, 1850.
45. *Ibid.*
46. *Staats-Zeitung*, April 27, May 11, May 18, 1850; *Tribune*, April 9, April 20, April 23, April 24, July 26, 1850; New York *Herald*, March 11, March 13, April 12, 1850; New York *Evening Post*, April 17, April 18, 1850; Schlüter, *Die Anfänge*, 79–80.
47. Schlüter, *Anfänge*, 79–80.
48. *Staats-Zeitung*, May 7, May 31, June 8, 1850; Wittke, *Utopian Communist*, 190; New York *Tribune*, April 24, July 3, 1850; Schlüter, *Anfänge*, 131; Foner, ed., *Sorge*, 91–92.
49. New York *Tribune*, April 24, August 15, 1850; Schlüter, *Anfänge*, 131.
50. Foner, ed., *Sorge*, 93.
51. *Staats-Zeitung*, March 2, July 27, August 2, August 10, August 17, August 24, 1850; New York *Herald*, July 23, July 25, 1850; New York *Tribune*, July 25, August 6, August 7, December 16, 1850.

52. *Staats-Zeitung*, August 24, 1850.
53. Wittke, *Utopian Communist*, 188–275.
54. *Ibid.*, Schlüter, *Anfänge*, 79–127; Foner, ed., *Sorge*, 89–94.
55. The *Turn-Zeitung*'s "History of the Turners" described the Turner membership in quite limited terms. Its opening, "We are united under the name of Turners, not as artisans, wage earners or as day laborers, but as spiritual people . . . ," did not even allow for the possibility of members who might be from other social strata. *Turn-Zeitung* 1 (1851–1852), 274–276.
56. Schraepler, *Handwerkerbünde*, 224–232.
57. H. C. A. Metzner *Geschichte des Turner-Bundes* (Indianapolis, 1874) 1–20.
58. The story was written by Wilhelm Schlüter, later editor of the *New Yorker Demokrat* and active Turner. *Staats-Zeitung*, October 17, 1846.
59. *Staats-Zeitung*, November 18, 1848.
60. Schlüter, *Anfänge*, 199–200; Metzner, *Turner-Bundes*, 21–23.
61. *Turn-Zeitung*, 1:297 (November 1, 1853).
62. *Ibid.*, 1:10.
63. *Ibid.*, 1:13–14.
64. *Ibid.*, 1:325, 329–348.
65. *Ibid.*, 1:329–348; 18–19; 294.
66. *Ibid.*, 1:187–188, 203–204.
67. Schlüter, *Anfänge*, 199–200; Metzner, *Turner-Bundes*, 21–23; and Turnverein records, Scholer Collection (New York Public Library).
68. New York *Tribune*, February 24, 1854; and Bruce C. Levine, "In the Spirit of 1848" (Ph.D. dissertation, University of Rochester, 1980).
69. At first the *Staats-Zeitung* simply took an anti-free-soil position and favored colonization, the resettling of freed slaves in Africa (April 1, 1852 and July 6, 1853), but it denied that it supported slavery (May 16 and June 6, 1855). When some southern Turners split with the national organization over its pro-abolition stand, the *Staats-Zeitung* tried to promote split in New York, too (November 11, 1855). By 1856, however, the *Staats-Zeitung* was referring to its opponents' "Niggerblatter" [Nigger Papers] (August 26, 1856) and to "black Republican Nigger love" (September 26, 1856).
70. Nadel, *Little Germany*, ch. 7.
71. Former Union General Franz Sigel, for example, was appointed assessor at the Internal Revenue Office in New York in the 1870s (Pickard Typescript [Scholer Collection, New York Public Library], 221A) and Dr. Scholer of the Turnverein, who was also a Republican Party activist, was later a New York County Coroner.
72. New York *Herald*, November 20, 1852; New York *Sun*, December 3, 1852; February 22, 1854.
73. *Staats-Zeitung*, April 15, 1853; New York *Times*, November 10, 1853.
74. Schlüter, *Anfänge*, 88–93.
75. *Turn-Zeitung*, 1:10, 18–19, 114–115.
76. Franz Mehring, "Neue Beitrage Zur Biographie von Karl Marx und Friedrich Engels," *Die Neue Zeit*, XXV (1907), 99.
77. Karl Obermann, *Joseph Weydemeyer* (Berlin, 1968), 270.
78. *Staats-Zeitung*, March 4, 1853; Wittke, *Utopian Communist*, 213.
79. *Staats-Zeitung*, March 3, April 1, April 8, May 6, 1853; Schlüter, *Anfänge*, 132–134; Obermann, *Wedemeyer*, 297–303.
80. *Staats-Zeitung*, March 18, 1853.
81. Obermann, *Wedemeyer*, 298; Wittke, *Utopian Communist*, 215.
82. Schlüter, *Anfänge*, 138.
83. *Turn-Zeitung*, 1 (June 1, 1850), 220–221; die *Reform*, October 12, 1853.
84. Schlüter, *Anfänge*, 135–139; Obermann, *Weydemeyer*, 298–300.
85. Obermann, *Weydemeyer*, 316.
86. Obermann, *Weydemeyer*, 318–340; Schlüter, *Anfänge*, 135–156.
87. *Staats-Zeitung*, December 21, 1854 and January 12, 1855.

88. *Staats-Zeitung*, January 9, 1855.
89. *Ibid*.
90. See excerpts from the Club's statutes in Obermann, *Weydemeyer*, 345; and Schlüter, *Anfänge*, 161–162.
91. New York *Times*, November 3, 1857; New York *Herald*, November 3 and November 6, 1857; New York *Tribune*, November 6, 1857.
92. On "Citizen" see, *Sociale Republik*, September 11, 1858. For an extensive glorification of Robespierre, see *ibid*., July 16, 1859.
93. Schlüter, *Anfänge*, 165–174, Obermann, *Weydemeyer*, 344–357.
94. *Staats-Zeitung*, April 26 and May 5, 1858.
95. *Staats-Zeitung*, March 7, April 21, August 3, November 10, November 26, 1859; New York *Sun*, March 11, March 22, March 25, April 2, April 29, 1859, New York *Tribune*, September 28, 1859; April 3 and April 30, 1860; Schlüter, *Anfänge*, 176–177.
96. Lawrence Costello, "The New York City Labor Movement, 1861–1873" (Ph.D. dissertation, Columbia University, 1967), 173; New York *Sun*, May 21, June 4, October 28, October 30, November 8, November 18, November 19, 1862; New York *Herald*, December 8, 1863.
97. Obermann, *Weydemeyer*, 347.
98. Samuel Gompers, *Seventy Years of Life and Labor* (New York, 1925), 47, 61; Lawrence Costello, "The New York Labor Movement," 165–185; Nadel, *Little Germany*, ch. 7.

PART TWO

Early Twentieth-Century
Immigration

SELMA BERROL

Introduction: Early Twentieth-Century Immigration

Summarizing and synthesizing immigrant history is dangerous. At the very least, it is essential to recognize that each group brought its own historical, cultural, and economic baggage and that their experience in the United States varied with the time at which they came and the place where they settled. But one generalization is valid; every group of newcomers, to a greater or lesser extent, had to cope with hostility from nativists in the larger American society, previous arrivals in their own group, more settled immigrant communities, or all three. Such conflict especially characterized New York City, which grew from just under two million people in 1880 to just under seven million in 1930. By this date, three-quarters of the city's residents were immigrants and their children, mostly from the great southern and eastern European exodus of the past five decades. The conflict that resulted is the theme these four studies have in common.

David Mauk's work on the Norwegian community of Brooklyn and Mary Elizabeth Brown's piece on Italo-Irish hostilities in the archdiocese of New York are examples of intragroup difficulties; Andrew Yox is more concerned with the pummeling of the German-American community of Buffalo at the hands of patriots during World War I. Where does James Dorman's work on the "Immigrant/Ethnic Theatre in Gilded

Age New York" fit in? His most interesting paper is not about conflict but rather its resolution, expressed by his idea that benign stereotypes (of the stage Irishman, Jew, etc.) blunted nativist and intergroup hostility and thus helped assimilation. The latter point is the link between Dorman and his fellow authors. Attacks from established members of their own group and/or the larger society as well as modifying influences such as the ethnic theatre hastened the newcomers' adoption of American values, attitudes and appearances, thus speeding up the all-important process of assimilation.

This is no small matter. One has only to look at the travails of other nations with large minority groups to realize how fortunate the United States has been. The reasons why we did not become permanently fragmented into hostile enclaves, of course, go far beyond the scope of these papers. But the pressure to accommodate, whether coming from Catholic leaders, more assimilated members of their own group, or American nativists, coupled with the image-making role of the theatre, undoubtedly hastened and eased the process.

Leaving Dorman's work aside for the moment, it would be safe to say that the first arrivals in each of the groups discussed here had to fight a two-front war. In addition to their difficulties with the Irish-controlled Catholic church, for example, Italian peasants from *Mezzogiorno* were often exploited and scorned by middle-class members of the established Italian community. This was even more the case for the working class Russo-Polish Jews who were often locked in combat with the settled bourgeois German Jewish community as well as feeling the effects of anti-Semitism. As Mauk found was true for the Norwegians, social class and old world experiences created a gulf between members of the same ethnic group that took years to overcome. But it did finally happen, and perhaps sooner than it would have if the earlier arrivals had unquestioningly embraced the newcomers and forged an ethnocentric solidarity that positioned them against the larger society.

Instead, members of the established group, in spite of the anger aroused by their criticism and snobbery, became role models for their less fortunate brethren. In an attempt to emulate the German Jewish garment manufacturers who were their employers (and often their exploiters), for example, Russo-Polish Jews saved their pennies and became contractors themselves. In other ways Brown's Italian Catholics and Mauk's Norwegians learned from the brethren with whom they fought but who were also their instructors. Dorman's ethnic theatre people were even better teachers; by using a most valuable tool, humor, they educated all Americans (or at least those lucky enough to be able to see a vaudeville show), about each other. Andrew Yox's Germans, unfortunately, were subjected to harsher pressures from outside their community during a period of war-induced hysteria. One hopes that such an experience will not be repeated. But one must also recognize that it had the same effect as gentler methods did for other groups, that is, to hasten their assimilation into the larger society.

4

Mobilization and Conflict: The Background and Social History of the Norwegian Colony in Brooklyn to 1910

The early 1890s saw the birth of community awareness in Brooklyn's Norwegian settlement. Previously, the elite of the older enclave in Manhattan had directed public affairs for metropolitan area Norwegians. In the 1890s, however, Brooklyn leaders formed a coalition of middle- and working-class groups to oppose the Manhattan leadership. During a protracted series of newspaper debates, the new leaders defined the Brooklyn settlement's social-economic values by attacking the other colony's elite. The Manhattan group, in their view, represented all that was outmoded and reactionary: old-country aristocracy, Norway's political subservience to Sweden, high-church Lutheranism, and patronizing charity to needy countrymen. Since Brooklyn's Norwegians rejected these vestiges of the past, coalition leaders claimed, they had to mobilize for their independence and assume responsibility for their own problem and institutions. Between 1890 and 1910, broadening public support for their coalition initiatives gave proof of the group's growing willingness to chart its own course. That support showed that the cru-

cible of conflict and mobilization had propelled the Brooklyn settlement into community awareness.

The small settlement that had developed near Manhattan's south-
eastern waterfront between the 1830s and the 1890s directly preceded
and crucially affected the evolution of the Brooklyn colony.[1] According
to an America-letter from the 1830s, the Manhattan group was so harbor-
related that the easiest way to make contact with compatriots then was
to go to the waterfront and shout, "Swedish Norwegian man." Soon
a Norwegian sailor would appear and direct the immigrant to colony
artisans and boarding houses.[2] Between the 1840s and 1860s the more
prominent or socially active joined in the creation of pan-Scandinavian
institutions — two newspapers, a social club, a Lutheran congregation,
and a Methodist seamen's mission. When the number of Norwegians
frequenting the city could support a separate associational life in the
1870s, resident leaders formed purely national organizations. Our
Savior's Norwegian Lutheran Church, the Norwegian Society, Nordmandenes Sangforening, and *Nordiske Blade* made the Norwegians a
much more self-sufficient group. The inter-Scandinavian societies continued to exist but for most Norwegians became a supplementary re-
source used when the exceptional amounts of money or manpower required could not be obtained from their own sources of support. [3]

The Norwegian settlements in the New York area grew rapidly between 1870 and 1890. The table below shows the Norwegian-born populations of New York (the incorporated section of Manhattan) and the
city of Brooklyn during those twenty years.[4]

	New York	*Brooklyn*
1870	372	301
1880	893	874
1890	1,455	4,508

Even in 1870 the Manhattan-based ethnic organizations and businesses could scarcely have survived without drawing on the Norwegian
population across the East River. During the next ten years both settlements more than doubled in size, but the Brooklyn group grew somewhat more rapidly. The turning point in the relative size of the two
enclaves came sometime in the 1880s. By 1890 the Norwegian population of Brooklyn had increased by a phenomenal 416 percent to more
than three times the size of the Manhattan settlement.

In 1874 Jørgen Gjerdrum, a visiting Norwegian who sent travel letters
to *Dagbladet* in Christiania, reported the claim of the local consul and
the Lutheran minister that New York and Brooklyn contained ten times

the Norwegians indicated in the 1870 census. The two local leaders' assertion might appear to be an unfounded boast unless, as seems likely, they had difficulty in distinguishing between permanent and temporary residents in the settlements. Gjerdrum noted that most countrymen he met in the city were either seamen or tradesmen serving them. Other observers confirmed his impression that mariners were the largest group of Norwegian wage-earners. Census enumerators could easily under-count a group whose occupation made their presence in the city inter-mittent. The crews of an estimated 1,200 Norwegian ships that entered the harbor annually added to the day-to-day population of the settle-ments. Moreover, thousands of Norwegian sailors jumped ship in Amer-ican ports. While only around 4,000 deserted in the United States be-tween 1856 and 1865, well over 19,000 did so from 1876 to 1890. As early as 1871, the Director of Norway's Central Bureau of Statistics, A. N. Kier, blamed most of the rise in Norwegian desertions on growing trade with just one city— New York. Finally, the 1880s witnessed the highest rates of Norwegian emigration to America before 1900, and the over-whelming majority entered the country through New York, where many remained at least temporarily with friends or relatives. Thus, the leaders' claim of a substantially larger population may have had a basis in fact.[5]

In Manhattan, Our Savior's congregation and the members of the Norwegian Society, representative of the more settled part of the colony, accepted the leadership of the most prominent local Norwegians. Gjerdrum's status as a well-known businessman from the old country gave him easy access to this elite, whose institutions he judged by the standards expected at home. His sense of superiority is evident in his remark that, although the Lutheran minister lacked "Latin training after Norwegian conceptions," he was *"mirabile dictu* — in possession of adequate culture to carry on his work." Because Gjerdrum thought such a small group might easily disperse in the metropolis, he approved of the Norwegian Society founded by tradesmen and professionals to knit the membership together by providing sick benefits, social affairs, and a Norwegian-language library.[6]

Disturbed by the seamen's immorality, Gjerdrum found some com-fort in the efforts of Baptist temperance men who ran a Manhattan boardinghouse for Norwegian mariners. In fact, the Methodist Bethel-ship mission and Our Savior's Lutheran Church, both purely Nor-wegian by this time, also attempted to reform the morals of Norwegians on the waterfront. In the 1870s and 1880s a group of reformers led by members of the Manhattan colony's business and religious elite com-bined to handle the mounting problems of unemployment, poverty, and sickness among Norwegian immigrants. By mobilizing the influence and assets of the Swedish-Norwegian consul, the Seamen's Mission Society in the old country, and the Norwegian Lutheran Synod in the Midwest, they founded a variety of social institutions with close links to orthodox state-church Lutheranism and shipping interests in Norway. A seamen's church, a temperance home, and a hiring office addressed the material and spiritual problems of the merchant marine. The Norwegian Relief Society provided temporary housing and job counseling for the needy and homeless. The Norwegian Lutheran Deaconesses' Home and Hospital concerned itself with the full range of medical, religious, and social problems.[7]

Several factors made Brooklyn the new center of the metropolitan area's Norwegian population. According to the colony's amateur historians, many Norwegian Manhattanites followed the movement of shipping across the East River, although documenting their assertion through the census materials is difficult. The transference of the city's main dock area from Manhattan was undoubtedly decisive for a community whose economy had always rested on maritime activity. Most of the new arrivals crowded into the cheap housing near the ship basins in the Red Hook-Gowanus district, a low-lying unhealthy area notorious for its shabby tenement houses, seamen's bars, and high crime rate. Here mariners spent their pay in drinking and carousing after coastal or deep-water voyages or fell into the clutches of runners and boardinghouse masters. Here runaway sailors came on land and joined other Norwegians seeking work on the waterfront or in the construction trades.

But if living conditions were poor, employment prospects were good. Despite local and national economic fluctuations, work remained plentiful for both the skilled and the unskilled because of the city's tremendous growth. Brooklyn's total population more than doubled during these twenty years. Through the 1890s the city remained the preeminent Atlantic freight depot, receiving the cargo of nearly four thousand ships annually. Between 1881 and 1885 alone the housing built was "the equivalent of a city larger than Albany."[8]

Work was available in Brooklyn. However, R. S. N. Sartz, a Norwegian employed at Castle Garden in the 1880s, learned from years of experience that certain categories of his countrymen were among the least likely to find or keep jobs. Greenhorns who had occupational training, some savings, and connections in the colony could expect employment although their wages would probably be low until they learned the language and American work habits. Worse off were those, such as students, who arrived with no salable trade. Sartz found many unsuccessful immigrants in this group.

Still more pathetic were the Norwegians who came as impoverished steerage passengers. Without money to travel further inland, many of these people completely lost their sense of purpose. Sartz later commented, "Some of these quickly disappeared, while others reappeared at Castle Garden in the course of the year following to get free meals or other assistance. Their highest wish was to return to Norway, even if they had to arrive penniless. Returning home, however, proved impossible, and it seems likely that most of them died in poverty and were buried in unmarked graves on potter's field." The unfortunates among the poor or untrained, plus seamen suffering from alcoholism or hard times, filled to capacity the social institutions established by the Manhattan Colony's elite.[9]

On May 17, 1889 The Norwegian Society in Manhattan convinced the mayor and alderman to raise its flag over New York's City Hall in honor of Norwegian Constitution Day. Brooklyn's City Hall would have been a more appropriate place to raise the flag, however, since the hub of Norwegian community life had moved there, and the influence of the Manhattan-based organizations was already waning. The old community's leaders had already recognized the migration by locating all the charitable institutions across the East River, but by the nineties the Brooklyn colony had developed its own business district and societies that competed with those in the first settlement area. Brooklyn harbored not only most of the laboring population but also a middle class and its own emerging elite. Our Savior's Norwegian Lutheran Church, Bethelship Norwegian Methodist Church, and two newspapers were also now in Brooklyn. Of the organizations once located in Manhattan only the Norwegian Society and the consulate remained.[10]

Conflict between the leaders of the two settlement areas characterized the period from 1890 to 1910. The foundation of the Manhattan community's economy was shipping and a more or less transient population of mariners, but its associational life was dominated by businessmen with important commercial connections in Norway, long-established artisan-shopkeepers, and the consular circle. The consul and his family represented a transplanted segment of the old country's office-holding class which was dependent on the Swedish king for its authority.

The second settlement area had no representatives of this upper class. Moreover, in Brooklyn the mariners' mutual benefit society, The Norwegian-American Seamen's Association, was the dominant secular force. Founded by sea captains and former mariners making their livings as ship-chandlers, builders, and boardinghouse masters, the Association only faintly resembled a modern labor union, but sailors *were* the majority in its membership. Its social affairs were often brawling, and its socio-political attitudes seemed radical enough to the Manhattan leaders.[11]

The small businessmen who constituted the leadership of Brooklyn's Norwegian Singing Society and the layman-oriented Norwegian Trinity Lutheran Church generally shared the Association's views. After a series of disagreements with the executive board of the singing society in Manhattan, the choir members living in Brooklyn formed their own society in 1890. Pious captains and workers founded Trinity after the Norway-based Seamen's Mission Society ejected them from its church to better concentrate on serving Norwegian nationals in the old country's merchant marine. Naturally, Trinity's membership had at best mixed feelings toward representatives of Norway's state-supported high church Lutheranism, a power in Brooklyn through Our Savior's and the Seamen's Church.[12]

The Norwegian Society and consulate in Manhattan, allied with the older of the Norwegian newspapers and all Brooklyn's Lutheran pastors but Trinity's, formed a conservative consensus to resist the demands for change coming from the newer socio-economic groups. Sigurd Folkestad worked in Brooklyn around the turn of the century both as a journalist and as an assistant minister at the Seamen's Church. In his opinion the divisions among local Norwegians represented an exaggerated form of class differences inherited from mid-nineteenth century Norwegian society. "A group of the maritime interests' overclass gathered in New York through the years," explains Folkestad, "and how completely this little elite agreed in condemning 'le peuple,' 'the social dregs from Van Brunt Street'— the whole mass of unenlightened 'simple folk,' who at home in Norway always had to stand with hat in hand for the great, but who over here wanted to 'be something special'."[13]

Van Brunt Street in Brooklyn was the home of the Norwegian popular party. The seamen, workers, and aspiring businessmen there felt especially bitter about their former superiors' snobbery because it contradicted the American democratic principles "which the 'popular party' most quickly and best assimilated," according to Folkestad. Starting in 1891 the opposition to the Manhattan elite found a voice in the columns of a new newspaper, *Nordisk Tidende* (hereafter *NT*). The Seaman's Association, itself only a year old, helped finance the establishment of this second paper in reaction to the unfair treatment it felt the older paper, *Nordiske Blade*, had given seamen and laborers.[14] A critical reading of *NT*'s first twenty years suggests that more than battling the other Norwegian paper for subscribers and an enjoyment of bombastic rhetoric lay behind its opposition to the established powers inherited from the Manhattan enclave. *NT* consistently aligned itself with the wage-earners, small businessmen, and low-church laymen in the Association, Brooklyn's singing society, and Trinity Church. In short, the coalition of upstart interests was *NT*'s constituency. Editorials and articles sent in by the paper's supporters reveal their agenda, as well as their targets and possible motivations.

NT's constituency portrayed itself as democratic and nationalist. Trumpeting its belief in freedom and self-determination, *NT* campaigned for "the clean flag"— Norway's flag with the rectangular symbol of the union with Sweden removed. The paper gleefully announced that the Seamen's Association had expunged the union mark from its flag and sent the offensive symbol of tyranny to the Norwegian parliament with a call for full national independence. Through *Nordiske Blade* the conservative consensus registered shock at such lack of deference for constituted authority and ridiculed the Association's belief that the parliament was interested in its opinion. Of course, these reactions suited *NT*'s constituency very well, since they provided "proof" that the local conservatives were mindless followers of aristocratic tradition.[15]

On the local front *NT*'s supporters agitated to have the annual Constitution Day celebrations moved across the river from Manhattan, claiming that was Brooklyn's right as the home of the largest colony. Their local patriotism was probably strengthened by the knowledge that their businesses would profit from having the metropolitan area's Norwegian population gather on their home ground for the festivities. After the Norwegian Society refused to move its celebration, they arranged their own and, moreover, initiated a Leif Erikson Day parade through the Brooklyn business district. When the Manhattan group predicted the failure of Leif Erikson Day in the columns of *Nordiske Blade* and declined to participate, *NT* called the Society and newspaper reactionary organizations. Trinity Church's most prominent layman, Gabriel Fedde, used *NT*'s columns to attack high-church theology and conservatives' opposition to religious crusades.[16]

NT's constituency also attacked the welfare institutions set up by the Manhattan group. Throughout its first decade *NT* frequently printed revelations of alleged mismanagement of funds or mistreatment of clients at the hospital, the seamen's home, and the shelter for the homeless. The root of these complaints was usually that the directors of the institutions behaved in an arrogant, patronizing manner towards seamen and poor immigrants, and showed more interest in the institution's welfare than the clients'. These stories not only sold papers but gained broad support from the enclave's working class, which often sent in letters confirming *NT*'s point-of-view. When the Seamen's church removed its announcements from *NT* and refused to have the "scandalous" paper in its reading room, *NT* reported the church's actions and insisted that institutions supported by public donations had to be open for the public's examination.[17] *NT*'s concern for the public may have been genuine, but both its editorials and the articles by its supporters create the impression of resentment for institutions outside local control. In 1894-1895, *NT*'s constituency established a home-grown hostel for the homeless and a seamen's employment office independent of the Seamen's Mission Society.[18]

During the next two to three years, the conflict between the conservatives and *NT*'s supporters grew more intense. Because the two newspapers were the public focus of debate, the conservative faction blamed much of the trouble on *NT*'s mishandling of colony issues. So, when *Nordiske Blade* began to fail economically in 1897 because of the competition for readers, its owner established a stock company and hired as editor the chief stockholder, a local physician, who promptly went into battle under the conservative banner. *NT* not only survived the assault but prospered. On the other hand, the doctor-editor tired of the fight and returned to Norway. The most concerted attempt to reduce *NT*'s influence came in 1906 after *NT* supported the crew of a Norwegian ship in their claim that assistant minister Folkestad had unfairly excluded them from the Seamen's Church. A group of conservatives headed by high-church ministers bought *Nordiske Blade* and installed Folkestad as editor. The new venture did not succeed, however, for a number of reasons. To the surprise of almost everyone, Folkestad weakened *Nordiske Blade's* usefulness as a conservative organ by attacking the Seamen's Church with arguments similar to *NT*'s. Probably the most important cause for the paper's failure was that *NT*'s constituency appealed to the majority of the colony's population, which was working-class and low-church. In 1910 *Nordiske Blade* stopped publication.[19]

These public conflicts between leaders of the community's most prominent groups represent only a small part of the divisions that made unity within the colony as a whole increasingly difficult as its population grew. Given the political, economic, religious, and regional differences that the immigrants brought with them, this increasing fragmentation of community does not seem surprising. The urge to gather with like-minded Norwegian immigrants for material and spiritual support produced a multitude of small-scale mobilizations, often in the service of quite specific community interests and not infrequently in conflict with each other.

By 1910 the Brooklyn enclave's associational life was rich and varied. Its religious denominations included a branch of the Salvation Army, two inner-city missions, two "free" churches, and a Baptist meeting house — in addition to the congregations already described. The political clubs included Democrats, Republicans, and Socialists.[20] Announcements in *NT* and anniversary booklets document the existence of these and twenty-six additional organizations that competed for the immigrants' allegiance. Among them were regional associations for Norwegians from specific parts of the old country, workmen's benefit societies, Scandinavian social clubs, choirs, athletic associations, women's clubs, half a dozen temperance lodges, and several Norwegian fraternal organizations. Almost annually, starting in 1891, various elements in the community set up a representative central committee to coordinate the colony's strength. Because the individual associations resisted any loss of autonomy, none of these umbrella organizations lasted more than a few months. Finally, the Norwegian National League (Det Norske Nationalforbundet) survived, perhaps because it seemed a monument to the burst of national patriotism during which it was created on Norway's achievement of full independence in 1905.[21]

Yet the majority in the community were probably not "joiners," either by inclination or because of the effort required in earning a living. Some occupational groups, such as seamen, were often out of town because of the nature of their work. Working people complained about long hours, exhausting working conditions, low pay, and difficulty in adjusting to the climate. The strain of everyday work routines is sometimes clearest in letters home. For example, on June 6, 1892, a young pharmacist's assistant who had worked in Brooklyn for six weeks apologized to his parents in Norway. "It's already late," he wrote, "so this won't be a long letter. I have long working hours — from 7 in the morning until 10 at night. When I know the language, even till 11." On June 15, he described the effects of a local heat wave. "It's terribly hot here now. . . . Here in the drugstore it was 93 degrees Fahrenheit in the middle of the day and that was at least a little cooler than outside. People who have to work outside fall dead of sunstroke. . . . Here in the store it's worst in the evening when the gas it lit. Last night it was 102 degrees when we closed." For a newcomer from a cooler Scandinavian climate, such weather must have been especially trying.[22]

But the effects of exhausting work were not merely a greenhorn's problem. Five years later the young man above was working at the same drugstore and had, he felt, mastered English. Yet on January 22, 1897, he protested perhaps too vehemently, "I have now got used to my long working hours, so I am not as a rule sleepy or exhausted, and the work in itself isn't really so strenuous, only that the long day over longer periods of time blunts one's energy, and most likely because of that it's such an effort for me, for example to write letters in the evening." Probably, many other immigrants striving to get established shared the fatigue he reluctantly admitted. Young and unattached, he came not as an unskilled worker but rather after some years' apprenticeship to a druggist in Norway. With such training he found employment within a week of his arrival. The physical demands of his job were minimal compared to factory or construction work. Yet if one accepts his own account of the situation, he had neither time nor energy for activities outside his work, even under such favorable conditions.

The assistant pharmacist's testimony may be somewhat extreme. For example, a women who arrived in 1895, writing a half century later, reported to *NT* that she was "soon disappointed over the long hard working day for small pay" but was nevertheless in a Norwegian women's club and attended ethnic choir concerts. Still, she indicated a more basic limitation on the social life of married couples when she stressed that she and her husband "did not have money for the theater and dances if we wanted to save something each month." Finally, she commented on the budget of working people in general: "Porterhouse steak or roast beef were meat dishes which the workingman never dreamed of. People did not have as much money in their pockets as they have in 1946."[23]

The New York State manuscript census of 1892 provides another way of putting the colony's public controversies and associational life in perspective. Since the 1890 federal manuscript census for Brooklyn was destroyed by fire, the state's canvass of the local population is one of the few sources available for facts about the great mass of the colony's population whose activities do not appear in the newspapers, the publications of ethnic organizations, or America-letters.[24]

Like all census materials, this state-wide enumeration has definite limitations. Enumerators made mistakes and had difficulties communicating with immigrants. The data collected reflects the facts on a particular day and does not take into account processes of change. The range of questions asked also narrows the possibilities for interpretation. The 1892 census gives the resident's name, sex, race, country of birth, citizenship, and occupation. On the other hand, it does not state family relationships, distinguish family members from boarders, make clear divisions of household units, or give the residents' street addresses. The analysis that follows comes from the information given by Norwegians living in the Brooklyn election wards close to New York Bay where the colony lay. The count done for this study showed 3,632 Norwegian-born adults in this area, when "adult" was defined as persons over fifteen years old. Since the published summaries for the Federal census two years earlier showed a *total* Norwegian-born population of 4,508 for all of Brooklyn, the analysis takes into account the overwhelming majority of residents in the colony.[25]

A reconstruction of the colony's occupational structure not only sheds light on the relative importance of newspaper debates and ethnic associational life but provides an approximate measure of the constituent groups leaders claimed to represent. Small business and professional men (including so-called semi-professionals) were the primary groups *NT* reports as the male leadership in such activities, yet those two groups totaled no more than 3.8 percent of the employed men. Adding ships' officers, an important element in the direction of the Seamen's Association, only increases the population pool of the colony's male leadership elite by 2.6 to a total of 6.4 percent.[26]

Skilled, semi-skilled, and unskilled workers accounted for the rest of the employed male population. Although the active participants in the colony's public life were a small minority, the numerical strength of the constituency the Seamen's Association could attempt to mobilize among men in harbor-related trades amounted to a little over a third (33.4 percent) of the total work force. More than one in four of the colony's workingmen (29.5 percent) found their livelihood aboard various kinds of ships. No less than 16.2 percent of the men reported their occupation as "seamen." It made good economic sense for a new paper like *NT* to maintain its loyalty to the Association and call itself "the seamen's" newspaper.[27]

The occupational structure of the colony shows that it was heavily dependent on the harbor economy. However, the size of other elements in the male working population prevents an easy assumption that the concerns of maritime groups could completely dominate public opinion in the enclave. Considered as a whole, skilled workers in land-based crafts (35.4 percent) comprised a slightly larger part of the total work force than the harbor economy did. In fact, carpenters (16.9 percent) were slightly more numerous than seamen. Still, these skilled workers probably had difficulty acting as a united interest group in the community. They were spread among a total of sixty-one different trades. Of all these job categories only three contained more than two percent of the male work force.[28]

Occupations categorized as low white-collar, semi-skilled, or unskilled comprised the bottom third of the male employment scale. These men also had very diverse kinds of work, but day laborers (17.5 percent) formed the largest single male job category in the community, constituting nearly one in five employed men. It would be a mistake to discount the influence of such men as potential readers of the colony newspapers. The average illiteracy rate of Scandinavians entering the U.S. at the turn of the century was under one percent.[29]

The reports of the Immigration Commission of 1911 suggest that the male occupational distribution in the colony remained relatively stable for several years. Based on data from the 1900 federal census, the Commission gave occupational information for New York City as a whole, using a somewhat different list of job categories. Nonetheless, a few comparisons are possible. The most striking is the percentage of seamen, 16.8 in 1900 and 16.2 in 1892. The closest possible approximation indicates that only five percent more men were employed in construction in 1900 than eight years earlier.[30]

The picture of women's socio-economic situation provided by the 1892 census shows how sharply female and male roles diverged in the colony. Of a population of 1,421 women, only 18.8 percent had jobs, and only a tenth of these were married. Most single women worked, but almost a third were listed as having no occupation. The work women got was in traditionally female occupations. Almost two-thirds (62.2 percent) were domestics, and the next most frequently-held occupations were seamstress and dressmaker (16.1 percent).[31]

The occupational elite of business and professional women (8.6 percent) seems large only because the percentage is relative to the number of *working* women. As a proportion of the adult female population, that elite was only two percent.[32] For the most part, housewives, rather than female professionals, were the active participants in colony organizations. Although excluded from membership, wives were essential to the economy of most male associations because their fund drives and bazaars usually paid a large part of the groups' expenses. The churches and temperance lodges had no restrictions on female membership and publicly recognized women's importance for their activities. The executive councils of these organizations were almost entirely male, but women founded many discussion groups and social circles through which they exerted considerable influence. *NT* regularly reported the affairs of the three women's clubs, which divided their efforts about equally between social and charitable projects. The clubs' membership, judging from newspaper accounts, was dominated by the wives of prominent men.[33] The Deaconesses' Home and Hospital provided the one important arena in which professional women influenced the colony as a whole. The day-to-day administrators at this institution were the five deaconesses, all of them trained as nurses and social workers in Norway. *NT* printed many articles attesting to their effectiveness in both the hospital and the community at large.[34]

The Brooklyn colony was probably attractive for female immigrants who wanted to marry. In 1892 the sex ratio for the total population was 1.6 men per woman. The imbalance was much greater among single adults where there were more than three men (3.2) to every woman.[35] Such sex ratios lend credence to the anecdotes told by elderly residents during interviews. One long-time resident insisted that in the first decades of the twentieth century seamen often married mail-order brides on board Norwegian ships docked in Brooklyn. Several women claimed that local wisdom had always advised staying in domestic service only until a suitable man proposed and that the Seamen's Church choir functioned as a "marriage bureau."[36]

The over-representation of men may also help explain the intermarriage statistics from the census. Almost a fourth of colony couples were "mixed." In 86 of the 125 marriages involved, a Norwegian man was married to a non-Norwegian. In other words, colony men were more than twice as likely to marry non-Norwegians. While the shortage of women within the ethnic group probably contributed somewhat to this situation, men's traditional role as the initiators of intimate relationships was undoubtedly an equally important factor. In over four fifths of the cases the marriage partners were both foreign-born. The immigration experience was apparently an even more important common background than cultural similarity. Norwegian women almost never married Americans; only one case appeared in the thirty-nine mixed marriages involving colony women. Most likely this is another indication of women's much more restricted freedom of association at the time. As might be expected, Norwegians who married outside the group usually found Scandinavian spouses, but again sex roles played a significant role. While about half of the men chose a Nordic mate, three quarters of the women did. In only two cases was a Norwegian married to a person originating outside of northwestern Europe.

The relationships between mobilization and conflict were complex in the Brooklyn colony between 1890 and 1910. Traditional sex roles played a part. Thus, for example, neither the deaconesses' nor the married women's marshalling of community resources through bazaars caused notable dissension because the only apparent motive of these women was assisting the unfortunate. The women were not competing for broader influence in the community nor attempting to change its fundamental economic priorities. Instead, they were engaging in the charitable enterprises that were an accepted part of women's role in society. Men were the colony's leaders in public matters. Through newspaper debates they strove to form coalitions that would address a variety of issues then considered to be men's province: economic and social rivalry between the Manhattan and Brooklyn settlements, high-church versus low-church Lutheran theology, Norway's struggle for independence from Sweden, and the politics of controlling social institutions that assisted newcomers, poor and homeless countrymen, and transient seamen.

The agenda set by *NT*'s constituency had an additional thought provoking dimension. The ideological nucleus of concerns that preoccupied *NT*'s constituency—local control, self-determination, a distaste for showing deference to authority—bear a striking resemblance to the rhetoric of the middle-class patriots who agitated for American independence. Was this a sign of their Americanization? As noted earlier, Folkestad believed that perceived class differences inherited from the old country and the greater Americanization of the popular party in Brooklyn lay at the root of the conflicts. The Seamen's Association *was* the first organization to put "Norwegian-American" in its name. The available sources are too meager to answer the question conclusively. However, since the material in *NT* identifies its constituency with Norwegian rather than American patriots, it is probably more accurate to say that these ideological emphases resulted from the general similarities between Norway's nineteenth-century relationship to Sweden and the American colonies' eighteenth-century relationship to Britain. As Sigmund Skaar has noted, American constitutions were among the most important models used for Norway's constitution in 1814.[37]

Table 1:   The Male Occupational Elite — 1892

	Number		Percentage of Work Force
	s	m*	
Professional			
Doctor	2	3	.23
Clergyman		4	.19
Draftsman	1	3	.19
Artist		2	.09
Photographer	2		.09
Civil engineer		1	.05
Nurse		1	.05
Musician	1		.05
Optician		1	.05
Druggist	1		.05
Reporter		1	.05
Interpreter		1	.05
Subtotal	7	17	1.14
Business			
Grocer	2	7	.42
Builder		6	.28
Cigar store proprietor	1	3	.19
Broker	2	2	.19
Miscellaneous**	6	29	1.61
Subtotal	11	47	2.69
Ships' Officers			
Captain	13	29	1.98
Mate	3	1	.19
Pilot	2	5	.33
Lighter foreman		1	.05
Quartermaster		1	.05
Subtotal	18	37	2.60
Grand Totals	36	101	6.43

* s = single, m = married
** miscellaneous: (job title and number of individuals) fish dealer (3), merchant (3), peddler (3), saloon keeper (3), storekeeper (3), cheese manufacturer (2), boarding-house keeper (2), ship-chandler (2), shipbuilder (2), dry goods dealer (1), speculator (1), insurance man (1), undertaker (1), furniture dealer (1), cigar manufacturer (1), contractor (1), stationery store proprietor (1), hardware dealer (1), liquor dealer (1), junk dealer (1).

Table 2:   Harbor-Related Occupations — 1892

Occupation	Number		Total No.	Percentage of Work Force
	s	m*		
Seaman	281	62	343	16.16
Lighterman	31	74	105	4.95
Boatman	36	68	104	4.91
Ship's officer	18	37	55	2.60
Dockbuilder	7	19	26	1.23
Ship's carpenter	4	15	19	.90
Longshoreman	2	13	15	.71
Rigger	1	7	8	.38
Sailmaker	1	7	8	.38
Steward	5	3	8	.38
Deckhand	2	5	7	.33
Stevedore		4	4	.19
Miscellaneous**	3	2	5	.24
Grand Totals	391	316	713	33.36

* s = single, m = married
** miscellaneous: (job title and number of individuals) fisherman (3), yachtsman (1), shipwright (1)

working on the docks rather than at sea: dockbuilders, ship's carpenters, longshoremen, riggers, sailmakers, stevedores, and shipwrights (.05 percent) *TOTAL* 3.84 percent

working at sea ("on board ships"): *TOTAL* 29.52 percent

Table 3:   Male Skilled Occupations – 1892
            (Land-based: excludes harbor-related occupations)

Occupation	Number		Total No.	Percentage of Work Force
	s	m*		
Occupation				
Carpenter	145	214	359	16.92
Framer	20	19	39	1.84
Housesmith	8	6	14	.66
Mason/bricklayer	3	3	6	.28
Miscellaneous**	6	3	9	.42
Sub-total	182	245	427	20.12
Other Skilled Occupations				
Machinist	25	33	58	2.73
Painter	20	28	48	2.26
Tailor	6	19	25	1.18
Shoemaker	10	13	23	1.08
Engineer	4	15	19	.90
Blacksmith	5	10	15	.71
Ironworker	12	2	14	.66
Baker	8	4	12	.57
Printer	8	2	10	.47
Watchmaker	2	5	7	.33
Tinsmith	2	5	7	.33
Engraver	3	4	7	.33
Cabinetmaker	1	4	5	.24
Jeweler	5		5	.24
Stonecutter	2	2	4	.19
Miscellaneous***	22	44	66	3.06
Sub-total	135	190	325	15.28
Grand Totals	317	435	752	35.40

* s = single, m = married
  miscellaneous: (job title and number of individuals)
** construction: plasterer (3), roofer (3), bridgebuilder (2), joiner (1).
*** other: factory worker (3), silversmith (3), plumber (3), woodcarver (3), bookbinder (3), mechanic (3), plater (3), electrician (3), polisher (2), sparmaker (2), gasmetermaker (2), oilermaker (2), boilermaker (2), cigarmaker (2), lineman (2), harnessmaker (2), furniture worker (2), moulder (2), car builder (1), tinker (1), boxmaker (1), box factory worker (1), pianotuner (1), caulker (1), varnisher (1), metal worker (1), millwright (1), compositor (1), wagonmaker (1), foreman (1), paperstainer (1), fur worker (1), lithographer (1), furrier (1), typographer (1), telegraph worker (1), hatter (1).

Table 4: Male Semi-Skilled and Unskilled Occupations — 1892
(Excludes harbor-related; includes low white collar)

| Occupation | Number | | Total No. | Percentage of Work Force |
	s	m*		
Low White Collar				
Clerk	49	26	75	3.53
Salesman	3	6	9	.42
Agent	1	4	5	.24
Bookkeeper	2	3	5	.24
Board of Immigration (Unspecified)		1	1	.05
Subtotal	55	40	95	4.47
Semi-Skilled				
Fireman	10	5	15	.71
Driver	3	11	14	.66
Bartender	5	5	10	.47
Watchman	5	4	9	.42
Conductor	2	4	6	.28
Barber	2	2	4	.19
Cook	4		4	.19
Miscellaneous**	9	4	13	.62
Subtotal	40	35	75	3.54
Unskilled				
Laborer	187	187	374	17.62
Porter	9	8	17	.80
Janitor	3	6	9	.42
Miscellaneous***	8	6	14	.66
Subtotal	207	207	414	19.50
Grand Totals	302	282	584	27.51

* single = s, married = m

miscellaneous: (job title and number of individuals)

** semi-skilled: butcher (3), apprentice (3), saloon (unspecified) (2), sexton (1), train-hand (1), railroad worker (1), wheeling (1), waiter (1).

*** unskilled: office boy (3), elevator operator (unspecified) (2), mailman (2), stoveman (2), stableman (1), newsboy (1), waterman (1), doorman (1), hostler (1).

Table 5:   Female Occupational Structure — 1892
           (All percentages are relative to the total female work force)

Occupation	Number s	m*	Total No.	Percentage of Work Force
Occupational Elite				
Professional				
Nurse	2	4	6	2.25
Lutheran sister				
(deaconess)	5		5	1.87
Music teacher	1	1	2	.75
Doctor	1		1	.37
Photographer	1		1	.37
Business				
Boardinghouse keeper	2	5	7	2.62
Cigar store prop.	1		1	.37
Subtotal	13	10	23	8.60
Low White Collar				
Saleslady	2	1	3	1.12
Typist	3		3	1.12
Clerk	2		2	.75
Telegraph operator	1		1	.37
Subtotal	8	1	9	3.36
Skilled				
Seamstress	23	3	26	9.74
Dressmaker	16	1	17	6.37
Factory worker	3		3	1.12
Sewing machine operator	2		2	.75
Milliner	1		1	.37
Silkworker	1		1	.37
Midwife		1	1	.37
Sailmaker		1	1	.37
Subtotal	46	6	52	19.46
Semi-skilled				
Domestic	164	2	166	62.17
Cook	6	3	9	3.37
Operator (Unspecified)	2		2	.75
Housekeeper	1		1	.37
Subtotal	173	5	178	66.66
Unskilled				
Laundress	1	1	2	.75
Washer	1	1	2	.75
Laborer		1	1	.37
Subtotal	2	3	5	1.87
Grand Totals	242	25	267	99.95

* single = s, married = m

Notes

1. The earliest Norwegian settlers migrated first to the Netherlands and then came with the Dutch in the seventeenth century to found New Amsterdam. When Norwegian immigration resumed 200 years later, their descendants, thoroughly blended into the American population, had no significant contacts with the newcomers. See Henry Isham Hazelton, *The Boroughs of Brooklyn and Queens, Counties of Nassau and Suffolk, Long Island, New York, 1609-1924* (New York, 1925), III, 1102-1104, 1150. For a detailed study of these earliest Norwegian settlers, see John O. Evjen, *Scandinavian Immigrants in New York, 1630-1647* (Minneapolis, 1916).

2. Johannes Nordboe to Hans Larsen Rudi, April 30, 1837, in "Johannes Nordboe and Norwegian Immigration, An 'America Letter' of 1837," Arne Odd Johnsen, ed., C. A. Clausen, trans., *Norwegian-American Studies and Records* (Northfield, Minn., 1934), VIII, 23-38. The quoted phrase is my translation of "Svedisker Norveisk Mand," which remains untranslated in the above article.

3. The brief interpretation of the Manhattan colony's institutional development between 1840 and 1880 builds on A. N. Rygg, *Norwegians in New York, 1825-1925* (Brooklyn, 1941), 6-13, 22-23, 36-38, 59-63, 75-76, 117, 133-134; Carl Søyland, *Skrift i sand* (Oslo, 1954), 15-16; and Karsten Roedder, *Av en utvandrer avis' saga, Nordisk Tidende i New York gjennom 75 år* (Brooklyn, 1966), I, 9-13. For evidence of continuing pan-Scandinavian activities and organizations, see John R. Jenswold, "The Rise and Fall of Pan-Scandinavianism in Urban America," Odd S. Lovoll, ed. in *Scandinavians and Other Immigrants in Urban America: the Proceedings of a Research Conference October 26-27, 1984* (Northfield, Minn., 1985), 159-170, and the announcements of pan-Scandinavian organization in *Nordisk Tidende*, August 11, 1898, p. 7.

4. The table of Norwegian-born populations in Manhattan and Brooklyn derives from U.S. Census, *Population*, 1870, 1: 386; 1880, 1:540-541; 1890, 1:675-676.

5. See Peter A. Munch, "Norwegians" in Stephan Thernstrom, et al., ed., *Harvard Encyclopedia of Ethnic Groups* (Cambridge, Mass., 1980), 754; and Einar Haugen, "Norwegian Migration," *Norwegian-American Studies and Records* (Northfield, Minn., 1954), 11-13, for the high rates of Norwegian immigration in the 1880s. Ingrid Semmingsen, *Veien mot vest: utvandring fra Norge til Amerika, 1865-1915* (Oslo, 1950), 280-284, uses both Norwegian and American government reports to show how important deserting seamen were to the rapid growth of the Norwegian population. Theodore C. Blegen, *Norwegian Migration to America, 1825-1860* (Northfield, Minn., 1931), 331-332, contains the statistics on desertions in the United States. A. N. Kier's remark comes from *Norges Skipsfart i Aaret 1871*, in *Norge's Offisielle Statistikk*, series C. No. 3 c, (Christiania, 1873), xiii. See "New York Station" in *Foreningen til Evangeliets Forkyndelse for skandinaviske Sjømænd i fremmede Havner i 50 Aar, 1864-1914. Festskrift utgit av Foreningens Hovedstyre* (Bergen, 1914), 191, for the estimated annual number of Norwegian ships in the port. Carlton C. Qualey, "Jørgen Gjerdrum's Letters from America, 1874-75, "*Norwegian-American Studies and Records* (Northfield, Minn., 1940) XI, 82-87, is the source for all Gjerdrum's remarks.

6. Rygg, *Norwegians*, 77-76; Qualey, "Jørgen Gjerdrum's Letters from America," 82-83, 86.

7. Beulah Folkedahl, ed. and trans., "Elizabeth Fedde's Diary, 1883-88," *Norwegian-American Studies and Records* (Northfield, Minn., 1959), XX, 170-196; Rygg, *Norwegians*, 88-90, 103-107; "Gjerdrum's Letters from America," 87.

8. Rygg, *Norwegians*, 22, 31-32, 66-67, 103-107; John S. Billings, *Vital Statistics of New York City and Brooklyn: 1890* (Washington, 1894), 171-172, 182-183, gives brief descriptions of the topography, population density, housing, and incidence of disease in Brooklyn election wards 6 and 12; 78 percent of the Norwegians found in the 1892 New York State Census lived in these two waterfront districts. Harold Coffin Syrett, *The City of Brooklyn, 1865-1898*: A Political History (New York, 1944), 138-140, 233-235,

242-243, documents the emergence of the area as the docking and storage center for the port of New York and supplies statistics on the growth of Brooklyn in general. In *The Golden Door: Italian and Jewish Mobility in New York City 1880-1915* (New York, 1977), 144-145, Thomas Kessner cites evidence of the district's long-term reputation as a working-class slum.

9. R. S. N. Sartz, "Fra Washington, D.C.," *Normands-Forbundet* (Kristiania, 1909), II, 181-186. Rygg, *Norwegians*, 88-92 and *The Norwegian Sailors' Home of Brooklyn, N.Y., A Condensed History of the Institution From Its Start in 1887 to the Present Time* (Brooklyn, 1939), 19.

10. Rygg, *Norwegians*, 36, 66-67, 117, documents the migration of organizations to Brooklyn. The description of the flag-raising over New York's City Hall is on page 76. See "Gjennem Hamilton Ave og Columbia St," *Nordisk Tidende* (hereafter *NT*), November 13, 1891, p. 3, for a description of the Brooklyn colony's business district.

11. Rygg, *Norwegians*, 77-79. *NT*, "Vore Foreninger," January 9, 1891, p. 1; "New York og Brooklyn," January 23, 1891, p. 2; "Hvad vi bør arbeide for," January 30, 1891, p. 1.

12. Gabriel Fedde, "Pennestrøg-Oplevelser" (unpublished autobiography), 114-122. Archivist Charlotte Jacobson at the Norwegian-American Historical Association Archives in Northfield, Minnesota, is currently editing a copy of the manuscript. The original is in the possession of Fedde's granddaughter, Alva Fedde Calvin, in Wilmington, Delaware. In *Trinity through the Years 1890-1965* (Brooklyn, 1965), 8-9, church historian Ingolf Olsen notes, "The Seamen's pastor did everything he could to persuade the people affected by the new ruling to join Our Savior's Church. But the High Church atmosphere in that congregation was quite foreign to the free, low church tradition to which the people had become accustomed." See also "Sjømandsmissionen," *NT*, 1, February 13, 1891 and Johannes Aardal, "Sjømannskirken i Brooklyn 1878-1953" in *Sjømannskirken i Brooklyn, N.Y. 1878-1953* (Brooklyn, 1953), 8-12. The cooperation between the Norwegian Singing Society and the Seamen's Association is evident in the *NT* articles cited in note 11. See also Rygg, *Norwegians,* 120, and "Vore Foreninger," *NT*, January 15, 1897, p. 8.

13. Sigurd Folkestad, "Norske i Brooklyn – New York," *Symra* (Decorah, Iowa, 1908), 4:79-97. My translations in this paragraph and the next come from 84-85.

14. Roedder, *Saga*, 1:12-15, 24-25, 28-35; *NT*, January 6, 1891, p 1; P. S. Christensen, "Lidt aviskronike. Skandinaviske blade i Østern" in *Symra* (Decorah, Iowa, 1914), 10:261-270.

15. "Til Stortinget" and "Skar Unionsmærket Ud, Men Blev Straffet" in *NT*, January 5, 1894, 1 and 4, document the patriotic action of the Seamen's Association and *NT*'s approval. In "Journalistisk Raahed," January 13, 1894, p. 4, and "Aktiv og Pasiv," January 17, 1894, p. 4, *NT* reprinted lengthy excerpts of *Nordiske Blade*'s satirical commentary on the Association's initiative. "Det Rene Norske Flag," November 9, 1897, p.9C, is an example of *NT*'s continuation of the campaign for the "clean" flag. See also Rygg, *Norwegians*, 143-144.

16. *NT*, "New York og Brooklyn," February 5, 1892, p. 3 and "En Stump af Koloniens Historie Med 17. Mai som Midtpunkt, " May 30, 1893, p. 1, show the Brooklyn leaders' desire to move the Constitution Day celebration. For *NT*'s description of *Nordiske Blade* and Manhattan's Norwegian Society as reactionary conservatives, see "Leif Erikson-Festen tat under behandling af 'Nordiske Blade'," August 28, 1891, p. 1A; "En Bagstraever-forening," September 4, 1891, p. 1A; and "Leif Erikson-Festen," October 2, 1891, p. 1A. *NT*, January 1 to February 19, 1897, contains the religious debate in a series of front-page articles. In "Pennestrøg-Oplevelser," 128-136, Gabriel Fedde describes his and Trinity's differences with Our Savior's and the Norwegian Lutheran Synod in the Mid-west.

17. *NT* published a multitude of complaints against the social institutions. For a sample, see the issues for September 2, 1893; February 1, 1895; and March 23, 1897. The following articles give detailed descriptions of the behavior and attitudes against which *NT* and readers protested: "Kjaeringen mod Strømmen," January 26, 1894,

p. 1; "Inserater," "April 6, 1894, p. 1; "Hittegods fra Sømandshjemmets Flytning," May 4, 1894, pp. 4–5; "Ud med Dem igjen," August 24, 1894, p. 1; and "Pastor Sårheims Farvel," November 16, 1894, p. 15.

18. "Hittegods fra Sømandshjemmets Flytning" and "Pastor Sårheims Farvel," listed in note 17, are actually revelations of the Seamen's Mission's hidden influence in other institutions. The following *NT* articles document the establishment of social institutions independent of the Mission: "Bra Gjort," October 19, 1894, p. 3; "Nattherberge Indviet," November 9, 1894, p. 1; "Rapport" and note on the Seamen's Association's own hiring service, March 1, 1895, p. 4; "Natherberget Overgaar til Emigranthjem eller Industri-Skole," March 8, 1895, p. 5.

19. Typical of *NT*'s attacks on *Nordiske Blade*'s doctor-editor are "En mystisk Redaktion" and "Nordiske Plage," and "End 'Nordiske Blad' selv da?," March 17, 1898, pp. 1A and 8A, respectively. Theodore Kartevold, "Da Skyskraperne manglet i New York" in "Nordisk Tidende's Jubilæumsnummer 1825–1925," October 8, 1925, p. 45, contains a brief description of the conservative cabal behind Folkestad's editorship. For understanding the Seamen's Church's and Folkestad's motivations, the best source is the correspondence between the Seamen's Church and the Mission Society's main office in Bergen, Norway, during 1906–1907. See "Korrespondanse og Aarsberetninger," Gruppe I: Stasjonene, New York 1901–1910, Den Norske Sjømannsmisjons Arkiv, (Regional Archives in Bergen). Roedder, *Saga*, 14–15, 22–23; and Rygg, *Norwegians*, 134–135 give short summaries of developments in New York's Norwegian press during these years.

20. During these years the Norwegians were far too small a group to have significant influence in politics or the labor movement on their own. Their ethnic political clubs functioned as semi-official branches of larger American party organizations. Colony men in the construction trades — over 20 percent of the male work force in 1892 — established no separate organizations. See Table 3. The extent of their involvement in American unions remains undetermined.

21. Rygg, *Norwegians*, 81–82; "Love for Det Norske Nationalforbund for New York og Omegn, Stiftet 1905" (n.p., 1936).

22. The quotations in this paragraph and the next are my translations from a private collection of America-letters covering the period from May 2, 1892 to November 28, 1906. All the information in the text comes from the dates cited there.

23. Quoted in Christen T. Jonassen, "The Norwegians in Bay Ridge: A Sociological Study of an Ethnic Group," (Ph.D. dissertation, New York University, 1947), 257–258.

24. Kings County Clerk's Office, manuscript census schedules, New York State Census for Brooklyn, 1892.

25. See note 4. The data in the ensuing analysis includes *all* Norwegian-born residents over fifteen years old residing in Brooklyn wards 1, 6, 8, 12, 17, and 22. The table below shows the absolute number and percentage of adults (relative to the total Norwegian-born population counted*) in each of those wards.

Ward	Number of Norwegian-born	Percentage
1	141	3.9
6	1,381	38.0
8	430	11.8
12	1,453	40.0
17	104	2.9
22	123	3.4
Total	3,632	100.0

26. To highlight the class conflicts and socio-political coalitions discussed a simplified list of broad occupational categories seems most appropriate. Except for the cate-

gory "harbor-related occupations," the classification system used in this study is a collapsing of the occupational status hierarchy in Stephan Thernstrom, *The Other Bostonians: Poverty and Progress in the American Metropolis, 1880–1970* (Cambridge, Mass., 1973), 289–302. Thus the "professional" category includes semi-professional workers, and "business" includes petty proprietors. For placing some occupations, Kathleen Neils Conzen, *Immigrant Milwaukee, 1836–1860: Accommodation and Community in a Frontier City* (Cambridge, Mass., 1976), 234–237 was also helpful. See Table 1 for the absolute numbers and percentages of the male work force among businessmen, professionals, and ships' officers.

27. See Table 2 for the distribution of single and married workers in harbor-related occupations according to the absolute number and percentage of the total male work force in each occupation.

28. See Table 3 for the distribution of skilled, land-based workers and notes 21 and 31 for additional information on colony construction workers.

29. Jonassen, "The Norwegians in Bay Ridge," 392.

30. "Occupations of Immigrants," *Reports of the Immigration Commission*, XXVIII (Washington, D.C., 1911), 181. The Commission found 27 pecent of the male Norwegian work force involved in construction. In 1892 the combined percentage of carpenters, framers, housesmiths, plasterers, masons and bricklayers, roofers, ships' carpenters, dockbuilders, and shipwrights was 22.2.

31. See Table 5 for the occupational distribution of colony women in 1892.

32. The male occupational elite was 6.4 percent of the employed men and 5 percent of the total number of adult men. These figures are so close because most men worked.

33. Rygg, *Norwegians*, 80–85, 173–176 and "Norske Kvinner i New York," *Normands-Forbundet* (Oslo, 1938), XXXI, 37–40. *NT*, "Frelseshæren Slaar Belzebub," April 21, 1893, p. 1; "En Virkelig Norske Landtur i Brooklyn fra Kvinneforeningen," August 1, 1893, p. 1; "Den Norske Kvinneforening Hjørdis," March 26, 1897, p. 10; "En Aandelig St. Veits-Dans," July 21, 1898, p. 1.

34. Rygg, *Norwegians*, 98–99. The Norwegian Lutheran Deaconesses' Home and Hospital, *Seventeenth Annual Report, 1899* (Brooklyn, 1900), 9, 28–30, and *Twenty-eighth Annual Report, 1909–1910* (Brooklyn, 1910), 11, 23–26. *NT*, "Brooklyn and New York," April 1, 1892; "Det Norske Diakonissehjem i Brooklyn," January 8, 1897; "Mathilde Madland," October 1, 1897.

35. In reality the thousands of transient Norwegian seamen who came through New York harbor probably made the overrepresentation of men even greater. On the other hand, the census population for the Brooklyn colony did not include the single Norwegian domestics who lived with their employers in more prosperous parts of metropolitan New York. Since a portion of these women most likely spent leisure time visiting the colony, their presence reduced somewhat the significance of the transient seamen for the sex ratio in the single population.

36. Interviews with Domestics, 2 and 3 (Brooklyn, January 23, 1986), names confidential; Interview with Hans Berggren, sailor, actor, and radio personality (Brooklyn, December 30, 1986); Interview with Hjordis Olsen Mortensen, daughter of choir director at the Seamen's Church (Norseville, New Jersey; May 10, 1986).

37. Sigmund Skard, *The United States in Norwegian History* (Oslo and Westport, Conn., 1976), 25–29.

5

'. . . The Adoption of the Tactics of the Enemy': The Care of Italian Immigrant Youth in the Archdiocese of New York During the Progressive Era

One of the most hotly-discussed issues facing the Catholic church in the United States between 1880 and World War II was the "Italian problem." Historians of Italian-American Catholicism have picked up the phrase, and have continued the discussion by examining the Church's response to one social problem in a particular setting. By close analyses of institutional developments in a local setting it will be possible to determine more precisely the Church's relationship with Italian immigrants.

In the late nineteenth and early twentieth centuries Italians came to the United States in steadily increasing numbers. In 1879, 5,791 Italians migrated to the United States; in 1880, 12,354 came. Between 1880 and

1899, the Italian-American migration numbered in the tens of thousands annually. Between 1900 and World War I, it numbered in the hundreds of thousands annually. War and the restrictive quotas of 1921 and 1924 finally brought one of the greatest movements of people in recent history to an end.[1]

Four-fifths of the Italians came from the *mezzogiorno*, the part of the peninsula below Rome, or from the island of Sicily. Over half were between fourteen and forty-nine years old, prime working age. Between 1881 and 1910, four-fifths of the migrants were male; between 1911 and 1930, about two-thirds were male.[2] Many of the immigrants were highly transient. They were landless, unskilled agricultural workers in the *mezzogiorno*, used to traveling in search of work, who extended their travels to the United States.[3]

New York City was the port of entry for most Italian immigrants, a temporary headquarters for many migrant workers, and a permanent home for hundreds of thousands of Italians. According to the 1910 federal census, there were 4,766,883 people in New York City, and over 700,000 of them were Italian: 310,000 on Manhattan, 235,000 in Brooklyn, 115,000 in the Bronx, 55,000 in Queens, and 20,000 on Staten Island.[4]

New York's Italians had many troubles besides earning a living. Progressives who sought to reform them possessed anti-Italian prejudices historians later echoed.[5] But even other Catholics, mostly Irish Americans, in the Archdiocese of New York were shocked by what they saw of Italian Catholicism. They, too, quickly labeled the Italians a "problem."[6]

According to the Irish-American clergy, the "Italian problem" had four characteristics. First, the Italians seldom attended Mass on Sundays or holy days, and seldom received Communion or went to confession. Second, they did not support the Church financially. Third, they were anti-clerical. Fourth, they were ignorant of the basic doctrines of Catholicism, and did not realize they were supposed to be doing better in all these areas.

The Italians have had their defenders. Contemporaries excused them by pleading poverty, explaining that the Italians came to the United States to make money to send home; thus, they worked rather than attend Mass, and hoarded rather than gave to the Church.[7] More recently, historians have explained that *mezzogiorno* Catholicism was organized differently than the legalistic, puritanical, Jansenist Catholicism of Irish Americans.[8] *Mezzogiorno* Catholicism was centered in the local community rather than abstract notions of "the Church." The men and women of the village had specific roles in communal religious life, which revolved around the village's relationship with its patron saint, or the Madonna, rather than around a set of rules to be observed. In short, the real "Italian problem" was the clash between *mezzogiorno* and Irish-American Catholicism.[9]

Some Irish Americans and most Italians saw national parishes as the solution to the "Italian problem." A national parish differed from a regular one in that regular parishes had territorial boundaries and ministered to all Catholics within those boundaries, whereas national parishes ministered to Catholics of a particular linguistic group, sometimes within geographic boundaries and sometimes with no regard to people's addresses. The first Italian national parish in New York City, St. Anthony of Padua, dates from 1859.[10] The first archbishop to make extensive use of national parishes was Michael Augustine Corrigan, coadjutor (auxiliary bishop with the right of succession) to John Cardinal McCloskey from 1880 to 1885, and archbishop in his own right from 1885 to 1902. Corrigan assumed Americanization was inevitable, and concentrated on keeping the Italians Catholic during the process. To that end, he authorized a number of national parishes, and gave generously of his energy and personal funds to establish Italian congregations.[11] John Cardinal Farley and Patrick Cardinal Hayes followed Corrigan's example, so that by 1941 there were about forty Italian national parishes in the City and Archdiocese of New York.[12]

The national parish system was just getting underway in the 1890s and 1900s when two new challenges arose. One was the increasing numbers of Italian children being born or raised in New York. The other was the Progressive Era. Together, the two posed a threat to the Italian Catholic community of New York.

The problem with the children was that the parents were trying to raise them according to *mezzogiorno* traditions, but their efforts were being thwarted by their offspring's exposure to American culture. This cultural conflict affected both sexes. *Mezzogiorno* girls were kept at home to assist their mothers and to learn housekeeping and child care. Adolescents were carefully chaperoned, for the choice of a husband was not the girl's alone, and the parents did not want her to meet anyone unsuitable. However well these techniques worked in Italy, they sabotaged the girls' chances for an American-style love match. If teenage girls contributed to the juvenile delinquency supposedly rampant in Little Italies in the 1920s, it was by their sneaking off for unchaperoned dates.[13]

Boys had traditionally been granted more freedom, in deference to their masculinity and to enable them to follow their fathers into migrant labor. Boys in America had the same freedom, but, as far as their parents could see, they put it to no good use. They rejected both

Italian and American culture, hung out with other boys caught between the two societies, and engaged in activities as frivolous as sports
or as potentially dangerous as crime.[14]

Both boys and girls were stuck between their parents' culture and
the allure of America. America became even more alluring during the
Progressive Era. Progressives took a special interest in urban, immigrant,
industrial working-class people, and organized institutions to assist
them. The best known of these was the settlement house. Other Progressive organizations which affected young people most directly were day-
care nurseries, kindergartens, youth recreation programs, and summer
camps.

Catholics regarded even secular-sponsored Progressive philanthro-
pies as attempts to convert immigrant Catholics to American Protestantism. This was not just a figment of Catholic imagination. American Protestants did pray "may American Christendom rise to its
opportunities" to convert those brought within its grasp.[15] They were
particularly interested in Italians. American Protestants regarded the
Italian migration as a second Exodus, from the Egyptian darkness of
the papacy to a land bathed in the pure light of the Gospel.[16]

Thomas Meehan, a Catholic layman and journalist, demonstrated
the connection between Protestants, Progressives, and youth in a 1903
article on Italian Catholics in New York. The Women's Branch of the
New York City Mission and Tract Society taught sewing, a popular
feminine accomplishment among Italian girls. The New York City Baptist Mission Society invited children to its summer Sunday School camp.
Meehan feared that these new methods of fun and games might succeed in converting the rising generation of Italian Catholics. He then
challenged his audience:

> [I]t seems that we need a more effective, general and practical system
> of Catholic organization, the abandonment of many old time methods
> fostered and continued through racial antipathies and traditions, and
> the adoption of the tactics of the enemy. We may scoff at 'settlement
> work' and the kindred varieties of modern professionally trained philan-
> thropy but their disastrous results stare us in the face on all sides. And
> what do we offer in their place as a practical substitute?[17]

The most complete history of a parish's adoption of "the tactics of
the enemy" came from the Jesuit mission to Lower East Side Italians
from 1891 to 1921. Here, clergy realized that Progressive reform could
be turned against itself to promote allegiance to Catholicism. The Jesuits'
first missionary, Nicholas Russo, was not a typical Italian immigrant.

He had come to the United States in 1875 to finish his Jesuit training, and for fourteen years after that had been teaching in colleges and universities and working in non-Italian Jesuit parishes.[18] His first contact with the mass migration came in 1889, when he and a *confrère* preached an Advent mission to a Sicilian congregation at an Irish church on the Lower East Side.[19] Russo took interest in becoming a pastor to these immigrants. In 1891, the Jesuits and Archbishop Corrigan agreed that Russo should open a chapel for Sicilians on the Lower East Side. Russo and a companion, Aloysius Romano, rented a barroom, renovated it for a chapel, and hung out a sign announcing *La Missione Italiana della Madonna di Loreto*. The first Mass was on August 16, 1891.[20]

Russo and Romano made house calls among their potential parishioners. "We were oftentimes received with the coldest indifference; not seldom avoided; at times greeted with insulting remarks." So, they began asking the parents to send their children for afternoon instruction. "[T]he children became so many little apostles," and soon Russo was looking for bigger quarters, since the chapel seated only 150. On September 27, 1892, Our Lady of Loreto moved into two renovated tenements across from its original site on Elizabeth Street.

Because Russo shared native-born Catholics' fears that public schools converted children to Protestantism, his next effort was to organize a parochial school. His first school was in his chapel's basement, which he divided into six rooms for 200 pupils. At first, parents objected to keeping their offspring in dark, unventilated rooms under gas light all day, but soon it was observed that public school made youngsters "less respectful and obedient, and more independent," and Russo won over the parents. When the two tenements adjoining his chapel went up for sale, he purchased them and renovated them for a school, which opened in October 1895.

Nineteenth-century pastors divided their parishioners into sodalities by age, sex, and marital status, so that each person might work on his spiritual life supported by a peer group. Russo made his boys' sodality serve social and recreational needs as well. He organized the St. Aloysius Club in the fall of 1892 or in 1893. In the beginning, Russo met with the boys himself every Saturday morning. He turned two of the basement classrooms into clubrooms, with checkers, dominoes, and tiddley-winks. He taught carpentry, coached dramatics, wrote plays, bought presents, and threw parties. By the time they reached nineteen or twenty years of age, some of the boys were firmly attached to the Church. They were then graduated to the Loreto Club, which had its own clubhouse and operated more independently.[21]

In 1899, Russo delegated responsibility for the St. Aloysius Club to a curate, who added light-blue sailor-suit uniforms and a pianola to the club's attractions.[22] But when Russo died on April 1, 1902, the boys' clubs were still part of the ministry to the whole Sicilian community. The youth ministry took on a life of its own under Russo's successor, William H. Walsh, who was assigned to Loreto on July 15, 1903.

Soon after his arrival, Walsh changed some of the parochial school's policies. Parents usually sent their offspring to Loreto's school only until they made their first confession and Communion. Then, the parents enrolled the youngsters in public school, thinking they would learn English better there. Walsh put a stop to this practice; consequently, the parochial school population increased. In 1904 Walsh introduced three Sisters of Jesus and Mary to teach in the Girls' Department. By 1917, the Girls' Department had fifteen teachers.

In 1905 a French laywoman, Miss Louise Rossi, took over as principal of the Boys' Department. Walsh kept in touch with the boys who graduated from Loreto and went on to St. Francis Xavier Preparatory School and Fordham University. The "College Boys" attended Mass in Loreto in the morning, studied there in the afternoon and early evening, and said the rosary with Walsh at night.

Music had long been a means of attracting boys to Loreto. One parish alumnus recalled that Russo had organized a uniformed brass band to play at entertainments. In 1905, when, in accordance with Pius X's *motu proprio* on the subject, male choirs replaced female ones, the choir became a vehicle of boy ministry. The choristers attended Loreto's school, took voice lessons from Miss Rossi, studied in the study hall, played in the courtyard, and said prayers with Walsh at night.

Walsh rearranged Russo's boys' clubs to suit his own interest in adolescents. Boys between seven and fourteen years old were organized into a sodality under the patronage of St. Stanislaus. Older boys remained in the St. Aloysius Club. Walsh was moderator of both clubs, but the latter was more active. It sponsored amateur theatricals, debates, a choral society (organized in 1912) and a newsletter (organized in 1910).

The Jesuits have a historic mandate to teach young men, but no such tradition regarding women. American Catholics segregated activities by sex, and Italians were even stricter about gender identification. For all these reasons, girls' work at Loreto was the province of the Children of Mary of Manhattanville, alumnae of the prestigious finishing school run by the Religious of the Sacred Heart of Jesus.[23]

The Children of Mary began their work in 1905, teaching manual arts to Loreto girls. Coincidentally, Walsh began teaching catechism in a former barbershop east of the Bowery from Loreto. Walsh could not persuade the parents to let their offspring cross the wide, curving Bowery, with its four lanes of trolley tracks, in order to come to Loreto. So, in 1908, he took steps to bring Loreto to the children. He purchased a house across the Bowery on Chrystie Street, and turned it over to the Children of Mary. The women opened a settlement named for Madeleine Sophie Barat, founder of the Religious Order of the Sacred Heart.

Barat's primary mission was catechetical. By 1912, it taught sixty boys on Tuesdays and Thursdays, and seventy-five girls on Mondays and Wednesdays. A priest heard confessions at the settlement on Saturday afternoons. Because none of the women who volunteered their time for Barat actually lived there, a live-in matron chaperoned the children at Sunday Masses. Barat also offered meeting space for children's sodalities, and celebrated religious events, such as first Communions and Madeleine Sophie Barat's feast day, with breakfasts and lunches.

The only secular subjects Barat taught were sewing and home economics. Probably its most important charity was its kindergarten, organized in 1912. The kindergarten supposedly operated from 9:00 a.m. to 3:00 p.m., but working mothers dropped their preschoolers off as early as 7:00 a.m. The kindergarten was full to capacity with eighty children. The experience with the kindergarten led Barat into day care. Walsh purchased the tenement adjoining the settlement, and the women renovated it for a nursery, which opened in 1915. It soon had eighteen infants and thirty-two toddlers in its care each day.[24]

The youth work closest to Walsh's heart, though, was the summer camp. Walsh was concerned about Protestants luring Catholics to their summer camps and thence to their faith, and began renting hotels to provide an alternative. In 1907 he purchased a hotel in Monroe in Orange County, New York.[25] At Monroe, the boys had luxuries they did not have on the Lower East Side, beginning with sixty-five acres of play space. There was also a ball field, a swimming pool, and, for rainy days, a movie projector.[26]

While Walsh was building his youth ministry, neighborhood changes were rendering Loreto a less satisfactory headquarters for his work. Loreto was technically a chapel for the Italians who lived within the boundaries of St. Patrick's Old Cathedral on Mott Street. When St. Patrick's made efforts to attract Italians, it siphoned them from Loreto.[27] In 1915 one of Loreto's curates applied for a transfer to the missions in India, claiming that things at Loreto were really rather quiet.[28]

Meanwhile, the Italian ministry at the Church of the Nativity, across the Bowery from Loreto, also lagged. Nativity was in poor financial shape, dependent upon entertainments and fund-raisers.[29] Its pastor had once referred to the Italians as "about the worst Catholics who ever came to this country." That same pastor did try to attract Italians to his church, but thought his efforts unsuccessful.[30]

Walsh already had a foothold in Nativity, as Barat was located within its boundaries. In 1917 he began a campaign to convince the chancery to give the Jesuits Nativity.[31] On May 11, 1917, Cardinal Farley made the transfer.[32] However, the archdiocese did not send a priest to replace the Jesuits at Loreto until 1919. For two years, Walsh was pastor of Loreto's chapel and school, Nativity, the Barat Settlement and Day Nursery, and the summer camp at Monroe.

Walsh collapsed in July 1919. Although he recovered and lived to be ninety, he never returned to the Lower East Side.[33] He was succeeded by Daniel J. Quinn, who served as pastor from August 1919 to summer 1921. Quinn's career at Loreto and Nativity provides a commentary on the wisdom of "the adoption of the tactics of the enemy."

Quinn was appalled by conditions at Loreto. The school was so run down that he closed it. The situation at Nativity was little better. The financial records were in disarray, the only certainties being heavy mortgages. Quinn concluded that Walsh had devoted all his time, money, and energy to the summer camp, at the expense of the rest of his parish. Quinn therefore closed the summer camp and set about trying to bring the parish back to basics.[34] He failed miserably.

The adult Italians were unresponsive. Quinn wrote his superior wearily: "These Italians were here before we came and they'll be here when we're gone and nothing short of a miracle of grace will ever bring them to the Church they hate and curse." They did not come to Mass or devotions, not even to the processions that were supposed to be their favorite pious practice. The collection reflected the small size of the congregation.[35]

Quinn's successor reverted to Russo's and Walsh's strategy, and reopened the summer camp. The pastors after him continued to emphasize youth ministry within the parish. "The tactics of the enemy" had indeed been adopted at Nativity. Were they adopted at any of the other Italian parishes in New York?

Loreto and Nativity were atypical Italian parishes in that their pastors were either Americanized Italians or Americans. Their pastors' use of Progressive techniques was motivated partly by a desire to convert the Italians to American Catholicism. William Walsh dismissed the Italians as ignorant, lax in their religious practice, and distrustful of the Church and its priests or ministers.[36] Russo excused the Italians' irreligion as the results of poverty and neglect by the American clergy.[37]

But both Russo and Walsh took steps to ensure Italian children would not grow up with the same bad habits as their elders.

Most other Italian parishes were staffed by Italian clergy. But most of these were northern Italians, of a different cultural background than *mezzogiorno* immigrants. Some parishes were staffed by diocesan clergy who had migrated from Italy. Most Manhattan parishes were staffed by religious orders, which sent steady supplies of missionaries. These parishes also experimented with Progressive techniques, adapted slightly to their own needs.[38]

The best example of adaptation is the settlement. Italian parishes had what they called "settlements" but which differed from the sort pioneered by Jane Addams.[39] No one lived in Italian settlements; they were usually staffed by sisters who lived in separate convents. Nor did the settlements offer extensive educational or charitable programs. Rather, they were places that provided facilities that did not fit into schools or churches.

For example, the parish of St. Anthony of Padua in Greenwich Village built a settlement in 1915. The settlement had all sorts of features designed to keep young men entertained under Catholic auspices. The basement had a swimming pool, billiards tables, two bowling alleys, and gymnastic equipment. The ground floor had a theatre and meeting space for sodalities.[40]

A little closer to the Progressive model was Madonna House, near St. Joachim's and St. Joseph's parishes on the Lower East Side. The sisters at Madonna House belonged to an American religious order, but they worked in two parishes staffed by Italian missionary clergy. Like other Catholic settlements, Madonna House had a nursery. Like non-Catholic settlements, it offered a variety of secular activities as well: classes in commercial art, dancing, dramatics, dressmaking, English, and "physical training," public lectures, entertainments, Boy Scouts, Girl Scouts, a military organization, a brass band, games, hikes and outings. Like traditional Catholics, the sisters distributed charity: food, fuel, clothing, free meals for children and the homeless, and advice to mothers.[41]

The most commonly adopted Progressive institution was the nursery. Of the Italian day care centers, that of St. Anthony of Padua has been most fully described. St. Anthony's nursery occupied the top, or second, floor of its settlement. It was staffed by two sisters from the same order which ran the parochial school. The nursery had eating, playing, and napping space for sixty children, two years old and up, and there was an after-school program for older children. The nursery menu, at least, was an Americanizing experience: oatmeal and milk at 8:00 a.m., soup and tea with milk at lunch, and cocoa and bread at 4:00 p.m. The nursery also supplied medical attention. There was a nurse on the staff, and a doctor came weekly to check on the youngsters.[42]

One priest even involved his parish in the expensive and time-consuming project of summer camps. This was Guiseppe M. Congedo, pastor of the Sacred Hearts of Jesus and Mary on East 33rd Street in Manhattan. Congedo began his "fresh air" ministry in the summer of 1918 by taking fifty or sixty children to the beach for a day. Having survived that, the next summer he rented a nine-room house in White Plains, New York, and gave vacations to 500 youngsters. The neighbors in White Plains complained about the noise and activity, and Congedo began looking for a place to buy for a summer camp. He settled on some property in Hackettstown, New Jersey.[43] By the early 1920s, St. Joseph's Summer Institute had room for 175 boys and girls, ages six through thirteen. It was staffed by Congedo and fifteen laity.[44]

Other Italian parishes maintaining Progressive institutions will be mentioned in passing below. These many scattered references indicate that the adoption of Progressive institutions by Italian parishes was fairly widespread. But why were Italian parishes interested in these ideas?

It seems that this interest did not stem from agreement with Progressive ideas on child-rearing, or on the cause and cure of poverty. The most succinct evidence of this comes from a survey taken of the churches in Depression-era East Harlem. East Harlem had four Italian parishes. Three participated in the survey. All of them offered at least something for youth. St. Lucy's participated in the Free Milk for Babies program. St. Ann's had a boys' club that sponsored boxing and other sports. Our Lady of Mount Carmel had a nursery and a social worker who helped the parishioners apply for welfare. But none of the clergy justified their parishes' activities on Progressive grounds. In fact, their assumptions that poverty resulted from either God's will or from an individual's own idle and spendthrift habits were quite traditional.[45]

A few Italian priests engaged in youth work as a way of practicing Christian charity. In some cases, youth ministry was part of the work of a religious order. The Salesians, for example, had been founded to work among delinquent boys in Turin. Salesian priests and brothers continued their apostolate when they took up work among Italian immigrants on the Lower East Side of New York.[46]

A frequently-cited motive for Italian pastors engaging in Progressive philanthropy was competition with the Protestants. Italian clergy were no different from Irish Americans in their suspicions of Protestantism. The Italian Franciscans at St. Anthony of Padua explained that they opened their nursery because otherwise working mothers would have to leave their babies in Protestant institutions, "with what dangers to these innocent creatures, one can only imagine."[47] The Italian clergy in East Harlem during the Depression recognized that an individual parish's efforts could not relieve the neighborhood's poverty, but they refused to join with Protestant or secular agencies to seek more effective measures.[48]

For some Italian pastors, Progressive philanthropy was a form of outreach. This was the observation of Caroline Ware, a social scientist who did an in-depth study of Greenwich Village in the 1920s. Greenwich Village had two Italian parishes. Both were faced with yawning generation gaps. Youngsters, seeking acceptance from their American peers, rejected their parents' Italian culture, including the Catholic church. The clergy retaliated by making the Church seem as American as possible. One parish had an amateur theatrical group, one pastor coached basketball teams for both boys and girls, and both parishes sponsored dances which took the place of parents as matchmakers for Italians looking for marriage partners. Though Italian themselves, the clergy strove to prove to the youngsters that one could abandon one's Italian heritage without abandoning one's religion.[49]

Other pastors used Progressive techniques to strengthen ethnic ties. The parochial school was already recognized as an efficient transmitter of Italian language, history, and literature, but other institutions could also help acquaint the young people with Italian culture or develop among them a sense of national solidarity.[50] For example, Ruggero Passeri, O.F.M., pastor of St. Sebastian's on the Lower East Side in the early 1920s, had his parish's amateur theatrical group perform Italian dramas.[51] Passeri also organized a baseball team, which defended Italy's honor by winning the archdiocesan championship.[52]

The case histories presented above raise some interesting questions about Italian immigrants, about the Catholic church in the United States, and about the way historians understand immigrant church history. Unfortunately, there is not enough data to answer all of the questions.

The most disappointing aspect of the work relates to the immigrants themselves. If those who were involved in these parishes were alive today, they would want to know whether their methods preserved the immigrant's religiosity. Did adopting "the tactics of the enemy" bind the Italians more closely to the Church?

It is notoriously difficult to measure whether the immigrant has kept the faith. The evidence is by and large the Italians did. They are among the most numerous of American Catholics today.[53] However, whether

Progressive philanthropy had anything to do with this persistence is impossible to say.

There are two major pieces of evidence against the effectiveness of Progressive Catholicism. One is the small number of persons reached by this form of ministry. For example, all of the Italian day nurseries in the Archdiocese of New York took care of 3,239 children in 1924.[54] Census records indicate that there were 802,946 Italian-born and American-born Italians in New York City in 1920.[55] Even when Brooklyn and Queens are excluded, there must have been more than 3,239 Italian mothers who could have used help with their preschoolers.

The other piece of evidence is the short life-span of some Progressive institutions. Very few of the establishments mentioned in this study survive today. Only one nursery which served Italians is still open.[56] Our Lady of Mount Carmel closed its nursery during the Depression.[57] The Barat Settlement and Day Nursery closed in 1945.[58] Other organizations are difficult to trace.

On the other hand, there is evidence to suggest that when settlements and summer camps did their job, they did more than just keep the kids Catholic. At least a dozen of the boys upon whom Nicholas Russo and William Walsh lavished their attention went on to become clergy themselves.[59] From 1927 to 1957, Nativity had four pastors, all of them Italian-American alumni of the Jesuits' boy ministry.[60]

Another observation has to do with adult Italians. The Italian clergy and adult laity did not watch passively while native Americans used Progressive institutions to convert their children to American Catholicism. The Italian parishes organized and gave financial support to settlements, day nurseries, summer camps, and youth recreation programs. Sometimes these institutions were used to keep the youngsters in the ethnic fold. Sometimes they promoted assimilation to American Catholicism.

The Progressive Era also left its mark on the institutional Church. Progressivism brought expanded notions of what parishes should offer their parishioners. Nineteenth-century parishes were considered complete if they had churches, rectories, schools, convents, and bank accounts. Progressive pastors added other buildings, and took on more responsibility for their parishioners' welfare.

Three aspects of the institutional life of the Church bear special mention. The first is the role of the Catholic sisters. As parish activities expanded, so did the roles of the pastor and his assistants, the parochial school sisters. Some sisters moved from traditional parochial school work to nursery work. New religious orders were created to take up settlement and youth recreation work.[61]

The second is the expansion of extra-curricular catechism classes. Throughout most of the nineteenth century, the parochial school was the preferred method of Catholic instruction, and outside of it catechism was taught haphazardly.[62] The new settlement houses served as after-school catechetical centers. The religious and laity who taught catechism in settlements pioneered the after-school programs which educate most Catholic children today about their faith.

The third is the need for greater centralization. Its reputation to the contrary, nineteenth-century American Catholicism was not highly centralized. Chancery (bishops') staffs were small, and parishes bore most of the responsibility for Catholic spiritual life, parochial school education, and charity. But once parishes started opening Progressive institutions, a need for sounder financing and for greater coordination between eleemosynary agencies became apparent. The Archdiocese of New York therefore created an umbrella organization, Catholic Charities, in 1922.

Finally, the research presented here adds detail and complexity to the concept of the "immigrant church." This phrase was coined by Jay P. Dolan, who used it as the title of his 1975 book on Irish and German Catholics in antebellum New York City. Dolan found that immigrant Catholics did not immediately melt into American Catholicism. Rather, they segregated themselves into ethnic parishes in which they preserved their various national Catholic cultures.[63] Other scholars have found that other ethnic groups followed the same patterns. Silvano Tomasi, whose book on Italians was published the same year as Dolan's book, discovered the same patterns in Italian communities in New York in the late nineteenth century.[64]

The research presented here suggests that using national parishes to conserve a European heritage was but one role of "the immigrant church," and a role which the immigrant churches may have passed through rather quickly. The immigrants and their clergy were carried along by the same social and cultural currents, such as Progressivism, that affected other Americans. Perhaps more important, the immigrants and their clergy were carried along by waves of generational change, forced to reassess community mores and community institutions in order to keep up with their offspring, and to keep those offspring in the ethnic and religious fold.

Notes

1. United States Department of Commerce, Bureau of the Census, *Historical Statistics of the United States: Colonial Times to 1970* (2 vols., Washington, D.C., 1975), I, 105–106.

 2. Silvano M. Tomasi, C. S., *Piety and Power: The Role of the Italian Parishes in the New York Metropolitan Area, 1880–1930* (New York, 1975), ch. 2. This book has a number of handy statistical tables.

 3. Robert F. Foerster, *The Italian Emigration of Our Times* (Cambridge, Mass., 1924), especially chs. 2–6 and 17–20.

 4. John Horace Mariano, *The Italian Contribution to American Democracy* (Boston, 1921), 19–22.

 5. There is no history of Italians in New York City comparable to Humbert Nelli's *Italians in Chicago, 1880–1930* (New York, 1970), but several aspects of Italian life in New York are covered in diverse books. For the economic position of Italians, see Foerster *Italian Emigration*, chs. 17–19 and Louise C. Odencrantz, *Italian Women in Industry* (New York,[1919]reprinted 1977). For housing, see Jacob A. Riis, *How the Other Half Lives: Studies Among the Tenements of New York* (New York,[1890]reprinted 1971), chs. 5 and 6 and Donna R. Gabaccia, *From Sicily to Elizabeth Street: Housing and Social Change among Italian Immigrants, 1880–1930* (Albany, N.Y., 1984). For family life, see Leonard Covello, *The Social Background of the Italo-American Schoolchild: A Study of the Southern Italian Family Mores and their Effect on the School Situation in Italy and America* (Leiden, 1967). For a collection of Progressive articles on Italians, see Lydio Tomasi, ed., *The Italian in America: The Progressive View* (New York, 1972).

 6. Henry J. Browne, "The 'Italian Problem' in the Catholic Church in the United States, 1880–1900," United States Catholic Historical Society *Records and Studies* 35 (1946), 46–72.

 7. Louis M. Giambastiani, "Into the Melting Pot — the Italians," *Extension* 7 (1912), 9–10, 20–21.

 8. Rudolph J. Vecoli, "Prelates and Peasants: Italian Immigrants and the Catholic Church," *Journal of Social History* 2 (1969), 217–268, and Vecoli, "Cult and Occult in Italian-American Culture: The Persistence of a Religious Heritage," in Randall M. Miller and Thomas D. Marzik, eds., *Immigrants and Religion in Urban America* (Philadelphia, 1977), 25–47.

 9. Robert Anthony Orsi, "The Madonna of 115th Street: Faith and Community in Italian Harlem, 1880–1950," (Ph.D. dissertation, Yale University, 1982).

10. *St. Anthony of Padua Church, New York City* (South Hackensack, N.J., 1967), unpaginated.

11. Stephen Michael DiGiovanni, "Michael Augustine Corrigan and the Italian Immigrants: The Relationship Between the Church and the Italians in the Archdiocese of New York, 1885–1902," (Ph.D. dissertation, Georgian University [Rome], 1983).

12. *The Official Catholic Directory* includes in its listings of New York parishes the dates of the parishes' foundations and the ethnic groups they originally served.

13. Dorothy Reed, *Leisure Time of Girls in "Little Italy"* (Portland, Ore., 1932).

14. Irwin L. Child, *Italian or American? The Second Generation in Conflict* (New Haven, 1943).

15. Frederick H. Wright, "The Italian in America," *The Missionary Review of the World* 20 (1907), 196–198.

16. Examples of Protestant interest in Italians abound. The Italian Mission of the Protestant Episcopal Church in the City of New York published annual reports in the 1880s and 1890s. Antonio Arrighi, pastor of the Broome Street Tabernacle and probably the best-known Italian Protestant in New York, prepared annual reports for the Italian Evangelical Church. Two contemporary articles are William Wynkoop McNair, "The Evangelization of our Italians," *The Assembly Herald* 11 (1905), 404–409, and Stefano L. Testa, " 'Strangers from Rome' in Greater New York," *The Missionary Review* 31 (1908), 216–218. There are also unpublished reports, such as Henry D. Jones, "The Evangelical Movement among Italians in New York City," (New York, 1935). Historians have begun to exploit this material; see John McNab, "Bethlehem Chapel: Presbyterians and Italian Americans in New York City," *Journal of Presbyterian History* 55 (1977) 145–160.

17. Thomas F. Meehan, "Evangelizing the Italians," *The Messenger of the Sacred Heart of Jesus* 39 (1903), 32.
18. "Father Nicholas Russo," *Woodstock Letters* 31 (1902), 282.
19. Nicholas Russo, S. J., to Michael Augustine Corrigan, New York, October 24, 1891, Corrigan Papers, microfilm roll #14, Archives of the Archdiocese of New York (hereafter, AANY).
20. The next few paragraphs rely on Russo's own account, "The Origin and Progress of our Italian Mission in New York," *Woodstock Letters* 25 (1896), 135–143.
21. "Father Nicholas Russo," 284.
22. The next few paragraphs depend on a memoir by some of the parishoners, "A Short History of the Mission of Our Lady of Loretto, New York," *Woodstock Letters* 96 (1917), 172–187. Astute readers will notice that the text spells Loreto with one T, the Jesuits with two. This paper follows the *Official Catholic Directory* and the sign above the door of the church, both of which have one T.
23. The next few paragraphs depend on *The Year Book of the Barat Settlement House* (New York, 1912).
24. *The Year Book of the Barat Settlement and Day Nursery* (New York, 1915), 15.
25. "Report of Fr. Zwinge" (typescript, January 22, 1913), Loretto-Nativity folder, Archives of the New York Province of the Society of Jesus (hereafter, NYSJ).
26. "Short History," 181.
27. Nicholas Russo, S. J., to Michael Augustine Corrigan, New York, February 22 and 24, 1898, Italian Americans and Religion, Series I, Box 1, Our Lady of Loretto folder, Center for Migration Studies (hereafter, CMS:IAR:Series:Box, folder).
28. D[enis] Lynch, S. J., to Father Provincial, New York, October (1915?), NYSJ:Loretto-Nativity folder.
29. Dominic Cirigliano, S. J., "Jottings on the History of Nativity Church in Preparation for the Centenary Celebration" (typescript, 1942), NYSJ: History of Nativity Parish, 1842–1917.
30. B[ernard] J. Reilly to John Cardinal Farley, New York, February 4, 1917, CMS: IAR:I:1, Nativity.
31. William H. Walsh, S. J., to Joseph Mooney, New York, January 22, 1917, and William H. Walsh, S. J., "Short Statement of Father Walsh to the Cardinal's Committe . . .," New York, February 16, 1917, both in NYSJ:Loretto-Nativity folder.
32. "Church of the Nativity Transferred to our Fathers," *Woodstock Letters* 46 (1917), 411–412.
33. William H. Walsh, S. J., to Father Provincial, St.-Andrews-on-Hudson, New York, March 17, 1942, NYSJ:Nativity, 1933–1947.
34. There is a batch of letters from Quinn to Father Provincial in NYSJ: Loretto-Nativity. The important ones for this paragraph are: September 21, 1919, October 1 and 29, 1919, April 15, 1920, and August 9, 1920.
35. Daniel J. Quinn, S. J., to Father Provincial, New York, October 13, 1920, NYSJ:Loretto-Nativity folder.
36. "Our Church for Italians," *Woodstock Letters* 34 (1905), 448–449.
37. Russo, "Origin and Progress," 138–139.
38. For more on other Italian clergy in New York, see Mary Elizabeth Brown, "Italian and Italian-American Secular Clergy in New York, 1880–1950," *U.S. Catholic Historian* 6 (Fall 1987), 281–300.
39. In fact, almost all Catholics used the word "settlement" to mean something a bit different from the Progressive model. The one exception as far as New York's Italians were concerned was Miss Marian Gurney, founder of St. Rose's Settlement on the Upper East Side. See Lawrence Franklin, "The Italian in America: What He Has Been, What He Shall Be," *Catholic World* 71 (1900), 67.
40. The next few paragraphs rely on *Note di Cronaca sull' Origine e Progresso della Chiesa di S. Antonio* (Naples, 1924), 17–18.
41. William R. Kelly, "The Cardinal of Charities," *Il Carroccio* 19 (1924), 447.
42. *S. Antonio di Padua*, 18.

43. *Golden Jubilee, Church of the Sacred Hearts of Jesus and Mary, 1914–1964* (South Hackensack, N.J., 1964), unpaginated.
44. *Report of the Catholic Charities of the Archdiocese of New York, 1924* (New York, 1925), 33.
45. Mae Case Marsh, "The Life and Work of the Churches in an Interstitial Area" (Ph.D. dissertation, New York University, 1932), 331–350, 417–434, 575.
46. "Cronaca della Casa di Santa Brigida in New York City" (manuscript, 1915), CMS:IAR:III:6, St. Brigid's, New York City, and "Cronaca della Casa Salesiana e Chiesa di Maria Ausiliatrice" (manuscript, 1939), CMS:IAR:III:6, Mary, Help of Christians.
47. *S. Antonio di Padua*, 18.
48. Marsh, "Churches in an Interstitial Area," 597.
49. Caroline Ware, *Greenwich Village, 1920–1930: A Comment on American Civilization in the Post-War Years* (New York, [1935] reprinted 1965), 311–318.
50. Joseph M. Congedo, "The Bearers of Rich Gifts," *Il Carroccio* 20 (1924) 471–473.
51. *Il Carroccio* 15 (1922), 151.
52. *Ibid.*, 15 (1922), 836; 16 (1922), 123; and 17 (1923), 726.
53. Harold J. Abramson, *Ethnic Diversity in Catholic America* (New York, 1973), 19. Of the 47.8 million Catholics in the United States in 1970, 10 million were of Italian extraction.
54. *Catholic Charities* (1924), 26. The statistics are as follows:

Nursery	Parish & Address	Children Per Year
Asilo Scalabrini	Our Lady of Pompeii Greenwich Village	150
Barat	Nativity Lower East Side	140
Keating	Mary, Help of Christians Lower East Side	609
Little Flower	Immaculate Conception North Bronx	35
Madonna	St. Joachim, St. Joseph Lower East Side	240
Mt. Carmel School	Our Lady of Mt. Carmel East Harlem	1,274
Our Lady of Loreto	Our Lady of Loreto Lower East Side	153
St. Ann's	St. Ann's East Harlem	93
St. Anthony's	St. Anthony's Greenwich Village	240
St. John's	Our Lady of Mt. Carmel East Harlem	75
St. Pascal's	Epiphany East 22nd Street	230

55. Ira Rosenwaite, *Population History of New York City* (Syracuse, N.Y., 1972), 203–204.
56. The remaining nursery is that of Our Lady of Loreto, which was opened after the Jesuits left that parish.
57. Marsh, "Churches in an Interstitial Area," 435.
58. *Catholic Charities in 1945* (New York, 1946), 32.
59. Gabriel A. Zema, S. J., "The Italian Immigrant Problem," *America* 55 (May 16, 1936), 129–130. Zema was one of these boys.
60. *Church of the Nativity, New York City* (South Hackensack, N.J., 1971) 5–7.
61. For example, Marian Gurney, founder of St. Rose's Settlement, went on to found a religious order, the Sisters of Our Lady of Christian Doctrine, dedicated to after-

school catechism teaching, youth recreation work, and parochial work. See the *New York Times*, February 11, 1957, p. 29.

62. For an idea of how haphazardly, see George A. Kelly, *The Story of St. Monica's Parish: New York City, 1879-1954* (New York, 1954), 38.

63. Jay P. Dolan, *The Immigrant Church: New York's Irish and German Catholics, 1815-1865* (Baltimore, 1975).

64. See note 2 above.

6

The Fall of the German-American Community: Buffalo 1914–1919

The German-American community before World War I was an institutionalized challenge to the nation's dominant culture. The group was massive. The German-American Bund alone, in 1916, claimed two million members. German-Americans' dedication to German culture was heart-felt and ingrained in organizations from banks to schools. But the war was jarring: by 1919 the Bund had collapsed along with the will of many German-Americans to resist the draft, prohibition, and the Americanization programs instituted during the war. The demise of the German counterculture is one of the most dramatic episodes of American ethnic history, and a popular topic of research.[1]

The German-American wartime collapse suggests that something occurred very suddenly, but what? The literature suggests that the superpatriotic crusade against German culture was crucial, that harassment forced the ethnics to erase their cultural trademarks.[2] On one level, the patriotic hysteria that made it very difficult for the Germans to maintain their newspapers and parochial schools cannot be denied. But on a deeper level, why did so many German-Americans let the war destroy them, and why were they so lackluster in capitalizing on the post-war disillusionment? As the problem involves group psychology, it is necessary to examine the most basic assumptions behind German-

American efforts. Wartime realizations not only undermined the visible signs of German culture, but also the beliefs and pretensions that sustained the community.[3]

To clarify this point, a case study seems appropriate. Generalizations at the national level still lack the perspective that is needed to establish basic arguments. One wonders, for instance, about the actual influence of the superpatriots, the numbers of German-Americans, and the degree to which Bund leaders, or any national German associations, represented them. A case study, unique in nature, cannot totally obviate these problems, but it can examine the question of representation at a grassroots level. A look at trends in Buffalo — an important German-American city in its own right and a representative one given the size and diversity of its immigrant/ethnic population — will not only reassess the war experience, but also will illustrate the mass appeal of the Americanization movement to Germans themselves.

The case of Buffalo shows that historians have tended to underestimate the size of the German-American community in the early twentieth century. Because of the availability of the New York State manuscript censuses and previous studies, one can attain a reliable estimate of the German-American population in this port city of the Great Lakes. The methods used to determine this population involved the use of a surname probability list and estimates of intermarriage, and the result is a logical extrapolation of nineteenth-century trends. Of the city's population of 352,000 in 1900, the Germans comprised about 130,000 or 37 percent.[4] This figure indicates that the proportionate strength of the German-Americans in the city had declined from a high of almost 50 percent in 1875. Still, the Germans remained a substantial group, more numerous than the immigrants from southern and eastern Europe, but not so numerous that they made Buffalo atypical as a recipient of German immigration. A simple albeit crude equation clarifies this point. In Buffalo there were about 3.6 residents of German descent for every German immigrant in 1900. As Buffalo had a representative proportion of immigrants for large cities and a relatively youthful German settlement, the equation can be used to estimate a German-American population of 194,000 in Milwaukee (68 percent of the city's residents), 615,000 in Chicago (36 percent), and 1,160,000 in New York City (34 percent) in 1900.[5]

By 1915, the appearance of an American-born generation of Poles, Russian Jews, and Italians lowered the proportion of German-Americans in Buffalo to about 30 percent.[6] Nationwide, the German-American population increased, but not in proportion to these newer groups. Despite this relative decline, the Germans continued to make up a large proportion of the nation's more established population. In Buffalo, the city's Main Street before World War I provided visible evidence of the German-American impact. In the central business district near the lake, the German Insurance Society building competed with D. H. Burnham's Ellicott Square Building and Louis Sullivan's Guaranty "skyscraper" as one of the city's tallest structures. Further "up" Main Street to the north, a dark stone bank, called the "German-American," gave way to German bookstores and restaurants. Of the four churches on Main Street, two were German: St. Louis Catholic and Holy Trinity Lutheran. The St. Louis congregation was built in the likeness of Cologne cathedral in 1889. They boasted that their spire was the tallest in the city.[7]

Every ethnic group had a stake in the city, but the bookstores of Ernst Besser and Otto Ulbrich on Main Street carried histories of the city that were written from a German point of view. Both *Geschichte der Deutschen in Buffalo and Erie County* (1898) and *Buffalo und Sein Deutschtum* (1912) argued that the Yankee village had been transformed into an industrial center by German industry and diligence.[8] As the author of *Buffalo und Sein Deutschtum* put it, the Germans of the city had "paved the streets," "contributed to the city's prosperity," and had defeated the anti-immigrant, nativist spirit of the Yankees.[9] In addition to such claims, the books documented a few basic facts. Solitary German traders had arrived in the 1790s, and the "German village" on the city's east side dated back to the canal boom in the 1830s. The community had endured the nativist period of the 1850s and the Civil War, but Gilded Age prosperity had ushered in a new era. German entrepreneurs and professionals became city leaders, serving as mayors and as members of the Board of Trade. A major wave of immigration from Germany in the 1880s delighted German businessmen. In 1910 Louis Fuhrmann became the sixth German-American mayor, and a clique of successful German families dominated such trades as tanning (Schoellkopf), flour milling (Urban), meat packing (Dold), and brewing (Lang and Beck).[10]

The east side community of Germans was defined by both "blood and culture" in the early twentieth century.[11] The political influence of the Germans was augmented by the German press that reached 32,000 subscribers — more than one for every household of German descent in Buffalo in 1915.[12] In the schools, a new generation of German-American principals nodded approvingly at German language courses. By 1915, Buffalo's German classes enrolled 20 percent of the city's primary school students. The total number of students in German classes was 12,406, the highest ever. In the high schools, the emphasis on German was more pronounced because it was thought essential to understand the scientific and commercial innovations of the early twen-

tieth century. Forty-five percent of the city's high school students were
in German classes.[13]

In 1914, nearly one of every two German-American household heads
in Buffalo had been born in the United States, but when Germany
declared war on England and France, both American-born Germans
and their immigrant parents looked with pride at early German victories. German military successes had dazzled the east side masses since
the 1860s. In 1914, the German Day celebration attracted 30,000 participants, the largest crowd in the city's history to gather for a single
German-American festival. Emotional support for Germany was un-
disguised and contagious. Industrialists such as the Dolds and
Schoellkopfs appeared. Buffalo-born members of the elite musical society, the Orpheus, sang "Germany Above the Nations." Even the
American-born leader of the English Lutheran movement in the city,
Friedrich Kahler, heralded the prospect of a German victory. The
German-American press encouraged the notion that the war would
resemble the glorious but brief engagements of the late nineteenth century, such as the Franco-Prussian War in 1871 and the Spanish-American
in 1898. "German precision" would prevail, and the German-Americans
would mediate the fortunes of the world's remaining powers, Deutsch-
land and America.[14]

This was the dream of 1914. Confident that Germany's victory was
imminent, the Buffalo Bund leader, Wilhelm Gaertner, dispatched a
note to the German Kaiser. The letter had the Bund seal, but it spoke
for "the German citizens of Buffalo." Gaertner promised the Kaiser
the "moral and financial support" of Buffalo's German Americans during
the crisis.[15] According to a reporter from the *Buffalo News*, a leading
progressive newspaper, the reading of the letter on German Day was
greeted with thunderous cheering and applause. After a few speakers
had urged German-Americans to take a more commanding role in
American life, voices joined in a lusty rendition of the German national anthem. Buffalo's German papers subsequently hailed the festival as a "triumphant sign" of German unity in the city.[16]

In retrospect, German Day, 1914, was a golden day for German ethnicity in the city. A self-conscious local following had promoted unity
with chauvinistic assessments of German culture and the German nation. But the surging applause, the wild rebelliousness of the singing,
and the unsupervised dancing were all based on assumptions. Would
the German armies justify their faith in things German? Was bilingualism feasible? Could German Socialists and capitalists work together
to forge a more perfect economic order as the festival speaker of 1914
implied? However they defined their loyalty to the Kaiser and each

other, they had already made structural choices that were inimical to the future of German culture. They had emigrated to a country 5,000 miles away from the homeland, they had learned English, and they had also expressed loyalty to a nation in which English was the dominant language. By absorbing the English language, they became members of a new communication network, and entered into the political life of a democratic nation. Their acceptance of English also cleared the path of instruction for the Americanization of their children.

Only one step remained to be taken, to drop German as a second language, This had not yet occurred. The German language was the key that unlocked the secrets of the German culture. Though one did not need it in America, one could always use it as long as the tie to Germany promised dividends. A constellation of minor provinces in the mid-nineteenth century, Germany had become perhaps the leading military power in the world by 1915. The Germans went on to proclaim their superiority in every area, and thus businessmen, scientists, merchants, musicians, and teachers had a reason to sharpen their translation skills. With a knowledge of German idioms, one might attain a competitive head start in the laboratories, stores, schools, and conservatories of America.

The tie between the German language and the German nation was fastened steadfastly by German-American institutions. The German organizations on Buffalo's east side (e.g. the Harugari lodges, the Turnverein gymnastic society, and the Sangverein singing society) imported literature from Germany and provided arenas for German speakers to meet and socialize. Rather than rely on the education of American doctors in a crisis, the east side also supported two German hospitals where German-speaking physicians applied recent techniques learned from German medical schools. The German churches, too, stood staunchly in support of the German language. According to the Reverend Edwin Mueller of Emmaus Lutheran Church, the English language might become the language of the world, but never of the church. In 1915, the overwhelming majority of Evangelical, Reformed, and Lutheran churches used German for their main Sunday services. Though Buffalo's German Catholic priests said Mass in Latin rather than German, the Catholic population on the east side was as supportive of their first language as the Protestants. The second and fourth most popular German newspapers, the *Volksfreund* and the *Aurora*, with a combined circulation of 13,000, both represented the interests of the German movement within the American Catholic church.[17]

The threat to Germany awakened the commitment for the culture of the homeland. But as the energetic forays of 1914 ebbed into the trench warfare of 1915, the conflict became more mundane and ugly. Faced with a war of attrition, both the Central Powers and the Allies blockaded each other's ports. The British, with a superior navy, contained the German fleet at Kiel, but the Germans, with the improvement of the submarine, had their own oceanic patrol. The details of these military procedures would have mattered little to Americans had it not been for the fact that the submarine was unable to follow traditional rules of naval warfare. Though a destroyer could intimidate and detain a neutral merchant ship to search for contraband, an emerging submarine was like a shark on land — passive and vulnerable. The submarine could not ask questions, and if the German blockage was to be effective, these undersea boats would have to fire at any ship that could aid the British war effort.

The German naval staff initially had dismissed the thought of destroying neutral vessels, fearing that indiscriminate shooting would shock world opinion. But with the British noose tightening, the Germans became more flexible. In the spring of 1915, the chief of the German naval staff announced a policy of unrestricted attacks. The sinking of the Lusitania, with a loss of 128 American lives, promoted reassessments of the German homeland. President Woodrow Wilson talked about the possibility of war. Those German-American leaders, such as William Gaertner, who had sympathized with the German naval policy, now found it helpful to disentangle themselves from the Kaiser's reputation. Some blamed the British for arming their merchant marine. Others faulted American authorities for not prohibiting trans-oceanic passages.[18] But the hoped-for vindication of "German precision" was frustrated. Submarine warfare marked the first major turning point in the German-Americans' retreat from their ethnic identity.

The Americanization Movement

Many German-American leaders across the country in 1915 began to pursue a strategy that seems remarkably self-defeating in hindsight. They attempted to camouflage the symbols of German ethnicity behind American patriotic festivals and slogans. On the one hand, the new approach was a concession to superpatriotic pressures. As the historian John Hawgood has pointed out, "Americanism" was a term that many German-Americans associated with the English language and nativist reform. In their patriotic utterances, the German-American leaders sometimes bewildered their own constituency, but they did fashion an intelligible response to the realities of Europe. Doubts that Germany could win a quick war made it necessary to reaffirm one's commitment to the United States. At the same time, by appearing as Americanized as possible, German ethnics could best influence the nation's policy toward Germany. American neutrality might ensure Germany's success, and affirm the political clout of the German Americans.[19]

Their opponents were a vocal minority in Buffalo by 1915. The preparedness parades in the years before 1917 were subdued affairs. According to one contemporary historian, most of the people "laughed" at the first efforts of "the Americanizers."[20] The most influential of these pro-war activists had the time to invest in the Preparedness Parade committees, the Committee on Americanization, and the Committee of One-hundred, groups in which over 80 percent of the members had Anglo-American surnames and only about 6 percent had German surnames.[21] These organizations, superpatriotic leaders such as Walter P. Cooke, Edward H. Butler, and Finley H. Greene, and newspapers such as the *News* and *Express* articulated the pro-British position of their Anglo-American constituency. Figures for 1915 are lacking, but for 1925, the entire Anglo-American population constituted only 15 percent of the city's population of 538,000. Germans that year made up 25 percent of the total, Poles almost 20 percent, and Irish 10 percent.[22]

The logic of the superpatriotic position exerted a force, however, that touched nearly all Americans. It was hegemonic in the sense that while it did not persuade the majority, it so expertly allied its advocacy of preparedness with "national interest" that counter-arguments appeared shrill and contradictory. German submarines had shed American blood. America was prospering as a supplier of the Allies. German spies were in America. Gustav Hitzel, the new leader of the Buffalo Bund, like many other German-American leaders, faced these realities and tried to embrace the nationalism of the superpatriotic position. A responsible leader had to swallow the pill and appeal to national interests. Hitzel, a leader of the Germans, subsequently supported the Americanization movement within German circles.[23]

The Buffalo-born physician was a robust exponent of what might be called hidden ethnicity. As a local politician, Hitzel believed that Gaertner's pro-German position was very dangerous. As the son of an immigrant he knew that the Kaiser had a limited audience in America. Never one to antagonize non-Germans, Hitzel nevertheless believed in the superiority of German culture. He was confident about the skills he had learned in Munich and about the quality of the city's German Hospital. His authoritarian personality was a product of this assurance, but his message was one of restraint rather than proclamation. In 1915, he believed that an era of German dominance would soon dawn in America. Until it did, the Germans could remain discreet. Excellence would always be rewarded, and the "secrets of German culture" would always be sought.[24]

The easy faith of local leaders did not lend itself to the writing of books or to a propaganda crusade, but merely to efforts to check the excesses of German aliens and radicals. After sidetracking the Bund's antiprohibition activities, Hitzel and a few like-minded colleagues visited the German-American clubs and urged that they moderate their affirmations of ethnicity. For the 1915 German Day, Hitzel introduced local newsmen to his patriotic countrymen. The color scheme stressed red, white, and blue. The Bund members distributed "Old Glory" buttons with the caption, "The Flag I Love Best." The love for America was rendered by a 250-voice children's choir that sang the "Star Spangled Banner." One speaker, Evangelical pastor Frederich Haas, characterized the Germans as the best of patriots. He had an "uncanny feeling that the United States was again becoming a colony of England."[25]

Haas insisted that neutrality was the historical ideal of the American people. Despite the secular character of the Bund, and its Protestant leaders, German-Catholics supported strict neutrality and hooted at the name of Wilson. The German Central Verein, a national organization for Catholics that had been established by Buffalo immigrants seventy years before, proclaimed its "love for the American flag" in its 1915 convention at St. Paul. The local *Aurora*, normally a devotional paper, responded eagerly to the claim expressed at the convention that the sympathies of the Anglo-Americans were "unAmerican." In its fatherly, didactic manner, the *Aurora* urged its readers to:

1. Give generously to German-American peace organizations such as the American Independence Union and Labor's National Peace Council.
2. Become a member of the Bund.
3. Work unremittingly for the cause of peace.
4. Show other Americans that you are men of action.[26]

The *Echo*, the *Aurora's* English-language equivalent for second- and third-generation German Americans shared these concerns. The Catholic paper accused the Anglo-Americans of trying to set up a racial oligarchy where the standards of Americanism would be tied to English customs.[27]

The movement to divert eyes from the *Lusitania* and stress the need for peace found a leader in Louis Fuhrmann, the city's mayor. The Buffalo-born politician successfully caricatured the Anglo-American reformers in his utterances and built his appeal among Buffalo's ethnics. The *News*, in turn, saw the Fuhrmann administration as a smear agency, and clamored that the mayor's chief talent was his evasiveness. When the mayor attended preparedness programs to enhance the national defense, he proved adept at answering irrelevant questions and dodging real concerns. For him, the American arms buildup had nothing to do either with his administration or the threat from Germany. When asked to speak at a conference of mayors in New York City, Fuhrmann reminisced that the Canadian border had been peaceful for 100 years, and that the American people "did not want war with any nation on earth."[28]

Fuhrmann believed that he had expressed the will of a majority in Buffalo. Irish nationalists who belonged to the fraternal order of Hibernians joined German-American groups to save America from the war propaganda of the English. German leaders claimed that those of Austrian, Swiss, Danish, and Swedish descent subscribed to the German point of view. Tacit support came also from other groups. Buffalo's Italian newspaper, the *Corriere Italiano*, provided its readers with favorable accounts of German-American leaders such as Herman Ridder of New York City and the Buffalo Bund leader, Gustav Hitzel. Buffalo's socialists, who had drawn over 4,000 votes for Eugene Debs in 1912, showed distaste for the German leaders, but supported their call for neutrality.[29]

Isolationism was a practical response to superpatriotic jingoism, but it soon became an uncomfortable position. The German community was bound inextricably with Germany's fate. How could the German leaders extinguish the chauvinistic slogans that alone could bridge the division within their community? Despite the Bund's emphasis on Americanism in 1915 and 1916, German-American crowds inevitably sang "Germany Above the Nations" with more feeling than the "Star Spangled Banner." Concert goers were shocked to hear German speakers projecting their native tongue loudly and authoritatively during intermissions. A few Germans still expressed their admiration for the Kaiser, and some had even hailed the sinking of the *Lusitania* as a victory. The German crowds appeared to hunger for recognition: festival speakers lamented that they either wanted to hear of Germany's greatness, or hear of nothing at all.[30]

The fire of German exceptionalism continued to smolder despite the measures of men like Hitzel. The lack of political realism among the masses has suggested to some that many immigrants and "soul Germans" were deluding themselves. Americanization policy crashed not merely against narrow beliefs, but against the hard realities of a culture that had integrated those beliefs. Many German-American families maintained an unassailable sense of pride and honor. The cultural aristocracy of the old German neighborhoods imbued, with *Gemütlichkeit* and the love of order, dismissed others as "low Germans," "Yankees," or "shanty Irish." Their arrogance rested not necessarily on their economic status, but on their claim to culture. To these urban Junkers, the term "American" signified something "cheap" or even "trashy." An American-made product was defective. Even "American democracy" was suspect. These "soul" Germans believed in German culture both because they doubted America's power, and because their own personalities were intertwined with the myth of German superiority.[31]

The German-American community was at war with itself by 1915. Americanizers such as Hitzel wanted the stragglers to wake up, whereas pro-German leaders such as Gaertner wanted the patriotic singing to die down. Thus, when anti-German elements in the United States began a campaign of harassment in 1915, part of the community was either sympathetic to the effort, or at least unwilling to oppose it. In his State of the Union Message of 1915, in which he referred to those foreign citizens who poured "poison" into the arteries "of our national life," President Wilson proclaimed the crusade against all things German.[32] Later in the year, two books, *The German-American Plot* by Frederic Wile and *German Conspiracies in America* by William Skaggs, showed that anti-German extremists had plenty of rhetorical ammunition.[33] Mainstream Protestant ministers joined in the fray against the hyphen, and one Presbyterian publication compared the *Lusitania* with the crucifixion of Christ as one of the most atrocious acts in history.[34] Before the end of the year, Buffalo's major English-language newspapers, the *Courier*, the *Express*, and the *News*, had joined the campaign to "swat the hyphen" and end Germany's influence in America.

For the German-American community of 1915, the anti-German campaign was embodied by an outbreak of ethnic suspicions and criminal acts on the city's east side. On German Day, 1915, 15,000 Poles gathered in a nearby park to review German atrocities in eastern Europe. Stories of rapes, murders, and looting in eastern Europe seemed to justify and explain violent actions against local Germans. The stabbing of the retired Mendel Eckert seemed a case in point according to the *Volksfreund*. Eckert's only offense was his attendance at a German lodge meeting. On this way home, "Polish terrorists" had pounced on the hapless old man. An even more vicious assault occurred on Frederick Winter after he had picked up a German newspaper at a grocery store on the lower east side. This time, an Italian immigrant, Giovanni Dilerenso, purportedly had exchanged insults with Winter before thrashing at the German with a knife. With Winter in critical condition, the *Volksfreund* bemoaned the rumor that Dilerenso would plead self-defense. The German newspaper subsequently printed Dilerenso's address as well as the names of the policemen who were thought to have bungled the case.[35]

Harassment and the fear of persecution are often cited as the key factors behind the demise of German-American institutions. But even with the charged atmosphere, local German-Americans remained defiant as an ethnic group in the years 1916 and 1917. The 1916 German Day, for instance, drew 25,000 partisans, 5,000 more than in 1915. Though Hitzel remained committed to Americanism, German-American speakers became more shrill in their denunciation of "English materialism" and the "servants of Satan" who sold American munitions to the Allies. As the British blockade tightened in 1916, German-American leaders became more forthright about the need to aid poor German families in the Fatherland. A national campaign identified by the use of a black German cross to record contributions made its way through the major German communities in 1916. The so-called Iron Cross, a nationalistic imposition on a Christian symbol represented the sacrifice and charity that German-Americans were willing to show towards the Fatherland.[36]

Not a strategy but a dream gripped German-America at the New Year dawn of 1917. The prodigal son would resuscitate the father through humanitarian aid. A member of the British war party would slap the American ambassador in the face. The Russian war machine would crack under the cold wind of the steppes. But a much grimmer reality intervened. The Germans had lost over a million and half men by the beginning of 1917. With civilian morale crumbling at home, military leaders gambled that the United States was too divided to intervene in time. The Germans announced the resumption of unrestricted submarine warfare. As Wilson already had issued an ultimatum against this policy, war with Germany appeared inevitable. The intercepted Zimmerman telegram, like an invitation to fight, described a German proposal to give American territory to Mexico in return for a Mexican alliance with Germany. The tables of democracy swung against the German-Americans as the vast majority of congressmen sided with the President's war declaration on April 6.

German-American Obstructionism

The spring of 1917 appeared as a logical time for the German community to sever its remaining ties to the German nation and its culture. As the *Aurora* warned, the Germans would have to hold their tongues because even "unintended words could lead to incarceration — or worse."[37] But the declaration lacked finality and the ethnic culture developed a new set of dreams and explanations, more fantastic than ever before. It seemed to many that Germany, in announcing its submarine warfare, was on the eve of victory. The Americans, meanwhile, were too disorganized to fight. Wilson's "peace mask had fallen," and his hypocritical effort to hide his English sympathies would soon be exposed to the American people.[38]

By the summer of 1917, the Buffalo Bund had reinterpreted its ethnic activities. It was now a "patriotic organization" dedicated to the peaceful resolution of the war in opposition to Anglophile interventionists. Hitzel thought in terms of a distant post-war future, but Friedrich Brill, a local socialist candidate, aspired to offer the east side voters something more concrete and immediate. The fight for neutrality was over, he said, but the struggle for peace had just begun. Americans had been duped by the munitions makers and a "puppet President." In a mass struggle against wartime legislation and the official jingoism, the people could obstruct a military response. And all of this could be done without sacrificing America's territorial interests.[39]

Obstruction of the war without hindering America's military interests made little sense. But this nonrational option was the only one German-Americans had left besides sedition and resistance to the draft. Brill's suave appeal for humanity was consumed eagerly by the masses who applauded his anti-war and anti-draft platform. High school principals and local businessmen passed the word that patriotic fund raisers and civic programs were merely vehicles of superpatriotic propaganda. In the midst of the war crisis, Reverend Friedrich Kahler of the English Lutheran Church excited his congregation by saying that a Christian could not go to war blindly for his country, a principle had to be at stake.[40] Such a moral purpose seemed lacking, and the Germans created a mood of apathy and resignation in the city. The *News*, ever sensitive to dissent, reported that the turnout of 2,000 participants for the first Liberty Loan parade in Buffalo was a municipal disgrace. In tune with its east side subscribers, the *Volksfreund* responded: "Why should we be excited to see our young men become the cannon fodder of the European murderers?"[41]

For many who had urged the Americanization campaign within German circles, such rhetoric was both illegal and dangerous. But realists such as Hitzel and not the "anti-war shouters" lost their audiences in 1917. A case in point was Mayor Louis Fuhrmann, who sensed that his political future depended on his support for America's entry. Unlike Chicago's mayor, Bill Thompson, who courted his German constituents by opposing the war effort, Fuhrmann met the superpatriots part way. His aides claimed that the mayor shook the hand of every soldier who left Buffalo after the conscription law was passed in September 1917. The mayor also wrote personal dispatches for the local newspapers that encouraged citizens to respond favorably to the Liberty Loan program. He selected committees staffed with superpatriots to oversee fund-raising campaigns.[42]

Fuhrmann, however, also continued to heed his moderate supporters, a point that frequently has been missed. He refused to ban the sale of alcohol to incoming soldiers. He entertained Jeannette Rankin from Montana in September, a representative noted for her vote against the war declaration in April.[43] Even so, the mayor seemed unable to defend his loyal east side constituency from the onslaughts of the Socialists. By October, the *Commercial* noted that Brill's following was "dangerously large."[44] The Socialists machine appealed especially to the blue-collar workers who constituted almost 70 percent of the German-American household heads, but also to staunch Catholics and Evangelicals. Even Frank Schwab, a Buffalo-born friend of the mayor and the head of an anti-Socialist Catholic fraternal order, worked for the Socialist machine in the fall of 1917.[45] With a general primary approaching that would narrow the field of mayoral candidates to two, the incumbent had to campaign strenuously merely to remain a contender.

The 1917 campaign generated an unusual amount of controversy in the city. The *Courier* wondered how large the "Kaiser's following" had become. Other superpatriotic newspapers such as the *News* staged vicious attacks against Fuhrmann, who was seen as an artificial patriot. The third force, the superpatriots, wondered if the city would become an embarrassment to the country. Their candidate, George Buck, was a competent businessman with solid credentials for reform. But Buck, who wore steel-rimmed glasses and had purportedly displayed a British flag in his office, appeared to have no chance among the city's ethnics. In such a charged atmosphere, the *Express* wondered if the "best man" could win.[46]

The "smiling patriot," Louis Fuhrmann astounded his many enemies by again staging an upset. The moderate German-American triumphed in the Irish first ward, the Polish Fillmore district, and in the west side Italian wards. But what was most distressing for the superpatriots was the early report that Brill had toppled Buck for second place. All of the old east side wards were solidly in Brill's camp, and the reigning assertion that the Germans had "snuggled up to the Socialists" was fundamentally correct.[47] Spearman correlations between

the percentage of German-Americans in a ward and the strength of
the Socialist vote are very high and positive both for the German immigrants (.900) and the American-born of German descent (.634). These
scores suggest that a majority of German immigrants and a plurality
of the American-born voters of German descent rallied for the Socialists
in 1917.[48]

The final returns gave Buck a 400-vote lead over the Socialist candidate, but the strength of the "anti-war" party seemed unbounded. Buck,
the lone non-German, had obtained only 25 percent of the vote. Brill
had won over 14,000 votes and the *Times* believed that the Socialist tally
was the visible sign of the "unpatriotic" movement. Superpatriots agreed
that the east side needed a "thorough lesson in Americanism," but that
the crusade could not end at home.[49] The climax of Socialism in the
United States came not with the Debs vote in 1912 but with German-
American resistance to the war in 1917 in places like Chicago, Milwaukee
and Toledo. In the centers of German settlement, obstructionism reached
formidable heights: 10,000 people attended an anti-draft rally in New
Ulm, Minnesota, and in Monroe, Wisconsin, 90 percent of the voters
registered their discontent with the war in a special ballot.[50]

The battle between Buck and Brill embodied the ideological struggle
of 1917. Buck had the moral force of the state and the law on his side,
but Brill, an aspiring local leader, appealed to vague generalities about
the "conscience of the American people," and the clout of the German-
Americans. With the defeat of the Socialists in 1917, the soaring ideals
of the German-Americans were exposed to ridicule and recrimination.
As the east side householders watched their sons march off to the training
camps from which they would be sent to Europe, many fell back into
what might be called an ultra-realistic position. The great myths about
their culture ceased to have meaning. Cynicism and malaise set in.
What mattered was whether their sons would survive.

The War Spirit

The ties with Germany, whether expressed by hyphens, iron crosses,
or anti-draft votes, could not stretch much further. When Americans
began to engage German troops in the spring of 1918, the life went
out of German-American institutions. External pressures at this point
were formidable, but most surprising was the way many German-
Americans gravitated toward the superpatriotic position. The term
Heinie, a German-American neologism, was used even by those of
German descent to harass suspected spies and traitors. In general, the
German-American press reversed itself, with the surviving organs hostile

to the "Kaiser's empire." The obstructionist, once seen as a life-saving patriot, became a back-stabbing traitor.[51]

The decline of German-American resistance was evident in the outcome of the 1917 election. In the runoff between Fuhrmann and Buck, the German east side ventured wildly into the Buck column. The Anglo-superpatriot, who supported the war and prohibition, won the election, taking nineteen of the city's twenty-six wards. Part of this shift occurred because Buck compromised his position to draw votes. With Fuhrmann aligned with the war effort, Buck claimed that the "sacred cause of patriotism" should not be dragged into a municipal election. This reversal disgusted the pro-Fuhrmann press which saw the Anglo-American compromising with the "unpatriotic vote." But Buck was also able to capitalize on the disenchantment that paralyzed the east side. Many of Brill's supporters refused to vote. Others decided to stop battling the wind. As the *News* put it, only "blind and foolish Germans" would continue to promote the Kaiser at the expense of American interests.[52] As the war dragged on, Americans wondered about their fate in the event of a German victory. The German-American effort to derail the war effort meant little in the light of their stand for "Americanism" after the *Lusitania* sinking, and their passivity in the face of conscription. The *Volksfreund* in 1918 called on its readers to accept the war spirit, just as one might adjust to the cold of a winter day:

> Face the fact . . . the war is here . . . When the Kaiser is victorious in Europe, will he not come here? Will he not kill the women and children of Buffalo, just as he murdered the blameless in Paris and London?[53]

Few expressed reservations. A prominent member of the local *Bund* conceded that there was now little time for beer gardens and German festivals. "The highest duty of every American citizen," he said, "was to promote the victory of the United States. In this effort one must give his full and unconditioned support."[54]

The anti-German impulse, supported in part by Americans of German descent, struck forcefully at the network of German language classes in Buffalo's schools. In February, 1918, the United States Department of the Interior released a study that encouraged the elimination of the German language from primary schools. The report suggested that Buffalo as well as fifteen other major cities in the United States should retain German only as an elective in the high schools. The study won immediate approval in Buffalo, and economy-minded educators moved quickly to end the $60,000-a-year German program. The chairwoman of the school board expressed her regrets about the layoff of more than sixty German instructors, but reported that the foreign language program in Buffalo had been fostered by "German propaganda." Uncertainties that existed before the war had given way to new convictions. The educators were certain that the primary schools should teach "one language, one nation, one flag."[55]

In full view of the German press, the school board eliminated the German program. In 1873 a similar proposal had ignited a raucous political battle that had ended the careers of anti-German aldermen and had reinstated the German program. In the aftermath of that fight, German aldermen had bragged that they ruled the city.[56] But now a dazed German press did little more than report the event. The *Echo* explained that the board's decision was in the "spirit of the times." The *Volksfreund* was fascinated by the case, but the paper's articles on the subject had the emotional tone of a scientific abstract.[57]

The change among German-Americans was not a case of repression so much as accession. The superpatriots controlled city hall, and their will would prevail. The educators, meanwhile, attempted to mollify the Germans. In their public statement, they pointed out that their budget cuts were not meant to insult the city's German population. School Superintendent Emerson insisted privately that the school board should encourage the patriotism of the foreign element rather than alienate them with accusations. Such an opportunity came when superpatriotic physicians on Buffalo's Academy of Medicine criticized the role of the German gymnastic programs in the schools. The doctors charged that Karl H. Burkhardt, the city's gymnastic supervisor and a member of the Turnverein, fostered standards that were unhealthy and un-American. The educators countered successfully that Burkhardt was an able instructor and a "loyal citizen." Eight principals testified on Burkhardt's behalf as well as the superintendent, Emerson, who called the allegations "scandalous."[58]

Superpatriotic agencies such as the National Security League aspired to uproot all the vestiges of German culture. The German newspapers were especially vulnerable because they had supplied readers with a stream of pro-German rhetoric before the war. But moderate voices again prevailed: an act of Congress in October of 1917 had required all German newspapers to file translations with the local postmaster. The tedious process of translation complicated the task of the German-American editor, but it also protected the press from the charge of sedition. Buffalo's major German dailies survived this requirement and continued publishing into early 1918.

The near-shutdown of the German-American press in Buffalo came in the spring and summer of 1918. The Catholic newspapers, the *Volks-*

freund, the *Aurora*, and the *Echo*, reported precipitous declines in circulation; the *Arbeiter Zeitung* and the community's most prestigious newspaper, the *Demokrat*, folded.[59] The demise of the *Arbeiter Zeitung* resulted from the decision of the local socialist party to reorganize and support the war effort. Martin Heisler, the new party leader, explained that the Socialists were whole-heartedly committed to the fight against the Prussian monarchy.[60] The *Demokrat's* demise proved especially disarming to the old German families of Buffalo. The paper had a lineage that dated back to 1837, and by 1915 it had attained a circulation of 11,000. In its final issue, the editor conveyed the hopelessness he felt as a leader of the German-Americans:

> We believe the German language paper in the United States has served its purpose. The prejudice against everything German is pronounced, and the desire of the German reading public to take up purely American ideals is so evident, that we believe nothing further can be accomplished in this field.[61]

The ultra-realistic stance was also a cynical position. If America lost the war, all would suffer. But if the Allies won, as was more likely, both Germany and German-America would be finished. Why then continue? In such a deflated spirit, German-Americans canceled their subscriptions to the *Demokrat*, voted for Buck, and let their clubs sag into nonexistence. For the Central Schuetzen Verein of Sharpshooters, the Old German Society, and the Freiheit lodges, the end was melodramatic as members simply failed to attend. In 1918, over half of the Harugari lodges also disbanded, and the Deutscher Humoristen club ran out of jokes. With the very name "German" arousing unrest, popular institutions of the east side community such as the German-American Bank and the two German hospitals hid behind a new identity. The bank changed its name in 1918 to "Liberty," and the hospitals dropped the term "German" from their titles.[62]

Local leaders of the German-American Bund viewed these developments with a mixture of horror and fascination. Their crusade to promote German culture had not only failed, their entire movement was being obliterated. Even the national office of the Bund in Philadelphia, appraised by locals as a German-American fortress, prepared to disband. Congressional critics charged that the Bund headquarters had advanced $800,000 to Germany in the months before America had declared war. Superpatriots claimed that the German government had siphoned this "humanitarian offering" into the coffers of their propaganda office. With the King Bill, passed by Congress on July 2, 1918, the charter of the national organization was revoked, and the Bund name equated with treason. Because the state office of the Bund in New York became a center of controversy, its leader, Henry Weismann, also dissolved the New York City unit in 1918.[63]

The national and state offices of the Bund were now silent, but the Buffalo branch plotted its survival. With Weismann and the national leader, Charles Hexamer, humbled, the American-born Hitzel attained the spotlight that he desired. His organization, to be sure, had an easier time escaping the glare of national suspicion, but the physician remained convinced that only the facades of ethnicity needed to change. The organization had to persist in some form. Thus the Buffalo branch planned to meet only four times a year, and to keep a low profile during the rest of the war. Instead of fighting prohibition, they would raise money for Liberty Loans and insure the prestige of German-Americans. Unlike other local branches of the Bund in Des Moines and Brooklyn that became American organizations, the Buffalo Bund wanted to hold to its "German-American" moorings. It would resume its fight for German culture when the war ended.[64]

For three months, the local cell functioned as a patriotic organization. Now a friend of the Allied cause, the local Bund no longer drew fire from the English-language press. But whereas its opponents in 1915 were the soul Germans, by 1918 they were the growing army of east side cynics. Many of the eighty-nine Bund delegates in Buffalo began to feel insulted and downgraded because of their affiliation. The most stoic of German leaders could endure slander from outside the community, but when the worst abuse came from fellow Germans, courage turned to apathy. The fact that the gymnast Karl Burkhardt had defended himself by attacking the Bund was one measure of ingratitude. The failure of the German press to report their activities was another. When the delegates met on July 26, they had seen enough. The Bund's 200-word resolution to disband claimed that the Americans of German descent had betrayed them.[65]

The liquidation of the Bund was a welcome development for the advocates of prohibition. Along with the collapse of German resistance in 1918, the states passed the Eighteenth Amendment to the Constitution, establishing prohibition. The law was billed first as a war measure, but when the amendment was ratified in January of 1919, it was as if the tomb of the German community had been sealed. German-American gatherings from backyard euchre parties to meetings in Turnverein Hall and outdoor singing festivals had always included beer on the agenda. German brewers had perfected the drink. The German workers depended on it with their starchy meals, and when the German band director wanted the audience to participate in a song, he held up his stein of beer. How natural to let this intoxicant stand as the symbol of the prewar community. But now this popular and vital element of *Gemütlichkeit* seemed forever banned from the United States.

The war spirit decimated the institutions and political power of the German-Americans, and tended to loosen the personal ties of ethnicity. About 90 percent of the 4,000 Americans of German descent who served in the armed services from the city survived the war. When they returned they showed little interest in ethnic activities. The percentage of German-American males marrying both endogamously and in German churches dropped precipitously from 60 percent before the war to about 35 percent in the early 1920s. Though church membership in German churches reached a high point in the 1920s, the attendance of two major Protestant churches that kept records dropped by about 10 percent during the war.[66] Dissimilarity indices that measure the extent to which a group's distribution among the city's wards changed over time also indicate that the rate of movement from German areas climaxed during the decade from 1915 to 1925.[67]

Significance of the War Experience

Ethnic solidarity waned during the war. The prewar counterculture was destroyed. German families and churches, however embattled, survived. But the challenge to American culture that had energized the German community before the war collapsed. America's victory over Germany proved that German hospitals, schools, and banks were unnecessary. The substantial commitment to the German language had been misplaced. With the fall of the prewar community, the German leaders could no longer subsist on the intoxicating rhetoric of national might, or the explosive predictions about German influence in America. The more sober group of postwar organizers had to revive interest in ethnic culture. They had to accomplish this task without a popular press, a central organization such as the Bund, or the financial backing of a city-wide German business network.

The war deflated the assumptions and dreams of the German movement at several crucial points. In 1914, German-American leaders such as Wilhelm Gaertner predicted a quick German victory and aligned their own movement with the fate of the Kaiser's armies. When German war measures stalled in France but kindled American antagonism through the sinking of the *Lusitania*, German-Americans spearheaded the neutrality movement and a hoped for German victory. With the American declaration of war, the most inflated vision of all prevailed that the German-Americans could obstruct the war movement. But when the brutal facts of confrontation with a militant majority emerged, there was nowhere else to leap. Over-reaching idealism gave way to cynicism as German-Americans supported the effort to crush the German armies.

The psychological fallout of the war helps to explain why a group as large as the German-Americans not only failed to maintain their culture, but actively sought Americanization by 1918. The pressure from the superpatriots, who engineered uniformity by weighting the scale of democracy against minorities, was indeed essential in providing direction to this process. But this study illustrates not only that the Americanizers were a minority at the beginning of the conflict, but that they were forced to compromise with moderate Germans in such cases as the 1917 election, the Burkhardt affair, and in the restrictions against the German press. The case of this turning point in American ethnic history thus points to the power of events in shaping American consciousness. The pressure for conformity was intense. But the response of those who were assimilated collaborated in the fall of Buffalo's German-American community.

Notes

This work has benefited from the criticism of Thomas Archdeacon, James Berquist, Kathleen Conzen, David Gerber, and Leonard Riforgiato.

1. Frederick C. Luebke, *Bonds of Loyalty: German-Americans and World War One* (Dekalb, Ill., 1974); Melvin G. Holli, "Teuton vs. Slav: The Great War Sinks Chicago's German Kultur," *Ethnicity* 8 (December 1978); Phyllis Keller, *States of Belonging: German American Intellectuals and the First World War* (Cambridge, Mass., 1979); Carl Wittke, *German-Americans and the World War* (Columbus, Ohio, 1936); Clifton J. Child, *The German-Americans in Politics, 1914–1917* (Madison, Wisc., 1939), 164–165; Guido Dobbert, "German-Americans Between New and Old Fatherland," *American Quarterly* 19 (Winter 1967), 678.
2. Luebke, *Bonds of Loyalty*, 321; Holli, "Teuton vs. Slav," 407–418.
3. I have argued elsewhere that the religious and class divisions of the German-American community narrowed the range of ideological possibilities for the group. By their appeal to German supremacy, community leaders found a way out of the dilemma. The myth of cultural superiority was one belief that united the factions of the German community. See Andrew P. Yox, "Bonds of Community: Buffalo's German Element, 1853–1871," *New York History* 66 (April 1985), 142, 149–150. For a similar argument, see Kathleen N. Conzen, "Die Assimilierung der Deutschen in Amerika: Zum Stand der Forschung in den Vereinigten Staaten," in Willi Paul Adams, ed., *Die deutschsprachige Auswanderung in die Vereinigten Staaten* (Berlin, 1980), 47.
4. See 1900 federal manuscript census schedules. The explanation of the methods used to determine the German-American population in Buffalo from 1855 to 1925 is given in Andrew Yox, "Decline of the German-American Community in Buffalo, 1855–1925" (Ph.D dissertation, University of Chicago, 1983), 364–378.
5. According to the federal census, proportions of city residents who were foreign-

born in 1900 are: Buffalo — 30 percent, Milwaukee — 31 percent, Chicago — 34 percent, and New York — 37 percent.

6. Yox, "Decline of the German-American Community," 385.

7. Richard C. Brown and Robert Watson, *Buffalo: Lake City in Niagara Land* (Woodland Hills, Ca., 1981), 119, 184–186; *Solemn Commemoration of the Centenary of the Founding of St. Louis Church* (Buffalo, 1929), 3.

8. [Ottomar Reinecke?], *Geschichte der Deutschen in Buffalo und Erie County* (Buffalo: Reinecke and Zesch, 1898), 114–116; *Buffalo und Sein Deutschtum* (Philadelphia, 1912), 1.

9. Ibid., 45–48.

10. Melvin G. Holli and Peter d'A. Jones, eds., *Biographical Dictionary of American Mayors 1820–1980* (Westport, Conn., 1918); *Buffalo 1908* (Buffalo, 1908), 55–237.

11. *Buffalo und Sein Deutschtum*, 1; *Buffalo Freie Presse*, October 3, 1904; *Buffalo Demokrat*, March 11, 1907.

12. J. R. Arndt and May E. Olson, *German-American Newspapers and Periodicals* (New York, 1965), 319–330; 1915 New York State manuscript census schedules.

13. Department of Public Affairs, *Buffalo: Its Schools* (Buffalo, 1916), 30.

14. 1915 New York State manuscript census schedules; *Demokrat*, August 10, 1914; Paul F. Bloomhardt, *Frederick August Kahler* (Buffalo; Otto Ulbrich Co., 1937), 37; *Buffalo Volksfreund*, June 6, July 10, August 8–12, 1914.

15. *Buffalo News*, August 10, 1914.

16. Ibid.; *Buffalo Commercial*, August 10, 1914; *Buffalo Express*, August 10, 1914.

17. *Buffalo und Sein Deutschtum*, 40–53; Bloomhardt, *Kahler*, 33; Yox, "Decline of the German-American Community," 285–287; Arndt and Olson, *German-American Newspapers*, 320–330.

18. *Buffalo Times*, May 8, 1915.

19. John A. Hawgood, *The Tragedy of German-America* (New York, 1940), 236. For most German-American authors, the term "American" had very positive connotations. What they disliked, however, was the attempt to reify the term. "Americanism" thus frequently was dismissed as a way of defining the national identity by English culture.

20. Daniel J. Sweeney, *History of Buffalo and Erie County 1914–1919* (Buffalo, 1919) 20–21.

21. Ibid., 7, 37–38, 49, 753. The German surname table was drawn from an alphabetized printout of the 1855 New York manuscript census schedules. See Yox, "Decline of the German-American Comnunity," 369–375.

22. Ibid., 385.

23. Cases of the German experience in eastern Europe and Latin America support the thesis that America's democratic system was peculiarly inimical to the maintenance of minority cultures. Eberhard G. Schultz, ed., *Leistung und Schicksal: Abhandlungen und Berichte ueber die Deutschen in Osten* (Koeln, 1967), 374–384; Donald C. Newton, *German Buenos Aires, 1900–1933* (Austin, 1977), 4; Martin N. Dreher, *Kirche und Deutschtum in der Entwicklung der Evangelischen Kirche Lutherischen Bekenntnisses in Brasilien* (Goettingen, 1978), 194.

24. *Buffalo und Sein Deutschtum*, 1, 12; *Demokrat*, January 20, 1915; *News*, August 9, 1915.

25. *Aurora*, August 13, 1915.

26. Ibid., August 6, 1915; *News*, August 9, 1915; Phillip Gleason, *The Conservative Reformers: German-American Catholics and the Social Order* (Notre Dame, 1968), 22.

27. *Echo*, June 17, 1915.

28. Sweeney, *History of Buffalo*, 27.

29. *Corriere Italiano*, October 2, November 6, 1915; *Volksfreund*, August 9, 1915; *News*, August 14, 1916.

30. *Volksfreund*, August 12 and 14, 1916; Luebke, *Bonds of Loyalty*, 121.

31. Interviews with Martha Murbach, Buffalo, August 13, 1979, and Emily Doell, Buffalo, August 8, 1979; Douglas C. Stenerson, *H. L. Mencken, Iconoclast from Baltimore* (Chicago, 1971), 52.

32. Luebke, *Bonds of Loyalty*, 146.

33. Ibid., 140.

34. *Ibid.*, 131.
35. *News*, August 9, 1915; *Volksfreund*, August 23, 1915, July 28, 1916.
36. *News*, August 14, 1916; *Volksfreund*, August 14, September 22, 1916; *Times*, August 5, 1915. The symbols of German nationalism were so potent for some German-Americans that they mixed them with Christian symbols decades before the pagan ritual of the Nazis. Friedrich A. Kahler, the Lutheran pastor in Buffalo, for instance, noted how some immigrants talked of a "teutonic Jesus." One Evangelical pastor in Cincinnati thought that the Fatherland had a special relation to God. Jokes and sayings that had God singing and speaking in German were not uncommon. Bloomhardt, *Kahler*, 28; Luebke, *Bonds of Loyalty*, 105; *Volksfreund*, August 7, 1915.
37. *Aurora*, April 20, 1917.
38. *Ibid.*; *Volksfreund*, April 23, 1917.
39. *Ibid.*, August 26, 1917; *Times*, October 10, 15, 16, 1917; *Commercial*, October 16, 1917.
40. Bloomhardt, *Kahler*, 37.
41. *Volksfreund*, March 15, 1917.
42. *Ibid.*, September 14, 17, 1917.
43. *Ibid.*; *Echo*, May 14, 1917.
44. *Commercial*, October 16, 1917.
45. *News*, July 26, 1943. Schwab later became mayor of the city from 1921 to 1929. The fraternal order he headed was the Knights of St. John.
46. *Courier*, October 15, 1917; *News*, October 11-15, 1917; *Express*, October 15, 1917.
47. *Times*, October 17, 1917.
48. The computation of the Spearman correlations was based on ward tabulations of the vote found in: *Buffalo Enquirer*, October 17, 1917. The procedures obtaining the statistics cited here are illustrated in detail in: Yox, "Decline of the German-American Community," 312-314.
49. *Times*, October 17, 20, 1917.
50. Luebke, *Bonds of Loyalty*, 206-239.
51. Interview with Emily Doell; *Volksfreund*, January 16, 1918; La Vern J. Rippley, *The German-Americans* (Boston, 1976), 185.
52. *Times*, October 20, 1917; *News*, October 18, 30, 1917.
53. *Volksfreund*, July 2, 1918.
54. *Ibid.*, July 27, 1918.
55. *Ibid.*, February 5, 6, 16, 1918; *Enquirer*, April 18, 1918.
56. *Demokrat*, May 20, 1873; *Freie Presse*, October 16, 1875.
57. *Echo*, February 14, 1918; *Volksfreund*, February 5, 6, 16, 1918.
58. *Ibid.*, July 1-2, 1918.
59. Arndt and Olson, *German-American Newspapers*, 319-330; "German Newspapers of Buffalo," Buffalo and Erie County Public Library.
60. *Enquirer*, April 19, 1918.
61. *Demokrat*, quoted in the *Express*, July 18, 1918.
62. *Buffalo Directory 1915* (Buffalo, 1915), 58-85; *Buffalo Directory 1919* (Buffalo, 1919), 56-74; *Volksfreund*, August 8, 1937; Interview with Martha Murbach.
63. Child, *German-Americans in Politics*, 168-173; *Volksfreund*, April 5, 1918.
64. *Ibid.*, April 27, 1918.
65. *Ibid.*, July 22, 27, 1918.
66. Sweeney, *History of Buffalo*, 497-510. German-American veterans caused the most serious physical confrontation with local Nazis in the 1930s. In 1938, veterans shoved uniformed Nazis down the stairs of the east side American Legion Hall. *Buffalo Courier Express*, January 14, 1944. For marriage statistics, see Yox, "Decline of the German-American Community," 320; Records of Christ Lutheran Church and St. Peter's Evangelical Church, now Zion United Church of Christ.
67. Yox, "Decline of the German-American Community," 408.

JAMES H. DORMON

7

European Immigrant/Ethnic Theater in Gilded Age New York: Reflections and Projections of Mentalities

Since its advent in the 1930s, the study of ethnic phenomena in the United States has been beset by definitional and conceptual imprecision.[1] In the essay at hand, for example, one need look no further than the title to discover the confusion that results when the terms "immigrant" and "ethnic" appear as adjectives modifying the noun "theater." "Immigrant" and/or "ethnic" theater might be at least two different things: theater produced *by* and presumably *for* immigrant and/or ethnic peoples, or theater produced *about* such peoples, intended for an audience composed of members of the group, outsiders, or, more likely, both. The two usages (and possibly a third, in which ethnic performers play ethnic character roles) apply to the theater history of several ethnic populations in the United States. Despite the perplexing terminology, however, each of these usages is significant, and there are implications in all three that reveal much about the process of ethnic group formation and maintenance as well as ethnic theater history during the era of the New Immigration (ca. 1880–1920).

In her introduction to *Ethnic Theatre in the United States*, Maxine Seller

contends that ethnic theater was among the most important institutions that "expressed and sustained the internal life" of American ethnic
communities.[2] Doubtless she is correct, perhaps even more so than
she may have realized. The theater of, by, and for ethnic communities
was a primary mechanism for the expression of ethnicity ("ethnicity"
in this context meaning the indvidual's attachment to and identification
with his or her ethnic culture) and for projecting aspects of the Old
World experience deemed worthy of honor and remembrance.

Ethnic theater thus functioned to maintain ethnic groups through
the ritual celebration of shared ethnic cultural values. It provided a
sense of belonging for the disoriented and dislocated. Finally, ethnic
theater provided "boundary markers" (the term was suggested by the
anthropologist Frederick Barth) indicating the boundary enclosing the
group and separating "us" from "the others."[3]

On the other hand, "ethnic theater" in the second sense marked the
cultural boundary from the outside. Ethnic groups in Gilded Age New
York were among the most popular subjects of the contemporary theater. In the semiotic system of the day, the stage ethnics represented
recognizable types that came to signify the group as a whole by way
of their emphasis on the most salient ascriptive qualities that "outsiders"
associated with the group. A "we-they" polarity thus resulted. Those
who provided this version of "ethnic theater" normally used crude, comic
caricatures to create essentially demeaning (though often very amusing)
images. Moreover, middle-class American audiences, whose direct contact with real immigrants and ethnics was at best limited, often came
to accept these images as reflections of reality. This process was most
evident in the last decades of the nineteenth century and the first decade of the twentieth.

That the immigrant/ethnic theater (usage one) was in fact an important ingredient in the ethnic experience has been well documented
by Seller and others. In this essay I will summarize that experience
as it occurred among the most notable groups producing ethnic theater; specifically, the Germans, the Italians, and the Yiddish-speaking
European Jews. I will then assess the significance of the tradition for
each of these peoples.[4] Finally, I will examine the ways in which the
mainstream New York stage depicted the same groups, and attempt
to determine how those projections formed ethnic stereotypes.[5] In all
cases I hope to demonstrate the functions of theater in boundary formation and maintenance; i.e., the means by which theater defined and
bolstered the boundaries dividing one group from others.

Although establishing chronological precedence in the introduction
of ethnic theater among the largest immigrant groups is difficult, there

can be little doubt that in the nineteenth century the German immigrants came first. They brought with them, as part of their cultural baggage, the best-developed theater tradition among the European immigrants. The latter half of the eighteenth century and first half of the nineteenth produced a remarkable flowering of German drama. Whether representative of the high culture or the popular culture, whether in the work of the great German romantics (Lessing, Goethe, Schiller) or of the popular melodrama (Kotzebue, for example) the German public claimed a remarkable dramatic heritage, and the emigrant population coming to America brought its taste for German drama with them.[6] Upon their arrival they quickly established German-language theaters — initially amateur, then professional — to provide the local German-speaking population with their beloved drama.

By 1854 the original "Stadttheater"— later to be known as the "Alte Stadttheater"— was offering semi-professional German-language repertory theater in New York. Ten years later the "Neue Stadttheater" (located at 45–47 Bowery) had established itself as a much improved, thoroughly professional company. The advent of the Irving Place Theater (in 1892) brought the German audiences an operation deemed outstanding by its contemporaries, capable of producing polished performances of the German favorites as well as Shakespeare and the French classics in translation.[7] In the words of one contemporary observer, the Irving Place Theater offered drama "on a higher plane than . . . in any other theatre in this city . . ."[8] Under the management of the talented immigrant actor, Heinrich Conried, the Irving Place featured a stock company offering up to sixty-five productions a year, all eminently legitimate, in its repertoire.

In 1882 Odell's authoritative *Annals of the New York Stage* began featuring "German Activities" under separate headings, carefully noting each program, including the numerous benefit performances (as, for example, those for the "German Emigrant's home," the "German Hospital," and the "German Ladies Benevolent Society," all in the season 1882–1883).[9] By this time the German-American theater had come to represent a major social and cultural dimension of German-American ethnicity. Throughout the 1890s the Germans of New York claimed three operating playhouses — the popular Germania and the Thalia, as well as the Irving Place — and could claim to have created a German-American theatrical tradition in their own right.[10]

If the Germans of New York enjoyed an earlier start in establishing their ethnic theater, the Italians began to compete immediately upon their arrival in the city. Once again, the immigrants drew upon their Old World experience to provide a new form of ethnic theater in their new homeland. If the Italians lacked the advantage of a major world dramatic literature, they boasted a tradition based in folk drama that could serve quite as well. Italian-American theater also began with amateur productions designed to provide a focus for community activities. The performances were normally held in churches and coffee houses as a form of amusement for the local population.[11] The establishment of the Filodrammatica Italiana di New York in 1878, however, inaugurated a more formal Italian-American theater tradition. This organization, which operated until at least 1902 on Mulberry Street in the heart of Little Italy, was the first of several companies providing the Italian community with drama in the mother tongue.

Each Italian company offered a somewhat different form of theatrical enterprise, the variations among them normally relating to Italian regional or provincial dialects and dramatic preferences. "La Compagnia Napoletana," for example, specialized in Pulcinello farces in Neopolitan dialect, and geared its performances to the tastes of working-class audiences.[12] "La Compagnia Comico-Drammatica Italiana," on the other hand, was a more professional organization that favored standard continental drama (including Shakespeare) in translation, and served the interests of more sophisticated immigrants. The "Circolo Filodrammatico Italo-Americano" specialized in contemporary Italian playwrights — Paolo Giocometti, for example — as well as melodrama, bourgeois comedy, and romantic tragedy. Some productions appealed to a middle class Italian-American audience, thus belying the notion that the community wholly rejected bourgeois aspirations and values.[13] Virtually all Italian audiences, however, recognized one popular stage figure, who in fact represented the proletarian immigrant. Known as "Farfariello," he was a stock character in the Italo-American *commedia dell'arte*. A humorous/pathetic figure in the Chaplin mold, he was poor, honest, hard-working, and "green" to the ways of America; unlettered but wise through experience; the typical Italian immigrant street vendor, laborer, rag-picker, organ-grinder; a type based in the realities of the immigrant experience with whom many identified. He was the product of ascriptive processes developed within the boundaries of Italian-American ethnic community. He also was portrayed in a rather different way by those outside the group, and the differences of characterization reveal much about the functions of ethnic semiosis.

There can be little doubt of the popularity and indeed the scope of Italian-American theater. The journalist/author Hutchins Hapgood, who wrote extensively (and perceptively) on ethnic theater in New York at the turn of the century, provided an excellent account of the contemporary Italian theater in an article published in *The Bookman* in

1900.[14] Hapgood suggested that the immigrant/ethnic community was divided in its theatrical preferences. Each segment of the population had its own favorite playhouse performing its own special line. Ranging in sophistication from elaborate puppet shows (the "Teatro delle Marionette" was located at 9 Spring Street) and variety entertainment through the popular melodrama to the Italian-language versions of the European classes, these companies offered a full spectrum of theatrical fare. The best-known company offering high drama was doubtless the Teatro Italiano (also housed on Spring Street). It featured the "Compagnia Comico-Drammatica Italiana," under the directorship of its leading players, Antonio Majori and Pasquale Rapone. This troupe offered Shakespeare. *Romeo and Juliet* and *Othello* were especially popular, though a production of *"Amleto, Principe di Danimarca,"* advertised for April 26, 1900, also attracted a following as did earthy melodrama and plays dealing with Italian social problems.

As with their German predecessors, the Italians obviously craved the ethnic identification and association represented by familiar theater in the old language and the excitement of new productions as they were introduced from the old country. And as he had done with the Germans, Odell began featuring a special category of "Italian Miscellany" in 1882, to serve as a supplement to the normal listings of Italian plays produced by the regular Italian-language houses.[15]

Hapgood contended that the Italians did not, however, offer much in the way of a domestic drama featuring local settings and situations. (The exception was a melodrama by Beniemino Ciambelli entitled *The Mysteries of Mulberry Street*, which, according to Hapgood "had a great success, running four successive nights.")[16] Apparently the Italian-American audiences preferred the original Italian product which served as a continuing link with their homeland. Notes Hapgood: "The audience, the actors, are just the same as they might be in a little theatre in Southern Italy, and the plays are imported, written by men in Italy."[17] But though the drama may have been imported, once again an immigrant/ethnic group proved its determination to maintain its theater tradition as a part of its ethnic culture.

If the Germans and the Italians used the theater to express their ethnic sensibilities, thereby reflecting their ethnic identities, the Yiddish-speaking Jews of the New Immigration based an essentially new theatrical tradition upon their ethnicity. The Yiddish theater, a veritable infant in the family of world drama when it was transported to New York in 1882, was raised to its maturity in America as a manifestation of the Jewish-American ethnic experience. Born in Romania in 1876, the Yiddish theater (in the words of its foremost historian, David Lifson) "became the pride of the Jews" in Europe and in America.[18] Its founder, Avram Goldfadn, drew on the folk experiences of the *shtetl* to produce a variety of essentially formulaic pieces; comedy, farce, history, and melodrama, that served as the basis for much of what followed later, often in more sophisticated forms (though his lesser imitators actually corrupted his work by way of their embellishments). Goldfadn ultimately came to America himself to participate in the American development of the tradition, albeit without much personal profit. In America the Yiddish drama took on a new dynamic largely through the efforts of his followers.

Yiddish-American theater began in New York in the "Turn Hall" on East Fourth Street in 1882, just six years after its birth in Eastern Europe.[19] It functioned as both entertainment and social benefit, to raise funds for the various ethnic Jewish fraternal and mutual support organizations as well as to offer psychological escape from the harsh realities of life in the ghetto. In the words of the immigrant Mosche Nadir, a self-proclaimed "Average Theatergoer": "I do not go to the theater to think, but to forget. I seek there to forget my wife, the children, the crowded tenement, the littered wash, the bad ventilation."[20] But whatever the motivation of the audience, from the outset, the Yiddish theater proved successful. The growing Yiddish-speaking population of the Lower East Side seemed insatiable in its craving for the drama in the vernacular language. As Seller observes, " . . . no immigrant community was more ardent in its support of theatre than the Eastern European Jews."[21] Consequently, there was profit to be made in the management of the Yiddish houses, despite the fact that their managers contributed substantial funds to assist the immigrant population in settlement, subsistence, and adjustment to a strange new culture. The two motive forces, profit and charity, produced a remarkable (albeit short-lived) flowering of a new addition to world drama, which provided a unique dimension to the ethnic experience of its devotees.

In the insightful *Spirit of the Ghetto*, Hutchins Hapgood described in detail the operations of the Yiddish playhouses, the responses of the audiences, the types of drama, and the inner working of the world of the actors and playwrights.[22] He wrote of the ghetto life in the late 1890s, some fifteen years after the advent of the Yiddish theater and during its "golden Epoch," as Lifson has termed it.[23] From its amateur origins it had rapidly developed into fully professional repertory theater. From the dingy little meeting halls that originally served as playhouses, real theaters came into use. There were three such theaters: the People's, the Windsor, and the Thalia (which apparently alternated between German and Yiddish productions), all in or near the Bowery. As with the Italian-American stage, each theater featured its own company and its own repertoire, and each attracted a specific audience, its appeal largely based on class preferences and education.

At the most popular level stood the variety shows, featuring comedians, singers, magicians, and burlesque entertainers. Most of these shows also offered popular drama as well, notably the works of Joseph Lateiner and Moshe Hurwitz, who specialized in plays from the European Yiddish tradition. Crude in construction, repetitious and imitative of each other, they included the traditional "culture plays" (based in the Jewish experience of yore) as well as historical and literary themes associated with the Old World. They also dealt with the problems of the immigrants themselves, sometimes by contrasting old World conditions with ghetto life. But fundamentally they represented, in Hapgood's words, "the conservative and traditional aspects of the stage."[24] They were also the most overtly commercial of the Yiddish offerings, and were clearly in enormous demand. Lateiner wrote over one hundred of them (Hapgood insists that none of them had either "form or ideas") to meet the demand. Despite the deprecatory assessments of the sophisticated Jewish intellectuals (who termed the genre "shund"; roughly "tripe" or "trash"), Lateiner saw his works as *Volksstücke* — the plays of the common people.[25] But whatever the literary merit of his efforts, he produced by himself a considerable portion of the entire Yiddish popular dramatic literature. Its rejection by the intellectuals only confirms that the elite tends to disparage the popular, usually to no avail.

Educated and more prosperous Jews supported Yiddish adaptations of the European classics (Shakespeare and Schiller were both offered in translation), as well as modern Yiddish originals or adaptations in the new realistic mode. The best of the playwrights to work in the latter milieu was surely Jacob Gordin, who has come to be identified with the "golden age of Yiddish theater." Gordin chose as his subject matter the experiences of the eastern European Jews and the Jewish immigrant community, which he treated in a realistic and honest manner. In such early plays as *Hard to Be A Jew* and *The Big Winner*, and in later efforts like *Siberia*, *The Jewish Priest*, *The Slaughter*, and *The Wild Man*, as well as his reworking of *King Lear* (*The Jewish King Lear*) and Ibsen's *Doll's House* (*Minna*), Gordin offered atmospheric renderings of the dark side of the Jewish experience and indeed, of the human condition.[26] Among those to follow him, only Sholom Aleichem (Solomon Rabinovitch), the "Jewish Dickens," dealt with the Yiddish tradition as sensitively as Gordin. The golden age also claimed the managers and performers capable of producing such difficult material. The best of them — Jacob Adler, Boris Thomashevsky, David Kessler, Bertha Kalisch — were formidable indeed.[27] But of equal importance were the lesser, sub-literary forms of Yiddish theater. Odell lists one such piece for 1889, a "local play" by Joseph Lateiner and Sigmund Mogulesko entitled *The Greenhorns*.[28] This musical problem drama dealt with the process of adjustment to America experienced by countless Jewish immigrants. The same was true of several other offerings, such as *The Green Shoemaker* (a "comic opera" with music by Max Abramovich), *The Mysteries of New York* offered by the "Russian Hebrew Opera Company," *Emigration from Russia*, and *The Polish Boy*, all produced between 1889 and 1891. As Odell observed, such plays constituted "the history of Jewish ideas and ideals . . . in America."[29]

Acculturation to American ways was another popular topic for local drama. Although few if any original scripts or prompt copies of such plays survive, their popularity suggests the ongoing fascination with the theme of acculturation, as well as the potential of popular theater for easing the immigrant adjustment process. By illustrating examples of problems familiar to all immigrants, the local ethnic drama sometimes provided solutions or (just as significantly) catharsis, by way of the theatergoers' identification with the beleaguered protagonists of the plays. In any case, the fact of their popularity has been clearly established. As Lulla Rosenfeld has noted, "whether they specialized in art or *shund*, the theatres downtown were the cultural center of [Jewish] immigrant life."[30] And the theater people took it upon themselves to interpret the Jewish ethnic experience to their audiences: "To be natural," as the great Adler put it, "to be real, to express the actual life of the people, . . ." such was their intent.[31]

So much, then, for the "ethnic theater" of and for the ethnic populations themselves. What of the second order of the phenomenon: The representation of ethnics on the mainstream stage? Whereas immigrant/ethnic theater attempted to maintain cultural continuity with the old country or to portray circumstances in the new, the mainstream stage tended to depict the new ethnic populations in the form of crude, normally comic, caricatures. Mainstream theatergoers, predominantly "outsiders" (though some were themselves ethnics), all too quickly accepted the caricatures as versions of reality — so much so that the caricatures became stereotyped. Both versions of immigrant life and character projected the images carried in the minds and hearts of their creators; both reflected mentalities as different as the cultures that divided the "we" and "they" along ethnic boundaries. But from group to group the particulars of the caricatures varied, thus necessitating observation of each image for purposes of analysis.

The Stage German made his appearance most prominently in the American popular theater in the late nineteenth century. But the "German Character," as Robert Dell has noted, began to emerge as "an identifiable type" even before the Civil War, though the particulars of the characterization had yet to be formalized.[32] By the 1880s, however, the fat, stolid, beer-loving dullard had come to be a standard stage image without which no vaudeville bill was deemed complete.[33] While mainstream theater offered an occasional German character, normally represented as hard-working, methodical, dependable and honest (if a bit stubborn and slow), the vaudeville "Dutch Act"—so known despite the fact that its protagonists were ostensibly German—defined the popular stereotype.[34] In the Dutch Act, normally either a single comic routine or a dialogue act between two characters, the humor typically turned on the combination of dialect farce and slapstick, knockabout action. The ascribed qualities of the "Dutch" type, in addition to boozy stolidity, ignorant buffoonery, and (inevitably) physical rotundity, included as well the butchered English associated with German immigrants in the minds of their beholders, the outsiders who provided most of the comedy material.[35]

The humor of the Dutch Act often turned on the misuse of language. The sketch entitled "Dig-ni-ty: A Double Dutch Cross-Fire," for example, features the characters Hans (a "German Houseman") and Hulda (his female equivalent). The opening lines suggest the nature of the dialogue for this and similar acts. Hulda speaks: "Hans-Kom hare! Kom frum dot room oudt! . . . Mach Schnell, und make it snappy."[36] Further action reveals the German vaudeville character in full bloom, in a wholly slapstick routine, the dialogue of which concerns the subject of dignity (neither character displays any) and portrays the protagonists as ignorant louts. With only minor variations, the same could be said of countless such sketches from the period: "Hans, the Dutch J. P.," for example, or "Der Two Subprises," or "the Dutchman's Picnic."[37] In the 1903 version of "Dutch Conversations," *Madison's Budget*, the most significant periodical publication featuring vaudeville and popular theater routines, provided more such material, virtually without variation from the earlier acts.[38]

Perhaps the fullest realization of the Dutch Act came from Joe Weber and Lew Fields, who gained enormous popularity in Manhattan's vaudeville houses with their "Mike and Myer" routine. Featuring knockabout and dialect humor, Weber and Fields brought to their roles a winning charm and comic timing that outdistanced all competitors. Nonetheless, their characters were based on the old "Dutch" stereotype. They simply did it better than others. One representative bit of dialogue will suffice as an example. In their "Pool Room Routine," the Weber character addresses the Fields character:

MIKE: I dond't know dis pool business.
MYER: Vatever I dond't know. I teach you.
MIKE: Dot seems fair.
MYER: To make der game more interesting, I bet dot I beat you.
MIKE: Oughtn't you to beat? Ain't you biggest?
MYER: Brains in der head, not bigness, vins in pool.

So the action commences, and continues in a similar vein through the full sketch.[39] Notably, Weber and Fields were themselves second-generation immigrant Jews whose parents had been forced to flee the virulent anti-Semitism of nineteenth-century Eastern Europe.[40] Though they did not normally write their own material, they performed their routine with no apparent sense that they were perpetuating demeaning stereotypes.

The German-American ethnic stereotype was, however, less demeaning than that of the southern Italians and Sicilians. Relative latecomers to the American stage, Italian immigrant characters began appearing in American plays only after the Civil War. But as the vaudeville stage developed its enormous appeal in the 1880s, Italian sketches came to rank among the popular "racial" comic routines of the period. Dell notes that in legitimate drama, the Italian "type" tended toward various forms of criminality and appeared largely in popular urban melodrama.[41] Typical of the genre was the social-comment play entitled *The Italian Padrone*: or *The Slave of the Harp* (author unknown), that had a brief run in 1880 and was occasionally revived thereafter.[42] A far more common Italian immigrant type, however, took on stereotypical proportions by way of vaudeville and burlesque performance. The dialect song came first, probably as a comic rendering of Italian street songs performed by caricature street peddlers or organ grinders as in this representative songbook selection from the early 1880s:

Vive a Garabaldi
I marry de Irish-a-girl,
We-a-got-two fine-a-kid,
One he-a-play de harp,
De oder he play-a-de-fid.[43]

Similarly, the Italian types common to the Edward Harrigan and Tony

Hart ethnic extravaganzas of the same period were mostly musicians and street vendors. They provided a consistent image through constant repetition. Harrigan's *The Investigation*, for example, featured an Italian in a minor role who described his circumstances, in song of course:

> I sella de fruit by de stand on de corner,
> I makea my living de best what I can . . .
> I likea de music I playa de harpa,
> When business is done I no sell anything . . .
> I gotta one brudder, he playa de organ,
> He gotta one monkey, a sweet little thing.
> He play a de alley he play a de streeta.
> He holda dat monkey with one little string.[44]

As the decade of the 1890s brought a substantial increase in the Italian immigrant population of New York, the stage version of the character became ever more popular and fully developed. By the first decade of the twentieth century the stereotype was complete. In the staging suggestions for this monologue sketch, entitled "A Sunny Son of Italy," vaudeville writer Harry Newton described the costume to be provided his "Sunny Son": "Rough sack suit, trousers rather short: large shoes; blue shirt; red bandanna handkerchief tied around neck; black slouch hat; brass rings in ears . . . , black wig; small black mustache [sic] . . . , make-up face dark."[45] By trade, the vaudeville Italian, like his prototype Farfariello, was still a peddler, organ grinder, or day laborer. But whatever his trade, he could always find time for enjoyment, most often through his beloved music.

To take a few cases in point: In an early twentieth-century routine entitled "The Italian's Goodbye," the subject, an Italian immigrant, sings of his experiences and aspirations in America:

> When I began-a,
> Me get-a banana,
> De peanut-a two,
> Me sell-a de few,
> Me push-a de cart-a,
> Me make-a good start-a . . .

He then gets ambitious and entrepreneurial:

[I] den get-a rich-a more,
An buy-a de store.
Me save-a de mon-a,
And have-a de fun-a . . .

But he plans at the end of his sojourn to return to "Italee,"

To bring-a Maree to dis-a countree.[46]

In another vaudeville sketch appearing in Madison's Budget in 1903, the organ-grinder/singer "Antonio Spaghetti" is involved in serenading a resident of a nearby apartment with a repetitious medley of "Sweet Violets" and the enormously popular (and apparently much overdone) "White Wings." When offered a nickel to cease the serenade, Antonio replies "I stoppa playing Sweeta Violetta for five centa, but Whita Winga, that costa ten centa."[47] Whether as an entrepreneurial street vendor or an extortionate street musician, however, gainful employment was something the stage Italian took lightly at best. In his description of the lead character in a "Wop Monologue" entitled "Just-a-Lak-a-Dat," sketch-writer Arthur Kazer notes "The free and independent wop has a genius for getting fired from every job he holds down: Even when he 'get-a in da fight' and is thrown into jail the judge fires him out!"[48] Indeed, one Italian character, "Tony Bragadello" in the monologue "As Tony Tells It," readily admits that he emigrated to America in search of its fabled bounty:

I leav-a da Italy 'cause I hear much-a bout United States America. Everybody say to me: "Tony, dat some country—great! It is a *free* country—everything free in United States America." I tell-a you I'm much obliged to come to place where I getta everything for nothing.[49]

And in truth the Italian newcomers often fared well in the United States, at least if the stage version of events prevailed in the real world. Another dialect song (ca. 1885) has its *buffo* performer describe a success story of the first order:

I came from Italy a short time ago,
This grand-a-place, America,
I came-a here to see.
I marry a lady with-a-plenta de monee,
We live all-a-time so happy.

On de harp I play for her music so grand,
The ladies it charm all-a-time,
It make-a-de heart bump-a-bump like a horse,
They say it was much-a-de fine.[50]

This ebullient immigrant found fortune by way of a fortuitous marriage. But things did not always work out so well for the stage Italian. America had its problems, as another newcomer, "Tony Macaroni," noted in 1908. In the "last war," says Tony, thousands of people "stood in the streets anxious to hold-up dis-a country's honor. Now in times of peace tink of de thousands dat stand in de streets at night waiting to hold-up de citizens."[51] Tony observes further that not even the vaunted public benefits afforded by the United States always served perfect ends. The country does provide "much-a charity," he notes, adding "If a man is hungry, he can go to some millionaire and get a library to read [in] . . . ; If a man starves to death de city will bury him for nothing."[52]

Such musings on Carnegie-style philanthropy, though noteworthy, are hardly typical of the stage Italian. Far more so was the immigrant "Joe" in the monologue "My Big-A-Brother Joe," remembered by his younger brother as "one smart-a fellow. He could play-a anything— piano, violin, craps,— he could play-a anything."[53] The great majority of Tonys and Joes were of a clearly established type: outlandish in attire, genial and easy-going (though sometimes quick-tempered and feisty), largely content with their circumstances, woefully ignorant and wholly without sophistication, given to indolence and the easy life in America; the good fellow, the happy, musical Mediterranean, always ready with a joke and a song. The type was pervasive, and especially so in vaudeville, the era's most popular form of theater. As was noted by *The Survey* in 1910, "[No] vaudeville or burlesque show . . . is complete without its Italian character actor and an Italian dialect song."[54] Once more, it would appear, an ethnic comic type had been formularized, with the ascriptive qualities of the character forming the basis of a caricature that came to be accepted as reality.

Even before Italian immigrants began appearing on stage in caricature form, the Yiddish-speaking, Eastern European Jews had become standard fare to the mainstream New York theater audiences, again most notably in vaudeville. As early as 1899, Epes Sargent, the vaudeville critic of the New York *Telegraph*, had observed (in a headline item) "Hebrews Have Been Chosen to Succeed Coons in Vaudeville." He added "After a Close Race for Popularity the Chosen People Triumph, and Children of the Ghetto are more in Evidence on the Stage than Residents of Doyers Street."[55] Sargent later made reference to "the

Hebrew craze" on the stage, and the editor of a major vaudeville gag-book added "The time is ripe for Hebrew dialect comedians. . . . stories illustrative of the traits and peculiarities of the Jewish race always create a laugh."[56] Shortly thereafter the *Budget* began carrying a full three-column page of "Hebrew Jokes and Monologues" in most issues. The emergence of ethnic comedian Joe Welsh as a top headliner at Tony Pastor's (in what Sargent termed an "exhaustive analysis of the east side Hebrew") provided a much-imitated model for literally dozens of "stage Hebrews," another standard bit in vaudeville's golden age.

The specific characteristics of the stage "Hebrew" are clearly in evidence in the typical routines. The character was, in the words of another vaudeville critic, "always" played in "the same stereotyped makeup, the same dialect, the same mannerisms . . ."[57] The routine varied but little from performer to performer and act to act, though some performers were clearly more talented and effective than others in their portrayals. What then were the primary qualities ascribed to "Hebrews" and emphasized in the act?

First, it was a male act, almost exclusively. The central character—the "Hebrew"—was invariably costumed in a long black frock coat, baggy pants, oversized shoes, and Derby hat. His clothes were perceptibly old, badly worn, and more than a bit grimy, as was his person. His beard was short and scruffy; his nose was decidedly protuberant and was normally accentuated by the use of nose putty.[58] He spoke in a stage Yiddish-English dialect that varied only with the style of the performer and often carried the burden of the act's humor. By occupation, the "Hebrew" was normally a pushcart peddler, an old-clothes dealer, or a pawnbroker. His major interests, his priorities, and his very value system were dominated by his concern for money. The acquisition and retention of money were his ruling passions, guiding his behavior and shaping his character. It was this preoccupation that formed the basis of the stage characterization. The "Hebrew" would, of course, marry for money, as is suggested by a bit of dialogue from a representative Hebrew "two-act." Cohen, seeking a wife, is informed by his friend Levi of a wealthy banker, Rosenheim, who has marriageable daughters:

LEVI: He's got von daughter sixteen years old to whom he vill gif $10,000 the day she is married.
COHEN: Ei Vei.
LEVI: Den he's got anoder daughter twenty-nine years old to whom he vill gif $15,000, und another daughter, forty-eight years old, to whom he vill gif $35,000.
COHEN: Haint he got an older von yet?[59]

Weddings also provided clear potential for acquisition. Irving Howe recalls a snippet of dialogue from a routine in which one character informs another (with reference to a wedding invitation) "RSVP means 'Remember to Send Vedding Present'."[60] But weddings could even provide bounty to the guests. The monologue "Cohen in Society" has Cohen offering to sell Levi an invitation to "a nice wedding":

> I says, "whose wedding is it?"
> He says, "what do you care. You have a fine time — get something good to eat and all it costs you is ten cents, including a hat check. And perhaps if you leave early you might even get a better overcoat, who knows."[61]

Preoccupation with money matters also dominated the marriage following the wedding ceremony. It even shaped matrimonial affection, as in the parody song "It Ain't No Lie," in which Moses and his wife Rebecca, vacationing at sea, encounter a gale. Rebecca becomes queasy. Then:

> Said Moses, as she rushed on deck,
> Here's where I get it in the neck;
> Vy couldn't my vife sea sick feel
> Before she ate that dollar meal.[62]

Children in their tender years were brought into the Hebrew's cash-dominant value system, as is suggested by the monologue "Abraham Cohen M.D." Jake Greenberg takes his son Ikey to Dr. Cohen for medical attention. Jake informs Ikey that the doctor charges $3.00 for the first visit and only $1.00 for each succeeding one:

> "So you know what to do —"
> When it was Ikey's turn he rushed in and said,
> "Here I am again, doctor." Replies Cohen,
> "Well, continue the same treatment as before."

But the lessons came hard at times, and fathers often despaired for their offspring. In the dialogue of "An Act for Two Hebrew Comedians," Cohen complains to Jake that his son has no head for business. Jake asks how this is so.

> COHEN: Yesterday Abe [the son] he jumped from in front of a trolley car and was hit by an automobile.

JAKE: Well, what's stupid about that?
COHEN: Doesn't he know it's much easier to collect from a trolley car company.[64]

Well might Cohen have been concerned, for the prospective benefits of insurance policies were not to be ignored. Indeed "Hebrew" business practices were *dominated* by the potential for collecting on insurance claims, especially fire insurance claims. Fire insurance routines were standard fare in the repertories of the racial comics, appearing with a monotonous regularity. A topical parody song, yet another take-off of "It Ain't No Lie," is typical. It opens:

Among those who to Cuba went [in the Spanish-American War]
Was Moses Cohen's Hebrew regiment

And the Cohen Regiment performed quite well prior to the first military encounter:

But When Moses shouted the word "fire!"
From the battlefields they did retire;
Each Hebrew to his home did flee
To get his insurance policy.[65]

Another popular parody, this one taking off "The Moth and the Flame," underscored the fundamentally dishonest aspect of the "Hebrew" fire insurance racket (as represented on the stage):

Ike Rapinsky kept a clothing store,
And though his stock was small,
He carried big insurance just the same.
You think that Ike was foolish
But he wasn't, not at all,
Not when you understand his game.

His "game" was, of course, arson, and Ike collected on his claims, one after another, until

After one more good fire, a rich man he'll retire.
That's the tale of the Cloth and the Flame.[66]

If fires were one sure way to business success, bankruptcy was another. In a 1903 monologue, the ubiquitous Cohen attributed his success to the famous "Five F's: Three fires and two failures." Later he notes that he "failed to make money, or in other words, I made money by failing."[67] Such repartee was commonplace in the period, as was the usury of the stereotyped Jewish pawnbroker. In another dialect monologue by yet another "Cohen":

> My store is a real curiosity shop,
> I take everything that they bring,
> An old broken bedstead, a rifle or clock,
> A diamond or gold-plated ring.
> I get thirty per cent on each dollar I lend,
> And with greenbacks I've papered my walls,
> So if short you should be, you can call upon me,
> At the sign of the three golden balls.[68]

One final feature of the stage "Hebrew" deserves mention. "Dirty" business practices found their counterpart in the physical uncleanliness ascribed to "Hebrews." Ethnic Jews were, in the semiotics of the popular stage, never really clean; indeed, they rarely bathed more than once a year. Dirty as children, they matured into dirty adults. Typical of the dirty children theme was a 1910 monologue on New York newsboys. The financier-philanthropist Jacob Schiff supported a project in which he sent all the newsboys to Coney Island each summer for a swim in the ocean. "At the last outing," the monologue contends, "little Ikey Epstein was just getting into the water when Mr. Schiff says to him, 'you look pretty dirty.' 'I know it,' said Ikey, 'I missed the train last year'."[69] Approaching adulthood, young "Cohen" and "Levi" (in a McNally's "Act for Two Hebrew Comedians") argue over which of them is the dirtier:

> COHEN: I'll bet you that I'm dirtier than you are.
> LEVI: Vell, why shouldn't you be dirtier than me, you're five years older.[70]

And in the skit entitled "Cheap Russian Baths," the mature "Hebrew inquires into the cost of a bath and is informed that they cost $1.00, but as a special attraction twelve may be purchased for $10.00. Replies the Hebrew: "Vat do you take me for; how do I know I am alive 12 years?"[71] Unwashed, unclean, untrustworthy; the association was patent.

The stereotypical stage "Hebrew" that emerged was thus a clever, manipulative, miserly, "dirty," fundamentally dishonest petty entrepreneur, comical in appearance and in language (again, the dialect was a staple of the bit), unsophisticated and clumsy in social demeanor, driven by pecuniary concerns (though a "ruthless underconsumer," in Stephan Thernstrom's apt phrase), whose values reflected a hopelessly distorted version of American achievement orientation. He was a caricature of a perceived type—an ascriptive type—the East Side Jew. But for all the fundamentally unpleasant aspects of the type, he was played as a *comic* figure, essentially harmless and not really predatory or threatening, in no way an object of fear (though surely unattractive and often obnoxious, always in humorous ways).

It must be stressed that audiences of the period deemed the "Hebrew" character absolutely *realistic*, at least if he was played well. One observer noted of the "typical" East Side Jewish immigrant (within the context of a comment on the stage version): "He has only to be himself and he is excruciatingly funny."[72] Similarly, critic/scholar Hartley Davis observed in 1905 that it was remarkable "how quick patrons of vaudeville are to recognize an act that comes near to truth." He commented further that a recent show—a "sketch of East Side life in New York" by Eva Williams and Jack Turner—was "very crude, yet very real and very human."[73] A bit later another critic referred to a Julian Rose performance as a "clever and correct study of New York types."[74] Rose was elsewhere designated "a finished artist" whose characterization "represents a type that does exist and is easily recognizable."[75] Yet another critic commented on a Joe Welsh performance: Welsh has the gift of being absolutely natural. He is a Yiddisher of the greatest American city's East Side."[76] A third commentator termed Abe Reynolds "one of the cleverest impersonators of Hebrew character the stage has even known . . ."[77] And so it went. By some complex social-psychological mechanism, the caricature had once again become the reality—the "impersonation"—in the eyes and minds of the beholders. The portrayal of an ethnic type had again come to reflect a mentality, predisposition to believe in the absolute reality of the stage immigrant/ethnic. The overwhelming popularity of the routines merely attested to the need for continuing reaffirmation of their subliminal message.

But what was the message, and what is its meaning to the social history of the phenomenon of the racial comic? Alas, such questions only point to the limits of the historian's craft. Yet informed guesswork— historical speculation if you will — might not be out of place in the conclusion to this essay on mind-sets and mental projections. It would seem safe to conclude, for example, that the boundaries established by "ethnic theater" (in both meanings of the term noted earlier) reflected (1) group needs to express their ethnicity and (2) rationalization needs

of outsiders to perceive the group's membership in essentially caricature forms. The boundaries, so marked, were thus more easily maintained and the "we-they" polarities confirmed. This appeared essential
to those who sought, however unknowingly, to preserve social order
through well-delineated ethnic boundaries.

Although surely demeaning, however, the qualities attributed to
America's Germans, Italians, and Jews were essentially *benign* in their
implications for the larger society. These stage ethnics were above all
comical creatures, comical in their simplicity, their naivete, their appearance, their language, their ignorance of American ways. Though
assuredly *different* from middle-class, white Protestant Americans, they
did not threaten the established bourgeoisie. They were safe, funny
creatures, who were not like us — such was the message of the stage
ethnics.[78] Because they were not like us, they could not be *of* us; they
could not and would not be assimilated into *our* culture, at least not
in their present form. Here was the sort of assurance that rendered
less ominous the potential threat to the social order — a threat that was
inherent in the sheer size of the New Immigration. The essentially
benign image of the stage ethnics attenuated American xenophobia,
ironically making the actual process of ethnic adjustment and accommodation somewhat less difficult and painful. In fulfilling the rationalization need of middle-class America for clearly defined ethnic boundaries, the stage ethnics paradoxically served to advance the process of
ethnic adjustment.[79]

Sadly, the need for ethnic theater as a means of maintaining ethnic
solidarity did not persist far beyond the accommodation process. That
process itself undermined the requirements of ethnicity — the mystical
bond of ethnos — by rendering the ethnic populations more typically
American. As such, the ethnic communities tended to lose their unique-
ness, normally beginning with the loss of the Old World languages.
Over time, other features of their ethnic cultures fell to the onslaught
of their — dare it be said? — "Americanization." Only the descendents of
the immigrants in later generations, those who consciously sought to
restore the old ethnic institutions, would be able to reconstitute features of the old culture. The efforts of the New York Jewish Repertory
Company to remount modernized versions of the Yiddish standard
drama constitute one remarkable example.[80]

Moreover, ethnic actors and actresses themselves tended to accommodate to the mainstream stage, frequently enacting the caricature
roles found so appealing by American audiences. Weber and Fields,
Joe Welsh, Sam Bernard, Julian Rose and many others performed essentially demeaning ethnic routines; indeed, they occasionally built

their careers on such routines. And those who followed them ultimately produced that third version of "ethnic theater" noted earlier: the version whereby ethnic entertainers played new kinds of ethnic roles, frequently neo-minstrel blackface song-and-dance routines, designed primarily for mainstream (or well-acculturated ethnic) audiences. The prime exemplar of this version would have to be Al Jolson, though Eddie Cantor, Sophie Tucker, and others advanced their careers with such routines. Jolson, Cantor, and Tucker were, of course, Jewish-Americans. Surely they were all sensitive to the potential for damage inherent in demeaning caricature. They were nonetheless quite willing to perpetuate black ascription in their enormously popular acts. It would appear that they never intended any affront to real-life blacks. They seemed to believe that their portrayals were funny and appealing, possibly even endearing reflections of Afro-American types. They meant no harm — nor did their predecessors, the "racial comics" of the Gilded Age — who created their own ethnic caricatures. Nor can they be blamed for the fact that their portrayals would advance popular racist assumptions. Indeed, black performers of the period also played neo-minstrel roles, even as Jewish performers played caricature Germans and Jews. And the portrayal of ethnic types would continue for years to come. That is, however, another story, best left to students of the social history of American popular entertainment, and more particularly the electronic media, of the twentieth century.

Notes

1. Werner Sollors has recently elucidated this point and endeavored to overcome the problems by assuming an essentially new perspective on ethnic things. The subtitle of his book suggests the direction of his tack. Sollors, *Beyond Ethnicity: Consent and Descent in American Culture* (New York, 1986). See also Jonathan Udell, *Toward Conceptual Codification in Race and Ethnic Relations* (Roslyn Heights, N.Y., 1979).
2. Maxime Schwartz Seller, ed., *Ethnic Theatre in the United States* (Westport, Conn., 1983), 3.
3. Frederick Barth, ed., *Ethnic Groups and Boundaries: The Social Organization of Culture Difference* (Boston, 1969), 2–18 and *passim*. For additional theoretical material on the matters of ethnic boundary formation and maintenance, see James H. Dorman, "Ethnic Groups and 'Ethnicity': Some Theoretical Considerations," *Journal of Ethnic Studies* 7 (1980), 23–36.
4. Limitations of space and the need to maintain thematic focus preclude the treatment of a fourth major immigrant group, the Irish, whose ethnic theater experience was unique to them (and atypical of other European groups) in salient ways.
5. For purposes of differentiation I have used the term "mainstream" to suggest theater intended primarily for English-speaking American (i.e., non-immigrant, non-ethnic) audiences. The primary locus of "mainstream" theater in the New York of the Gilded Age was a section of Broadway between Madison Square and Forty-second Street known as "the Rialto." See Lloyd Morris, *Incredible New York* (New York, 1951), 182.

6. Christa Carvajal, "German-American Theatre," in Seller, ed., *Ethnic Theatre*, 176–177.

7. *Ibid.*, 178–182. On the early years of the German-American Theatre, see Fritz A. H. Leucks, *The Early German Theatre in New York* (New York, 1928). A good contemporary assessment of the state of German-language theater in New York is in Norman Hapgood, "The Foreign Stage in New York: 2. The German Theatre," *The Bookman* 11 (July 1900), 452–458. See also Hapgood, *The Stage in America, 1897–1900* (New York, 1901), 235–248.

8. Hapgood, "German Theatre," 452.

9. George C. D. Odell, *Annals of the New York Stage*, 15 vols. (New York, 1920–1949), XII, 74.

10. Hapgood, "German Theatre," *passim*. See also Robert M. Dell, "The Representation of the Immigrant on the New York Stage, 1818–1916" (Ph.D. dissertation, New York University, 1960), 80.

11. Emelise Aleandri and Maxine S. Seller, "Italian-American Theatre," in Seller, ed., *Ethnic Theatre*, 239.

12. *Ibid.*, 253–255.

13. *Ibid.*, 251. The Circolo Filodrammatico Italo-Americano was among the Italian-American organizations that financed the erection of the Columbus monument at Columbus Circle in 1892.

14. Hutchins Hapgood, "The Foreign Stage in New York: 3. The Italian Theatre," *The Bookman* 11 (August 1900), 545–553. Hutchins Hapgood was the brother of Norman Hapgood. Both contributed to the *Bookman* ethnic theater series.

15. Odell, *Annals*, XII, 78, 281–282, 489–490.

16. Hapgood, "Italian Theatre," 553.

17. *Ibid.* Hapgood provides several plot synopses of such popular, ephemeral Italian plays, as for example, *A Young Man's Heart* (author unknown). He notes that this play was "typical of those in which the actors are seen to best advantage . . ." and proceeds as follows:

> In a poor cafe in Naples several ragged young men are drinking together. A quarrel ensues, and one of the two bosom friends calls the other a bastard and names a certain priest as the man best able to prove it. Knives are immediately drawn, but the others interfere. An affecting and exceedingly well-acted scene follows between the young man and his mother. He asks her if the charge is true. She does not deny, but refuses to tell who the man was with whom she had sinned. The priest comes in, and the young fellow picks a quarrel and is about to shoot when his mother cries out that he is the father. . . . The horror-striken son leaves his parents and seeks the friend who revealed to him the truth, tells him that he was right and falls in his arms. As friends they agree to die together, and embracing, they shoot one another. Then the other personages of the drama rush in, and the old priest says penitently that he is the cause of it all.

Hapgood observes that "The action here is as simple and passionate as it is in Cavelleria Rusticana." Hapgood, "Italian Theatre," 547.

18. David S. Lifson, "Yiddish Theatre," in Seller, ed., *Ethnic Theatre*, 552–553. For the expanded account, see Lifson, *The Yiddish Theatre in America* (New York, 1965).

19. Lifson, "Yiddish Theatre," 549.

20. Mosche Nadir, "I, the Theater Goer," translated by Etta Block in the "Prologue" to her *One Act Plays From the Yiddish* (2nd series, New York, 1929).

21. Maxine S, Seller, "Introduction," in Seller, ed., *Ethnic Theatre*, 5.

22. Hutchins Hapgood, *The Spirit of the Ghetto*, ed. by Moses Rischin (Cambridge, Mass., 1967; first ed., New York, 1902), 113–176. The series of essays constituting this collection was originally published between 1898 and 1902 in *The Atlantic Monthly*, *The Bookman*, and the New York *Commercial Advertiser*, among other periodicals.

23. Lifson, "Yiddish Theatre," 562.

24. Hapgood, *Spirit of the Ghetto*, 129. There was also a correlation between the length

of time an immigrant had been in the U.S. and his/her theatrical preferences. The "green" ones tended to prefer less sophisticated fare.

25. *Ibid.*, 121.
26. Hapgood suggests that *Minna* (subtitled *The Yiddish Nora*) was "One of the plays most characteristic" of the Gordin-Jacob Adler collaborations (Adler was the leading Yiddish actor of the day). The play, he continues, succeeded in "at once presenting the life of the Ghetto and suggesting its problems." He then provides the following synopsis:

> The first scene represents the house of a poor Jewish laborer on the east side. His wife and daughter are dressing to go to see *A Doll's House* with the boarder—a young man whom they have been forced to take into the house because of their poverty. He is full of ideas and philosophy, and the two women fall in love with him, and give him all the good things to eat. When the laborer returns from his hard day's work, he finds that there is nothing to eat, and that his wife and daughter are going to the play with the boarder. The women despise the poor man, who is fit only to work, eat, and sleep. The wife philosophizes on the atrocity of marrying a man without intellectual interests, and finally drinks carbolic acid.

Lest the desparing wife be construed as a sort of Jewish-American Emma Bovary, however, it is important to note that her husband (the Adler role) was played as a character bordering on "bestiality" in his greed, his foul temper, and his "filthy manners." Hapgood concludes "This Ibsen idea is set in a picture rich with realistic detail: the dialect, the poverty, the types of character, the humor of Yiddish New York." Hapgood, *Spirit of the Ghetto*, 142-143.

27. *Ibid.*, 139.
28. Odell, *Annals*, XIV, 79; Lifson, "Yiddish Theatre," 564.
29. Odell, *Annals*, XIV, 80. See also 82, 310.
30. Lulla, Rosenfeld, *Bright Star of Exile: Jacob Adler and the Yiddish Theater* (New York, 1977), 335. Werner Sollors has observed:

> Works of ethnic literature—written by, about, or for persons who perceived themselves, or were perceived by others, as members of ethnic groups—may thus be read not only as expressions of mediation between cultures but also as handbooks of socialization into the codes of Americanization (*Beyond Ethnicity*, 7).

So it was for ethnic *theater* as well, of whatever type.

31. Hapgood, *Spirit of the Ghetto*, 156.
32. Dell, "New York Stage," 81.
33. Paul Antoine Distler, "The Rise and Fall of the Racial Comics in American Vaudeville" (Ph.D. dissertation, Tulane University, 1963), 98. The term "racial comic" was routinely applied to vaudeville performers specializing in ethnic material. The misnomer has been carried forth in the scholarship on the subject despite its technical inaccuracy.
34. As early as 1879, the New York *Dramatic Mirror* advertised the appearance of "Watson and Ellis, the best team of German speciality performers now before the public." *Dramatic Mirror*, January 11, 1879.
35. The question of the authorship of the "racial" comedy sketchs is clearly pertinent to the matter of ethnic ascription in that their authors were the conduits of the ascriptive process. Ascribed characteristics were applied to the caricatures by the creators of the routines. Unfortunately, the creators' identities are not easily established. Normally, vaudeville performers either wrote their own material or, more often, paid comedy writers for routines, seldom providing public credit for their work. Once used on stage the jokes, skits, or whatever, fell into the public domain and frequently reappeared in popular collections of such material, again without author identification. Of those writers known to contribute stage material, however, few were themselves ethnics. They were usually outsiders, writing for mainstream audiences that frequently did include ethnic members. Among the most

active of those who provided such comedy routines were James Madison (Publisher of *Madison's Budget*), Leslie Carter (*Carter's Vaudeville What-Nots*), William McNally (*McNally's Bulletin*), and T. S. Denison (*Denison's Vaudeville Sketches*). Madison was scriptwriter for, at one time or another, Al Jolson, Ed Wynn, Joe Welsh, Nora Bayes, and Eddie Cantor, all of whom were "ethnic" comics. See Lida Rae McCabe, "How Vaudeville Sketches are Written," *Theatre Magazine* 7 (April 1906), VI, 103; Brett Page, *Writing for Vaudeville* (Springfield, Mass., 1915), *passim*; Albert F. McLean, Jr., "U.S. Vaudeville and the Urban Comics," *Theatre Quarterly* 1 (October-December 1971), 47–52. See also Distler, "Rise and Fall," *passim*.

36. "Dig-ni-ty—A Double Dutch Cross-Fire," in Carter, ed., *Vaudeville What-Nots* 1 (1929), 54–56. While the *What-Nots* collection began publishing in 1929, the material Carter included came from much earlier performances.

37. For these acts, see *Ames' Series of Standard and Minor Drama* (Clyde, Ohio, 1878), numbers 49, 66 and 379 (unpaginated).

38. "Dutch Conversations," in *Madison's Budget* 9 (1903), 15. For the full dialogue of a longer Double-Dutch Act, see Joseph Laurie, *From the Honkey-Tonks to the Palace* (New York, 1953; reprinted, Port Washington, N.Y., 1972), 444–464.

39. The sketch is reprinted in full in Distler, "Rise and Fall," appendix A, 196–199.

40. Ada Patterson, "A Dual Interview with Weber and Fields," *Theatre Magazine* 15 (April 1912), 113–116.

41. Dell, "New York Stage," 222–233.

42. Odell, *Annals*, XI, 700.

43. From J. K. Emmet, "Love of the Shamrock Songster," n.d. [ca. 1882] unpaginated.

44. Edward Harrigan, *The Investigation*, 11–12. Manuscript copy, Harrigan Collection (New York Public Library).

45. Harry Lee Newton, "A Sunny Son of Italy. An Italian Monologue," *Denison's Vaudeville Sketches* (Chicago, 1908), 2.

46. Eulalie Andreas, "The Italian Good-Bye" (published by the author, 1905) unpaginated.

47. *Madison's Budget* 9 (1903), 26.

48. Arthur LeRoy Kazer, "Just-a-Lak-a Dat. A Wop Monologue," *Denison's Vaudeville Sketches*, n.d. [ca. 1907], unpaginated.

49. Harry Lee Newton, "As Tony Tells It," *Vaudeville Monologues* (n.p., 1917), 85.

50. William J. Scanlon, "Peggy O'Moore Songster," quoted in Dell, "New York Stage," 223.

51. Newton, "Sunny Son," 7.

52. *Ibid.*

53. *McNally's Bulletin* 2 (1918), 5.

54. "Enter the Italian on the Vaudeville Stage," *The Survey*, 24 (May 7, 1910), 198–199.

55. New York *Telegraph*, August 28, 1899. The "Coon" reference reflected the enormous popularity of the ubiquitous "Coon Song" of the same period.

56. New York *Dramatic Mirror*, October 16, 1899; *Madison's Budget* 5 (1900), 1.

57. New York *Telegraph*, June 17, 1900. See also Pittsburgh *Post*, February 10, 1910. Clipping in Robinson Locke Collection, Abe Reynolds File (Library of the Performing Arts, New York Public Library, Lincoln Center).

58. Vaudeville handbooks of the period often provided descriptions of the stock characters. See, for example, Brett Page, *Writing for Vaudeville* (Springfield, Mass., 1915), 23; Frederick LaDelle, *How to Enter Vaudeville* (Jackson, Mich., n.d.), unpaginated. See also Distler, "Rise and Fall," 80.

59. *Madison's Budget* 9 (1903), 33.

60. Irving Howe, *World of Our Fathers* (New York, 1976), 404.

61. *Madison's Budget* 16 (1915), 8.

62. *Ibid.*, 4 (1901), 2–3.

63. *Ibid.*, 16 (1915), 5.

64. *McNally's Bulletin* 3 (1919), 61.

65. *Madison's Budget* 3 (1900), 3.

66. *Ibid.*, 5 (1899), 2. David A. Gerter has noted that the Shylock image of the mid-nineteenth century featured "the arsonist cheating his insurors." This ascriptive quality was thus already established by prior stereotyping (as were many other such qualities). Gerber, "Cutting Out Shylock: Elite Anti-Semitism and the Quest for Moral Order in the Mid-Nineteenth Century American Market Place," *Journal of American History* 69 (December 1982) 629.

67. *Madison's Budget* 8 (1903), 16; 10 (1905), 37. In another context, Michael N. Dobrowski has noted (of the period 1885–1905) "fire insurance and failure jokes were the vogue." Dobrowski, *The Tarnished Dream: The Basis of American Anti-Semitism* (Westport, Conn., 1979), 60. The "fraudulent bankrupt" was another feature of the earlier "Shylock" stereotype, according to Gerber. See Gerber, "Cutting Out Shylock," 629.

68. "Three Golden Balls," in Thomas Joseph Carey, *Hebrew Yarns and Dialect Humor* (New York, 1900), 20.

69. *Madison's Budget* 15 (1900), 20.

70. *McNally's Bulletin* 3 (1919), 59.

71. Carey, *Hebrew Yarns*, 11.

72. Alexander Carr, "Perlmutter Speaks," *Theatre* 14 (March 1, 1914), 38, quoted in Distler, "Rise and Fall," 82.

73. "In Vaudeville," *Everybody's Magazine* 24 (August 1905), 238.

74. Spokane (Washington) *Spokesman*, April 26, 1914. Clipping in Locke Collection, Julian Rose File. The comment pertained to a New York performance.

75. Unidentified clipping, Locke Collection, Rose File.

76. Minneapolis *Journal*, April 13, 1911, quoted in Distler, "Rise and Fall," 162.

77. Pittsburgh *Leader*, December 21, 1906. Clipping in Locke Collection, Reynolds File. Emphasis added.

78. This is not to suggest that the results of ascriptive stereotyping were wholly beneficial to European immigrants and ethnics. Clearly there were negative results as well. Stereotypes functioned to mark the boundaries for years, thus maintaining ethnic distinctions and divisions. But the impact on the immigrant adjustment process was likely salutary.

79. Even the Italian immigrants, often represented in popular literature as dangerous — the omnipresent stiletto was the prime signifier — were normally comic characters on the mainstream stage. Note the contrast between this circumstance and the knife scene in *A Young Man's Heart*, an original Italian drama, summarized in note 17. See also William Boelhower, "Describing the Italian-American Self: Type-Scene and Encyclopedia," *In Their Own Words* 2 (1984), 37–48.

80. One thinks, for example, of the recent revival of Goldfadn's *Kuni Leml* by the Jewish Repertory Theatre.

PART THREE

The Post-World War II City

RANDALL M. MILLER

Introduction:
The Post-World War II City

New York City long has prided itself as America's city of immigrants. Cast in the metaphor of the melting pot, New York was the great crucible out of which poured the rich alloys of American character and genius. As the golden door, New York promised access to the American dream. Even the city's song made New York the mecca for those with vagabond shoes. If you could "make it there, you could make it anywhere," Frank Sinatra crooned. America, the immigrant nation, was embodied in New York, the immigrant city, and popular culture seemed to confirm New York's conceit that all the world was New York.

Since World War II, however, those images and realities of New York have lost their lustre. Immigrants now go elsewhere, and New York's smoke-stack industries that once provided ladders for the upward movement of immigrant workers and choked the city's air with the black smoke of "progress" now stand idle. On the face of it, the new immigrants prefer the burgeoning sunbelt, especially California and Florida. Immigrants now arrive via airplane rather than in steerage, and few greet (or are welcomed by) the Statue of Liberty that once beckoned Europe's "huddled masses." Indeed, the "Lady" seems to be looking in the wrong direction for those to embrace, for since World War II the sources of immigration to the United States have shifted from Europe to Asia and the Western Hemisphere, especially the Caribbean region, and both geographical proximity and chain migrations have favored the southern rim over New York as the point of destination. In the

1980s Los Angeles eclipsed New York City as the nation's principal port of entry. Ever sensitive to popular trends, television and news weeklies now focus on California and Florida as the nodes of the new immigrant America. New York survives no longer in popular imagination as the golden door or the great crucible (an image scholars now reject anyway as contrary to the realities of the persistence of ethnic culture and associations among the immigrants and their children). It is, rather, a big apple gone wormy, rotten with economic and social decay and no longer attractive to those who hope for success in America. Seemingly, New York's day is past and the sun rises farther south and west.

In fact, New York remains an immigrant city and continues to reflect and affect the character and direction of American immigration. The New York City metropolitan area, sprawling over 3,600 square miles, claims more than 16 million people in the 1980s. According to 1983 federal census figures, 36 percent of the city's five-borough population is foreign-born—a proportion that compares with 42 percent foreign-born in New York in 1910 when the "new immigration" was at floodtide. While this proportion is not quite so dramatic as the higher foreign-born percentages in Los Angeles and Miami, it does suggest New York's continued importance as an immigrant city. Like the new immigrant cities of the sunbelt, New York is also a Hispanic city, at least in part. Indeed, Hispanics constitute 20 percent of the city's population in the 1980s, but more than just proportions, the sheer numbers of Spanish-speaking immigrants and migrants make New York an important Hispanic city in the United States, if not in the Americas. Puerto Ricans, who are not immigrants, have been coming to the city in large numbers since mid-century, and in recent decades large numbers of immigrants from the Caribbean region and South America have given the city an Hispanic mix equal to that of any sunbelt city. So, too, New York is an Asian city. Despite its distance from western ports of entry, New York continues to attract a significant and diverse Asian population. In that way New York further shares in one of the major population influxes of the post-war era that is, in the popular mind, generally associated with western sunbelt cities alone.

New York, of course, is not Los Angeles or Miami or Houston. It is an older city, suffering the general flight of its middle-class white population to the suburbs or beyond and the influx of poor and low-income blacks, Puerto Ricans, and new immigrants to the Bronx, Manhattan, or elsewhere in a city burdened with old or substandard housing, un- or underemployment in an economy adjusting fitfully to "deindustrialization," rising crime, and declining city services. Between 1945 and 1980 roughly two million middle-class people left New York City, while approximately the same number of poor and low-income people moved in. Pushed by higher costs for welfare and social services, while teetering on a shrinking tax base, the city almost fell into bankruptcy during the mid-1970s; its financial resources have remained precariously gerry-rigged throughout the 1980s. For all its promise and glitter, New York could not escape the consequences of suburbanization, the shift to the post-industrial service economy, and rapid population turnover. Still, the people came, and come.

In Part III of this book three themes emerge in the essays. One is the persistence of New York as the point of destination for immigrants and migrants in recent years. New York's size and population diversity offer an environment of anonymity and toleration inviting to many recent immigrants (legal and otherwise) and migrants, and its mystique as the arena of opportunity, though tarnished somewhat, still lures those who want to wake up in a city that never sleeps. By the 1980s New York was no longer the principal point of entry or point of destination for immigrants, but it has remained both for very many immigrants/migrants throughout the post-war era and still remains so today. Even subtracting the number of immigrants/migrants who "repatriated" or returned to their original homes (return migration being a significant, though not wholly unique, aspect of the post-war immigration/migration), the net in-migration has been substantial. Remigration patterns point to the fluidity of movement, and the importance of attitudes in directing migration and settlement. Large numbers of individuals who come with no intention of remaining for long will affect (and have affected) the city in different ways than those persons who planned to stay.

A second theme is the role public policy plays in directing the patterns and defining the composition and character of immigration/migration. Changes in immigration laws since World War II coincided with shifts in the sources of immigration to encourage the large immigration from Western Hemispheric and Asian peoples, thereby broadening the ethnic range in the city of immigrants, as in America. Though policy-makers neither anticipated nor wanted these newest immigrants, the economic and political convulsions in developing nations and the pull of America, made accessible by a tradition of receiving immigrants and by relatively inexpensive air transportation, combined to fuel the movement of so many people to New York and elsewhere. In the case of the Puerto Ricans, as Michael Lapp shows, mass migration to the mainland was in part the product of a conscious policy by the Puerto Rican government to encourage and manage such movement to (and in) New York. Unlike previous immigrations, the post-war experience in America included large numbers of refugees — a reflection of the circumstances driving people to migrate but also of American immigration policy which offered refugee status as one crack whereby an individual might pass through a wall of restrictions. Public policies sometimes worked at cross purposes or had contradictory effects. New York's generous welfare and social services influenced people's decisions to move or stay there. In contrast, federal enforcement of immigration and naturalization laws drove some immigrants to seek out the city's anonymity, while simultaneously discouraging those same people from claiming any public benefits and services lest they be discovered. As the authors in this section of the book remind us, laws and public policy have social consequences.

A third, though less explicit, theme of these essays is the retention of immigrant or ethnic identities. One implication of Elliott Barkan's discussion of remigration is that the ease and frequency of travel between the "homeland" and New York both reflected and reinforced the immigrants' (and one might add the Puerto Ricans') ability to resist assimilation into the dominant "American" host culture. Chain migrations and clusters of immigrant and ethnic groups in a city large enough to contain them further retarded assimilation and kept alive older cultures and social associations. In that regard, the city functioned in the post-war era much like it did in the late nineteenth and early twentieth centuries.

A close look at recent population data reveals that New York appears as it always was — an ethnically diverse metropolis. What is not so clear from head counts is the process of cultural and political mitosis and metamorphosis whereby New York becomes many cities. New York's many and varied, even contradictory, poses, born of the city's myriad faces and cultures, in part explain New York's persistent magnetism, drawing numerous and different people(s) unto her. But they also confound attempts to place New York in neat categories for sociological analysis. New York City defies easy description or summary. To discover the immigrant/ethnic city, it is necessary to stake off the boundaries of the city's whole immigrant/migrant population growth while simultaneously getting down to cases in looking at the factors compelling and/or propelling each particular people to choose New York. Charting the flows and measuring the dimensions of population movement to New York, and then suggesting the implications of that movement for New York's immigrant/ethnic character — that is the subject of the three essays in this section.

8

Recent Third World Immigration to New York City, 1945–1986: An Overview

When Daniel Moynihan and Nathan Glazer published *Beyond the Melting Pot* in 1963, they claimed that the melting pot did not occur in New York. They wrote that "the notion that the intense and unprecedented mixture of ethnic and religious groups in American life was soon to blend into a homogeneous end product has outlived its usefulness, and also its credibility. . . . The point about the melting pot . . . is that it did not happen. At least not in New York."[1] They insisted that New York's major ethnic groups — Jews, Italians, Irish, Puerto Ricans, and blacks — had changed but still maintained their ethnicity in important ways. Their account omitted discussion of those, like the original Dutch, eighteenth-century French Huguenots and large numbers of nineteenth-century Germans, who did not fit their thesis. They modified their conclusions in a 1969 edition, but kept their broad interpretation.[2]

Looking back to the 1960s one might wish to qualify their arguments further. Yet something else seems more noticeable today. At the time of their writing, changes of another sort were occurring in New York City. The post-1960 migration of so many immigrants from the

Caribbean and Asia has given the city new ethnic dimensions and renewed its image as a city of diverse peoples, this time from the Third World.

Small numbers of Third World immigrants found their way to New York before 1945. The city's Chinatown, in roughly its present location, dates from the late nineteenth century. However, it numbered only a few thousand before World War II and was mainly a bachelor society, which because of racial discrimination, was largely isolated from the mainstream of New York's social, political, and economic life.[3] Several thousand Japanese also emigrated to New York City during the same period. Again, their numbers were not large. Although more geographically dispersed, they too lived a segregated existence.[4] Other Asians were minuscule in number before 1941.

More significant — or at least more numerous — were people from the Caribbean. Some had arrived as early as the 1790s, and immigrants from French, British, Dutch, and Spanish colonies and former possessions continued to arrive after that time.[5] The most visible of these immigrants were English-speaking West Indians, who because of their concentration in New York City, made it the center of West Indian life in the United States. Of New York's 60,666 blacks in 1900, about 5,000 were West Indians. By the time of the Great Depression they numbered over 50, 000, about one sixth of the city's black population. They were located chiefly in Harlem, with another settlement in Brooklyn.[6] West Indians were often political and economic leaders in black New York City.

When the United States Congress began to ban Third World immigrants, the legislators first singled out the Chinese (1882), next Asian Indians (1917), and then the Japanese (1924). These Congressional Acts virtually barred further immigration from Asia, and also prohibited Asian foreigners from becoming American citizens. These laws limited the growth of Asian-American communities in New York City, though a few new immigrants occasionally arrived. A second generation, born in the United States and hence American citizens, grew up in the years before World War II.[7]

The situation differed for Caribbean migrants. When Congress enacted the restrictions, independent nations in the Western Hemisphere were not given numerical quotas, and immigrants from European colonies could enter under the quota of the mother country. In the case of the English-speaking colonies, this meant the largest quota of all, that of Great Britain, All newcomers were subject to restrictions on a long list of those the legislators considered undesirable, such as persons with certain diseases or those likely to become a public charge.

In 1952, as part of the McCarran-Walter Immigration Act, the colonies were granted quotas of only 100 each, thus cutting their potential immigration severely.

While the immigration restriction acts drastically reduced emigration to New York City, many American citizens still migrated there. From the American South came blacks, beginning in the nineteenth century and especially after 1910. One group migrating to New York City from the Caribbean had no restrictions whatsoever: Puerto Ricans. By virtue of the Jones Act of 1917, Puerto Ricans became American citizens; hence, they could move freely to the mainland. Driven largely by poor economic prospects at home and pulled by the hope of better conditions in New York, Puerto Ricans began moving to the city in growing numbers. They numbered over 7,000 there in 1920, and over 44,000 in 1940, thus making them the largest Hispanic group in the city.[8]

After the end of World War II both blacks and Puerto Ricans continued to migrate to New York City and they were joined by many immigrants from the Western Hemisphere. Because of the lack of numerical quotas for the Western Hemispheric independent nations, the advent of cheap air travel and better communication between the United States and Central and South America, and the availability of jobs especially in the city's service sector, migration from the Caribbean increased after World War II, even before the enactment of the 1965 immigration reforms.

Colombians were the largest group to enter from South America. They migrated partly to escape deteriorating economic conditions, but also because of rural unrest and violent turmoil during the 1950s. They were not necessarily the poorest elements of society. The largest Colombian settlement in the United States was in Queens, New York. While small in numbers, this early exodus formed the nucleus for the post-1960 migration.[9] Other scattered groups of South Americans, including some physicians and professionals, also entered New York during these years.

While the McCarran-Walter Immigration Act of 1952 cut British West Indian migration (West Indians headed for England after the 1952 act), it did not end it entirely. Spouses of United States citizens and their minor children were able to enter above the newly imposed quota, and some did so. Independent Dominican Republic and Haiti had no quota, only the list of prohibited groups. Dominicans generally settled in Manhattan.[10] Economic factors explain their migration to the United States, but Haitian immigration was triggered by both poor economic conditions and the repressive regime of the Duvalier family which began in 1957. Hence, some of the first Haitians to New

York were political exiles who fled for their lives. Mostly middle-class professionals, they usually settled in Brooklyn.[11] Even though the numbers of these Caribbean and South American immigrants were not large, they became the nucleus for future migration. As they settled and found employment and housing, they sent news back home to their families and friends; because of cheap air fares, they journeyed back and forth between New York and the Caribbean.

Emigration to the United States for Asians between World War II and 1965 proved more difficult. Yet Congress modified the nation's immigration policies in ways that permitted new Asian immigration. Most immediate post-World War II immigration liberalization eased the quota restrictions on European countries to allow displaced persons and refugees from communism to enter above small national origins quotas. In the process of admitting refugees, the legislators allowed a few thousand Chinese to enter and permitted some of those stranded in the United States, following the 1949 communist victory in China, to remain here. In addition, President John F. Kennedy used the parole power to admit about 14,000 Chinese refugees from Hong Kong.[12]

Congress also amended the basic immigration laws during and after the war to remove some discrimination against Asians. This made increased Asian migration possible. In 1943, as a gesture of wartime support for its ally, Congress repealed the Chinese Exclusion acts, gave China an annual quota of 105 persons, and permitted Chinese immigrants to become American citizens. This made it possible for some Chinese living in the United States to become naturalized citizens and bring in their spouses, in many cases after years of separation.[13]

At the end of the war, Congress passed the War Brides Act, which waived some restrictions on persons married to American military service personnel. The law affected mainly Germans and English, but also several thousand Chinese. In 1946 Congress gave India and the Philippines token quotas of 100 persons, annually. Then in 1952 the legislators repealed the ban on Asian immigration, gave most Asian nations an annual quota of 100; and placed a ceiling of 2,000 on South and East Asia. Spouses and minor children of American citizens were exempt from these limitations.[14]

All of these exemptions did not lead to radical new patterns of migration, but they did open the possibility for growth of New York City's Asian population, especially among the Chinese. As the city's Chinatown grew, it became the basis for future immigration from China. Small numbers of Indians, Filipinos and Koreans also migrated to the city during these years. They, too, began to develop networks for the larger, post-1965 immigration.

The various laws passed after the end of World War II undercut the national origins provisions of the 1952 McCarran-Walter Act. By the early 1960s about two thirds of all immigrants were arriving outside of the quotas. Those wishing to reform immigration restrictions claimed that the exceptions proved that the McCarran-Walter Act was unworkable. These reformers, composed of congressional liberals and religious and ethnic groups working with immigrants, urged Congress to replace the 1952 law with a system doing away with discriminatory national origins quotas and severe limits on Asians. Reformers also insisted that the McCarran-Walter Act injured American foreign policy by insulting many of our European and Asian allies.[15]

In the early 1960s racial and ethnic discrimination was under attack from a wide variety of Americans. Responding to black demands and following the landslide victory of Lyndon Johnson and many new congressional liberals, Congress passed sweeping civil rights laws in the mid-1960s. The time had obviously arrived when it was possible to amend drastically the 1952 act. By a lopsided vote the legislators junked the national origins quotas and replaced them with a new preference system for admitting immigrants.

In abolishing the national origins quotas in 1965 and replacing them with a preference system based on family unification, skills needed in the United States, and refugee status, Congress wanted to make it possible for southern and eastern European countries to send more immigrants. Such a change did occur in the decade after the 1965 immigration act's enactment. Many Italians settled in Brooklyn while a sizeable Greek community grew in the Astoria section of Queens.

In reshaping the law, Congress also desired to cut the flow of immigration from the Western Hemisphere (excluding Canada). Yet the restrictions did not seriously affect Caribbean migration. Indeed, in some ways, to be explained below, they made it easier for West Indians to enter the United States. Moreover, the new law had an unintended result of greatly increasing Asian migration. Thus, total immigration increased substantially after 1965.

While Los Angeles replaced New York as the city with the most newcomers, New York remained a major abode for immigrants, largely from the Caribbean and Asia. By 1980 the borough of Queens held the largest number of aliens, followed closely by Brooklyn, then Manhattan, and the Bronx. Richmond had only a small number of newcomers.[16] About 800,000 to 850,000 immigrants came to New York City during the 1970s. For the entire period 1965 to 1985, the figure was close to one and one half million.[17] How many immigrants returned home is not known because the Immigration and Naturalization Service (INS) stopped keeping such records in the late 1950s; nor is it known how many left the city for other locations in the United States. One thing is certain: the Third World newcomers were changing the city.

The presence of large numbers of undocumented immigrants and refugees make it difficult to generalize about the size of New York's growing Third World communities. There are widely divergent estimates about the size of this population and its impact upon American society. This was the center of discussion concerning the Simpson-Mazzoli bills in Congress and much public controversy. Many scholars and ethnic leaders believe that New York's minorities are undercounted, because of a lack of thoroughness by the Bureau of Census, suspicion on the part of minorities about the government, and the wish of undocumented aliens to remain undetected; hence, they avoid being uncounted.

Just how many illegal aliens reside in New York City in the mid-1980s? In 1978 Evelyn Mann of the Population Office of the New York City Planning Department told a United States House committee that there were 750,000 undocumented aliens in the city, but she admitted she had no data on which to build a precise estimate.[18] Other officials as well as some scholars have used similar figures. Mayor Edward Koch, in discussing the subject in 1985 put the figure between 400,000 and 750,000.[19] The Bureau of the Census estimated that it counted around two million illegal aliens in 1980 and put the number in New York State (mainly in the city) at 234,495.[20] How many were not counted the Bureau did not know, but in 1980 it did estimate the national total at between 3.5 and 5 million, which indicated that several million were not counted. In 1988, results of the amnesty offered by the Simpson- Rodino Act showed that only about 100,000 aliens applied from New York City.[21]

Regardless of how many undocumented aliens were in the city, counted or not, most observers believed that once in New York it was relatively easy for them to live and work. Though fearful of INS, these migrants were usually not discovered and deported. INS had limited resources and concentrated its efforts along the United States-Mexican border to halt the flow of illegal immigration. The New York office of INS, as in most large cities with many immigrants, was overwhelmed with case work, and lacked resources to find and deport undocumented aliens. According to New York police, for example, illegal Senegalese immigrant vendors were among the city's rapidly growing street peddlers. In early 1984 the police and INS rounded up and deported seventy-five of them. But officials believed the action was too expensive, and took away important resources for more serious violations. As one INS investigator said, "Our resources are focused on criminal aliens—aliens involved in drugs and benefit frauds....Which of those do I let go, to work on the Senegalese? Murders and drug peddlers?"[22] Moreover, fraudulent documents, such as birth certificates and social security cards, were relatively easy to obtain, which further complicated the work of INS.[23]

Compounding the problem of counting new immigrants was the issue of refugees. The post-1960 exodus of Third World refugees generally did not head for New York City. Cubans settled in Florida (especially in Miami) and New Jersey, with some spill over into New York City. About one-third of the Indochinese lived in California and only about 20,000 settled in New York in the mid-1980s. Refugee Iranians, Haitians, Salvadorans, and Nicaraguans also resided in New York City, and the city contained a sizeable Soviet Jewish community located in the Brighton Beach section of Brooklyn.[24]

These groups had been officially admitted as refugees by the United States government or were part of the small number (only a few thousand annually in the mid-1980s) who had come to the United States and then been granted asylum. Thousands of other New Yorkers lacked official status but considered themselves refugees. Many Haitians and Salvadorans, for example, were not technically refugees, but considered themselves as such and were part of their communities, even though INS and the census counters did not find them. The United States government did grant some groups, such as Poles and Iranians, extended voluntary departure status and allowed them to stay beyond the expiration date of their visas. Others simply slipped into the city, perhaps originally crossing the United States-Mexican border illegally or entering on student or visitor visas and simply staying on. If caught, they applied for asylum. As a result, the backlog of asylum cases grew rapidly following passage of the Refugee Act of 1980, but petitioners found it difficult to convince INS that they had a well-founded fear of persecution if they returned. Appeals often followed rejection by INS, and thousands of New York immigrants managed to postpone their deportation because of the backlog in asylum proceedings.[25]

One such case concerned a group of Afghans. While the United States did admit some Afghans under its quota for refugees, more wanted to come than places were available. In 1984 INS seized thirty-three Afghans who had entered illegally (mostly with bogus passports). When they requested asylum and refused to return home, they found themselves interned for nearly a year and a half. The government said they could be released if they went home, but the Afghans refused. Civil liberties groups and the intervention by New York's two United States senators and a representative eventually obtained their release and allowed them to be free pending the outcome of their asylum case.[26]

Regardless of this individual case, and the many others tied up in the courts, the total of undocumented aliens, claiming to be refugees or not, remains unknown. Certainly more immigrants lived in the city than the 1980 census takers found. Moreover, even for those with documents, in 1981 INS stopped requiring them to report their addresses annually. Thus, while the 1980 census found that one in four New Yorkers was foreign-born, the number was undoubtedly higher by the mid-1980s.[27] Keeping in mind that immigration to the city was about 800,000 in the 1970s and remained heavy in the early 1980s and that substantial numbers remained uncounted, some scholars and city officials estimated that 30 percent or more of New Yorkers were foreign-born by the mid-1980s.[28] That figure was the highest since the 1940s and represented a reversal of the pattern begun with the curtailment of immigration beginning in the 1920s.

The largest source of post-1965 flow to New York was the Caribbean, including Hispanics, English-speaking West Indians, and Creole-speaking Haitians. About half of all immigrants from the Caribbean to the United States came to New York during the 1970s.[29] Cheap air fare, the existence of older ethnic communities, plentiful news about New York, and the hope for a better life than found in the poor Caribbean countries all combined to trigger increased immigration to New York.

Hispanic immigrants came from the Dominican Republic, El Salvador, Guatemala, Cuba, Honduras, and Nicaragua as well as a substantial number from Colombia and other nations in South America.[30] The increasing Hispanic immigration led to a growth in the city's Hispanic population, to about 1.4 million according to the 1980 census. Puerto Rican migration to the mainland slowed in the 1960s, and after that many more may have left than came to New York. Thus while the great bulk of the city's Hispanics were Puerto Ricans in 1960, that proportion dropped to approximately 60 percent by the 1980s.[31]

Dominicans and Colombians were the two largest Hispanic groups arriving in New York between 1965 and 1985 and formed the largest settlements of Dominicans and Colombians in the United States. The center of Dominican life was Manhattan's upper West Side, with other settlements in Queens and the Bronx.[32] Colombians settled near their fellow countrymen in Queens.[33] New York City was the center of Dominican, and to some extent, Colombian life in the United States. Evidence exists that many Dominicans, as well as other people from the Caribbean, traveled back home frequently, in a circulatory migration pattern. Some even entered on visitors' visas, worked temporarily, and then returned home.[34]

While both the Dominican Republic and Colombia experienced economic difficulties and much poverty, Dominican and Colombian emigrants were not necessarily from the poorest strata of society. Upon arrival in New York, however, they usually could not find high-paying employment. As a result, many Colombians and Dominicans worked in the city's low-paying service industries. Dominicans also worked in the city's growing garment shops. These newcomers, because of their relatively cheap labor, helped New York slow the garment industry's deterioration.

South American newcomers were frequently highly educated, medical professionals. Their major settlements were found in Brooklyn. They obviously had an advantage over the poor Hispanic population. Perhaps those with the worst experience were the illegals, many of whom were escaping Central American poverty and the violent turmoil there. As noted, many Salvadorans, Guatemalans, and Nicaraguans considered themselves as refugees, but the federal government admitted few of them as refugees and granted only a handful the right to stay. In 1983 and 1984, for example, INS gave asylum to only 1,112 Nicaraguans and 375 Salvadorans, of whom a small number lived in New York, especially in Queens. The INS turned down most applications.[35] For those without documents or asylum status, life was difficult, often a shadow existence, living in fear of deportation.[36]

The 1965 reforms removed the 100 quota limit on newly independent countries in the Caribbean, which greatly aided emigration from Jamaica and Trinidad and Tobago to the United States.[37] Immigration from these two countries increased substantially, with New York being the center of this flow. In 1980, about half of all Jamaicans in the United States lived in New York City. Brooklyn claimed the largest settlement of Jamaicans; many lived in Manhattan as well. Jamaican emigration was often initiated by women who could find jobs as nurses or domestics in the city. On the whole, Jamaican immigrants had higher education levels than Dominican and Haitian migrants, though they, too, experienced racial discrimination in New York. West Indians had higher incomes and better educations than most native-born blacks, and because they were immigrants, they formed their own organizations.

The city's Creole-speaking community also grew after 1965. Haitians lived in the poorest country in the Caribbean (with a per capita income of only $300) and until the collapse of the Duvalier regime in early 1986, under one of the most repressive dictatorships. Following the early movement of middle-class professionals, many poor Haitians came to New York. Because of their poverty, many could not enter legally, and they chose to enter illegally by boat to Florida. Others entered on temporary visas, and then stayed on. Because so many lacked proper documents, estimates varied widely as to the number of New York's Haitians. They were probably the largest undocumented group in the city. Estimates of the city's Haitian population vary from 200,000 to as high as 500,000, mostly concentrated in Brooklyn.[38]

Like Salvadorans, Haitians had great difficulty convincing the government that they were refugees. INS considered those without papers as illegals who should be deported. They had friends in the United States who joined them in court battles attempting to win their freedom.[39] Like others awaiting asylum decisions, they tried to avoid the authorities and found employment and housing in Brooklyn's large Haitian community. Because of language barriers, little or no education, and racial discrimination, Haitians mostly found work only in low-paying occupations.

Although outnumbered by immigrants from the Caribbean, Asians made up a large proportion of the nearly one and a half million newcomers coming to New York from the time of enactment of the 1965 immigration act to 1985. The 1980 census reported about 230,000 Asian aliens in the city, and INS added that many Asians were continuing to locate in New York after that date. In 1982, for example, INS reported that over 13,000 new Asians claimed New York as their intended residence.[40]

Of this group, the Chinese were the most numerous. The Chinese headed for San Franciso and other cities with substantial Chinatowns, but New York City's Chinatown became the nation's largest in the 1970s. Official figures recorded about 35,000 persons living there, but community leaders said that was a gross undercount, and that as many as 60,000 lived there by the mid-1980s.[41] The new immigrants crowded into what housing was available. Housing prices spiraled upward, and Chinatown expanded east to the Lower East Side and north into "Little Italy."[42] More than half of the city's Chinese population lived outside Manhattan's Chinatown, principally in the Flushing section of the borough of Queens.[43]

Unlike the overwhelmingly male pre-World War II immigration, the new Chinese immigrants were often family groups, with women and children making up a majority. Chinese immigrants came from Hong Kong and Taiwan and were sometimes originally refugees from mainland China, which did not have a quota until 1982. These family migrations changed the bachelor society that dominated Chinese life in New York for so many years before World War II. As a result, the Chinese community became increasingly worried about schools and youth gangs as well as traditional concerns about jobs, crime, housing and discrimination.[44] The new immigrants stressed the value of education, and they quickly became known for their academic achievements in the city's public and private colleges and universities. Elite high schools like Stuyvesant and Bronx Science had disproportionately Asian and Chinese enrollments by the 1980s.

Among the post-1965 immigrants were a number of well-educated professionals, including physicians and scientists, who were part of the Asian "brain drain" to the United States. Yet because the new law gave preference to family members, many of the Chinese immigrants were poorly educated and lacked financial resources. Of course, some wealthy persons from Hong Kong had funds to invest, but the limited resources of many immigrants compelled them to take available employment.

Finding adequate employment for many was compounded by lack of English-language skills. For males this often meant working long hours in the hundreds of Chinese restaurants in Chinatown and Manhattan, and for the women low-paying jobs in the mushrooming sweatshops in or near Chinatown.[45] Because these sweatshops required little capital, some Chinese immigrants hoped to open their own shops, and a few did so. A few waiters and chefs (better paid than waiters and in demand) learned English and saved enough to open their own restaurants. Yet rapidly, rising real estate prices and other costs drove the price of opening a new restaurant to around $300,000 in 1986, clearly beyond the reach of the vast majority of immigrants.[46]

Thus, while the new Chinese acquired reputations for high academic achievement and entrepreneurial skills, many others found life in America hard, requiring long hours at low wages. This meant that Chinatown contained many poor families, not only among the elderly, but also among the new immigrants.

Only a few Koreans lived in New York City before passage of the 1965 immigration act. These were medical professionals or students, along with a few war brides. Passage of the 1965 act coincided with the growing shortage of physicians and nurses, and Korean medical and nursing schools were quick to send their graduates to staff New York hospitals. Once established, these first newcomers sent for their families and friends, many of whom were eager to leave Korea because they saw greater opportunities in America. The New York Korean community was second in size to that of Los Angeles.[47] The Korean immigration was thus of an elite — the educated and urban, and frequently Christian and middle-class — who because of the Korean War and the American penetration of their land, had heard a great deal about the United States.[48]

Koreans were most visible as greengrocers. Sociologist Illsoo Kim, who in 1981 published an excellent book on New York's Koreans, said the first greengrocers had migrated in 1971 from South America. Once these businesses became established, they were rapidly followed by others and numbered 350 seven years later.[49] A journalist estimated the Korean fruit and vegetable stores at 900 in 1982, and in 1984 the Korean Produce Association used about the same figure and said that these stores sold 85 percent of the fresh produce in the city.[50] Koreans also began opening other businesses such as liquor stores, manicurist shops, and stationery shops and began moving their operations to surrounding communities.[51]

Many of these storeowners were college graduates, but lacked English or had skills that were not in demand in the United States.[52] They turned their hands to these small entrepreneurial activities. They sometimes took other jobs at first, worked hard, and saved the small amount of capital needed to become a greengrocer or stationery shop owner. By working exceptionally long hours, the owners and their families won a well-earned reputation for high quality stores. While the fruit and vegetable stores were visible, Koreans were less visible as a distinct community. One large settlement existed in Queens, but the city lacked a "Koreatown." Koreans lived scattered throughout the city.

Smaller in numbers were Filipinos, Indians, and Pakistanis. The New York area's Filipino community may have numbered around 75,000 in the mid-1980s. Filipinos at first entered as medical professionals and worked as nurses and physicians in the city's medical centers. These medical professionals had been trained in American methods and had been taught in English. They found better opportunities in the United States. In addition, many were unhappy with the Ferdinand Marcos regime at home. Some took an active interest in Filipino politics, organized human rights groups, and hoped to go home again.[53] They settled throughout the city, but Queens probably claimed the largest settlements.

Of all the post-1965 newcomers, Asian Indians were the most highly educated and skilled. The 1980 census revealed that these newcomers had a high income compared to America's latest Third World immigrants. Indians had a mean family income of $26,145 compared to $25,200 for Koreans, $17,547 for Chinese, $11,719 for Dominicans, and $13,512 for Mexicans.[54] Asian Indians frequently entered as medical professionals, or as accountants, engineers, and scientists. Universities, hospitals, and private businesses recruited this elite. Once established, they sent for their families, who sometimes were less educated.[55]

While many Indians found employment in universities, medical centers and private enterprise, they became entrepreneurs in their own right. A number opened shops along Lexington Avenue in the 20s of

Manhattan and gave that neighborhood a reputation as "Little India."[56] Others opened restaurants which proved to be popular among New York's diners.[57]

The largest Indian business operation was begun by two brothers, Suesh and Bawnesh Kapor, who arrived in the early 1970s. One was an accountant, the other a New Delhi police officer. With little initial capital, they purchased and ran newsstands, in the subways, in the Port Authority, and along railroads. They also acquired licenses and funds to build new ones. In 1983 they successfully won a contract to operate 143 of the Transit Authority's newsstands. The brothers hired other Indians and Pakistanis to run their expanding news empire.[58] Like the greengrocers, running newsstands required long hours of work, with relatively low pay at first.

While Chinese, Korean, Filipino, Indian, and Pakistani immigrants were the most numerous of the newcomers from Asia, others from the Eastern Hemisphere also benefitted from the 1965 immigration changes. From South Africa a few whites and blacks sought a new life in the United States. The whites were largely professionals, many of whom lived in New York's suburbs. The two South African communities apparently had little to do with one another.[59] Following the Marxist takeover in Ethiopia, thousands fled to the United States, and a few won political asylum.[60] The Iranian turmoil after 1979 and the wars in the Middle East led many Iranians and others — Israelis, Palestinians, Syrians, Lebanese, and Egyptians — to emigrate. Some entered the United States as visitors or students and then overstayed their visas. Of those applying for asylum in the mid-1980s, Iranians were most successful, with nearly 7,000 being granted it in 1984-1985. These people feared persecution under the revolutionary regime in Iran.[61]

These diverse newcomers from Asia and the Middle East worked in a great number of occupations, not infrequently at employment beneath their educational training. A study by the New York Taxi Drivers Institute showed that of 4,396 new applicants for hack licenses in 1984-1985, three quarters were immigrants. They came from eighty-two different countries, and the survey said that more than half had completed two years or more of college.[62] Whatever their jobs, they frequently clustered around various community organizations, some of which took a great interest in political affairs in their homeland.

Only a small number of Vietnamese refugees, around 20,000 from 1975-1985, found their way to the city. According to the New York Association for New Americans, these included about 13,000 from Vietnam, with most of the rest hailing from Cambodia.[63] With aid from the federal government, and in cooperation with religious and secular relief organizations, they attempted to cope with their new environment. Like all refugees they experienced many problems in starting life anew. But for the Indochinese boat people, the exodus had been especially difficult. In some cases they spoke of horrible ventures at sea in escaping Indochina.[64] Not a few of the newcomers leaving in 1978 were ethnic Chinese, and some settled in Chinatown. In spite of their hardships, some did well. In 1984, one refugee, Chi Luu, became the valedictorian of his graduating class at City College.[65]

How will the new immigrants fare in New York City? Although it is too soon to tell, certain patterns stand out. While many Chinese are taking low level jobs available in New York's garment economy, others are finding employment as professionals and small businessmen. Moreover, Chinese—and in general, Asian immigrant youth or the children of Asian immigrants are flocking to the city's elite public schools and its colleges and universities. It appears that many Asians, like Jewish immigrants before them, will use education for social mobility into the city's better paying positions. It is a good bet that the children of Korean greengrocers, for example, will not work in these enterprises with their long hours, but rather will find employment in the professions or technical fields.[66]

For the other recent immigrants the future is not so bright. Unlike the elite Indian professionals, or even the Koreans or Chinese, most Hispanic immigrants do not have high levels of education and their drop-out rates in the city's schools are considerably higher than Asians. Whereas most Asian immigrants appear to want to stay in the United States, and sink their capital and roots here, it is not yet clear what many Hispanics will decide about eventually settling in New York City. Koreans and Indians, for example, are investing their capital in small-scale (but successful) enterprise. If Caribbean immigrants continue to return home in circulatory patterns, they might be unwilling to invest the necessary effort and funds for mobility here rather than looking home.

Black West Indians have a long history in the city, and compared to American blacks, have generally achieved higher levels of education and better paying jobs. They appear to be continuing this pattern. But West Indians face racial discrimination, which though less than during the 1940s, is still a fact of life for all blacks in the United States.

For those immigrants (such as Central American refugees and Haitians) who lack proper documents, there is the additional problem of status. Hence, undocumented Haitians, for example, not only suffer from racial discrimination, the lack of skills, and inability to speak the English language, but they also fear being caught by the INS and are careful about seeking out opportunities that might lead to their deportment.

How will these newcomers fare politically? Thus far, the new immigrants have not yet moved up politically. In individual cases, West Indians, such as former Congresswoman Shirley Chisholm, have been important in the city's politics. But for the present, the immigrant Hispanics and Asians have not been organized effectively. In Queens, for example, the home of many Hispanic immigrants, only a handful of Hispanics served on elected community boards in 1986, and no Hispanic had been elected as a state official. Haydee Vambrana, the Puerto Rican leader of the Concerned Citizens of Queens, summarized the problem: "The Hispanic community, from top to bottom, needs an education on how to use the American political system."[67] The newcomers first will have to master English, obtain citizenship, and then organize to win elections or gain concessions from the city's political leaders.

Asians appear to take out citizenship at a much higher rate than Hispanics.[68] While this might aid Asians politically, even then, problems exist. The number of Asians is considerably smaller than Hispanics or the older European groups or blacks in the city. To win would require more than massing ethnic voters. In 1986 Dorothy Chin Brandt, a Chinese American, successfully won the Democratic nomination for Civil Court judgeship in Manhattan. The nomination, tantamount to election in Manhattan, marked the first time that an Asian American had won a statewide election in New York. Her victory margin of only 150 out of nearly 70,000 votes cast was very close; obviously, she needed support outside the Chinese community for victory.[69] Mayor David N. Dinkins, then the Manhattan Borough President, said:

> I believe that the key to electing minorities to office in greater numbers lies in coalition politics. The ability of blacks, Hispanics, Asians and other minorities to come together will determine to a large extent our ability to impact on New York City politics in the years ahead.

What are the implications of the new immigration for New York City? While it is too soon to tell, especially since the precise numbers of immigrants are unknown, certain factors are obvious. The new immigrants have helped revitalize an economically declining city. Indeed, the paradox is that while New York City lost population (mainly whites to the suburbs) and employment from 1960 to 1980, it experienced a substantial amount of immigration.[70] Some of the economic "revival" of New York in the early 1980s was due to the low-cost labor that the new immigrants supplied. If unskilled or lacking English, immigrants have been willing to take low-paying entry-level jobs in the city's expanding service sector that many Americans seem to reject. Whether this labor has had an adverse impact on New York's American-born minorities remains to be seen.

In addition, the newcomers have opened many small businesses in the city's neighborhoods. The fruit and vegetable stores, newsstand operations, restaurants, and great number of new shops and enterprises are all evidence of the positive impact of the new immigration. As the city's medical services expanded after the 1960s, vacancies developed. Third World professionals have taken these jobs, supplying much of the staff for the city's hospitals. Some municipal hospitals count on Asian physicians and nurses for over half of their staff.

The diversity that the newcomers bring to the city has also enriched New York's cultural heritage, especially musically and artistically. A rejuvenated foreign-language press attested to the vitality of this latest wave of immigration. While the old Yiddish, Italian, and German press declined or disappeared, the Chinese, Arabic and Spanish press experienced new life. In 1985 the city contained more Chinese-language newspapers than English ones.[71] As noted, the newcomers have not yet changed the city's politics, but as many become citizens they no doubt will have an impact.

These new immigrants certainly have generated controversy over bilingual education, and make a significant impact on the city's social services. While some national leaders and INS spokesmen have called for limits on immigration, New York's leaders have generally not done so. In October 1985, Mayor Koch ordered city employees not to report illegal immigrants living in the city to INS. The mayor also said that undocumented aliens should not be discouraged from using services to which they are entitled. He concluded, "For the most part these aliens are self-supporting and law-abiding residents. The greatest problem they pose to the city is their tendency to underuse services to which they are entitled, and on which their well-being and the city's well-being depends."[72]

The larger and long-run effects of the new immigrants on education, the economy, politics, and culture will be seen in the future as more of them enter the city and a second and third generation grows up. Their experiences will no doubt be different from those in the past, but at the same time, it appears that we will all benefit by the new immigration.

Notes

1. Daniel Moynihan and Nathan Glazer, *Beyond the Melting Pot* (Cambridge, Mass., 1963 edition), p. v.
2. *Ibid.*, preface, 1969 edition. See also the comments of Thomas Kassner and Betty Boyd Caroli, in *Today's Immigrants: Their Stories* (New York, 1981), 22–25.
3. Bernard P. Wong, *Chinatown: Economic Adaptation and Ethnic Identity of the Chinese* (New York, 1981), 5–8.
4. Mitzi Sawada, "Dreams of Change: Japanese Issei to New York City, 1891–1924" (Ph.D. dissertation, New York University, 1985), especially last chapter.
5. See Ira De Reid, *The Negro Immigrant* (New York, 1939).
6. Gilbert Osofsky, *Harlem: The Making of a Ghetto* (New York, 1965), 3 and 131–135 and Harold Connolly, *A Ghetto Grows in Brooklyn* (New York, 1977), 76.
7. For a general discussion of restrictions against Asians see David M. Reimers, *Still the Golden Door* (New York, 1985), ch. 1.
8. Virginia E. Sanchez-Korrol, *From Colonia to Community: The History of the Puerto Ricans in New York City, 1917–1948* (Westport, Conn., 1985), 22.
9. Elsa Chaney, "Colombian Migration to the United States, Part II," *The Dynamics of Migration: International Migration* (Washington, D.C., 1976), 107–III.
10. The standard work on New York's Dominicans is Glen Hendricks, *The Dominican Diaspora* (New York, 1974). A general discussion of Caribbean migration to the United States is Virginia Dominguez, *From Neighbor to Stranger* (New Haven, Conn., 1975).
11. Martha Lear, "New York's Haitians," *New York Times Magazine*, Oct. 10, 1971. An excellent general discussion of Haitians in New York is Michael Languerre, *American Odyssey: Haitians in New York City* (Ithaca, N.Y., 1984).
12. Reimers, *Still the Golden Door*, 26, 27–28.
13. *Ibid.*, 11–15.
14. *Ibid.*, 15–22. See also Robert Divine, *American Immigration Policy* (New Haven, Conn., 1957) for a general discussion of immigration changes right after World War II.
15. The discussion of the 1965 immigration act is based on Reimers, *Still the Golden Door*, ch. 3.
16. U. S. Bureau of the Census, *Census of the Population: 1980 Characteristics of the Population* (New York), vol. I, ch. C, pt. 34, table 172.
17. *Time*, July 8, 1985, p. 46; Thomas Muller and Thomas J. Espenshade, *The Fourth Wave: California's Newest Immigrants* (Washington, D.C., 1985), 16 and Emanuel Tobier, "Foreign Immigration," in Charles Brecher and Raymond Horton, eds., *Setting Municipal Priorities, 1983* (New York, 1983), 171–175.
18. U.S. Congress, House, Select Committee on Population, *Immigration to the United States*, Hearings, 95th Cong., 2nd sess., 175–179.
19. *New York Times*, Oct. 18, 1985. Emanuel Tobier, a careful scholar, estimated the figure to be 400,000 to 500,000. See Emanuel Tobier, "Population," in Charles Brecher and Raymond Horton, eds., *Setting Municipal Priorities, 1982* (New York, 1982), 49–50.
20. *New York Times*, June 19, 1983.
21. U.S. Department of Commerce: Bureau of the Census (1980), *Illegal Residents*, 19.
22. *New York Times*, Nov. 10, 1985. When the New York City Police Department moved against the Senegalese, a Manhattan judge dismissed the charges against them, saying that the department had selectively enforced the city's laws on street peddling. Judge Bonnie Wittner claimed that such enforcement was an impermissible standard of race and nationality. *Ibid.*, July 31, 1986.
23. *Ibid.*, July 23, 1984 and Aug. 7, 1984. See also Milton Morris, *Immigration: The Beleaguered Bureaucracy* (Washington, D.C., 1985), ch. 4 and Reimers, *Still the Golden Door*, 203–209.
24. For a general discussion of refugees in New York City see Anita Shreve, "Exiles:

New York's Newest Refugees Have Fled Torture and Death," *New York*, April 30, 1984, pp. 34–40.

25. See Patricia W. Fagen, "Applying for Political Asylum in New York" (Paper, Center for Latin American and Caribbean Studies, New York University, 1983).

26. *New York Times*, Sept. 27, 1985; Nov. 23, 1985; Dec. 1, 1985; and Jan. 10, 1986.

27. During the 1970s New York City received more immigrants than any city except Los Angeles. Muller and Espenshade, *The Fourth Wave*, 16.

28. *Time*, July 8, 1985, p. 47 and Samuel G. Freedman, "The New New Yorkers," *New York Times Magazine*, Pt. II, Nov. 3, 1985, p. 24.

29. Emanuel Tobier, "Foreign Immigration," 178–179.

30. *Ibid.*, 174 and *Time*, July 8, 1985, p. 47.

31. One difficulty in estimating the Puerto Rican proportion is that several hundred thousand persons gave "other" Hispanic as their nationality, rather than naming a particular group.

32. See Hendricks, *Dominican Diaspora*; Philip Kayal, "Dominicans New York," *Migration Today* 3 (1978), 11–15; and U.S. Bureau of the Census, *Census of the Population, 1980: Characteristics of the Population* (New York), vol. I, ch. C, table 172.

33. Fernando Urrea Giralde, *Life Strategies and the Labor Market* (Center for Latin American and Caribbean Studies, New York University, 1982) and Chaney, "Colombian Migration to the United States, Part I," 55–64.

34. Antonio Ugalde, Frank Bean, and Gilbert Cardenas, "International Migration from the Dominican Republic: Findings from a National Survey," *International Migration Review* 12 (Summer 1979), 235–254.

35. Data from INS as reported in the *New York Times*, May 5, 1985.

36. See Anita Shreve, "Exiles."

37. The new law placed no limit on individual countries in the Western Hemisphere, only a total ceiling of 120,000 excluding spouses and minor children of United States citizens. In 1976 Congress placed a 20,000 per country limit on Western Hemisphere nations, which hurt Mexico more than the Caribbean countries. Two years later the lawmakers made the immigration system uniform and gave all nations a 20,000 limit, excluding immediate family members of U.S. citizens.

38. See the estimates in *Time*, July 8, 1986, p. 46. The best discussion of New York's Haitians is Laguerre, *American Odyssey*, especially 24–25, who estimates the Haitian population, including immigrants and their children to be about 800,000. Nearly three quarters of them reside in New York City.

39. See Jake Miller, *The Plight of the Haitian Refugees* (New York, 1984); and Namoi Zucker, "The Haitian Refugees versus the United States: The Courts as a Last Resort," in John Scanlon and Gilburt Loescher, eds., Global Refugees, *Annals of the American Academy of Political and Social Science* (May 1983), 151–162.

40. About 111,000 immigrants entered through New York in that year, of whom 74,000 stayed in the city. INS, *Statistical Yearbook, 1982*, pp. 64, 69, and 74.

41. See the comments of Betty Lee Sung in *Chinese Population in Lower Manhattan*, 1978 (Washington, D.C., 1981), 1–3, about estimates of the Chinese population. The *New York Times* reported in 1986 that the Chinese population of New York had doubled from 1981 to 1986 and stood at 250,000 in 1986. *New York Times*, Feb. 21, 1986. This agreed with the estimate of David S. Chen of the Chinatown Planning Council. *Ibid.*, Feb. 7, 1986. This figure included both immigrants and native-born Chinese Americans.

42. John Wang, "Behind the Boom: Power and Economics in Chinatown," *New York Affairs* 7 (Spring 1979), 77–81.

43. *New York Times*, April 14, 1984.

44. *Ibid.*, Aug. 19, 1984; Jan. 13, 1985; Feb. 19, 1985; and May 26, 1985 and Bergen (County) Record, May 26, 1985.

45. *Columbia Spectator*, Oct. 25, 1984; *New York Times*, Sept. 30, 1984; Ringer Buck, "The New Sweatshops: A Penny for Your Collar," *New York*, Jan. 29, 1979, pp. 40–46; and Emanuel Tobier, "Foreign Immigration," 195–196.

46. *New York Times*, Feb. 5, 1986.
47. An excellent study of New York's Koreans is Illsoo Kim, *New Urban Immigrants: The Korean Community in New York* (Princeton, 1981).
48. See Kim's discussion in *New Urban Immigrants*.
49. *Ibid.*, 112.
50. Marlys Harris, "Making It: How the Koreans Won the Greengrocer Wars," *Money*, March 1983, p. 192 and *New York Times*, Aug. 11, 1984.
51. *Bergen (County) Record*, Feb. 5, 1986 and *New York Times*, Feb. 21, 1986.
52. Demetrios G. Papademetriou, *New Immigrants to Brooklyn and Queens: Policy Implications, Especially with Regard to Housing* (New York, 1983), 120.
53. *New York Times*, Feb. 21, 1986.
54. U.S. Bureau of the Census, *Census of the Population, 1980: Characteristics of the Population, Detailed Population Characteristics*, vol. I, sec. A, table 255. See also Parmatma Saran, *The Asian Experience in the United States* (Boston, 1985), 27-30.
55. Reimers, *Still the Golden Door*, 114-115.
56. *New York Times*, Aug. 25, 1985.
57. *Ibid.*, March 4, 1981.
58. *Ibid.*, Sept. 20, 1984 and Jan. 3, 1986.
59. *Ibid.*, May 5, 1985.
60. Anita Shreve, "Exiles," 36; *New York Times*, Jan. 7, 1985 and Feb. 25, 1985.
61. *Ibid.*, Feb. 10, 1985.
62. *Ibid.*, Jan. 23, 1986.
63. *Ibid.*, Sept. 17, 1985.
64. *Ibid.*, May 24, 1984.
65. *Ibid.*, May 24, 1984 and May 10, 1985.
66. For an excellent discussion of Asian Americans and education, see Fox Butterfield, "Why Asians Are Going to the Head of the Class," *New York Times* (Education Supplement), Aug. 3, 1986.
67. *New York Times*, Aug. 15, 1986.
68. For discussion of Asian citizenship, see Elliott R. Barkan, "Whom Shall We Integrate?: A Comparative Analysis of the Immigration and Naturalization Trends of Asians Before and After the 1965 Immigration Act (1951-1978)," *Journal of American Ethnic History* 3 (Fall 1983), 29-57.
69. *New York Times*, Aug. 15, 1986; Aug. 18, 1986; and Sept. 11, 1986.
70. For a general discussion of immigrants in New York's labor market, see Marcia Freedman, "The Labor Market for Immigrants in New York City," *New York Affairs* 7 (Nov. 4, 1979), 94-111.
71. *New York Times*, Sept. 15, 1985 and Feb. 21, 1986. The Chinese paper with the largest circulation was published in Queens, reflecting the growing Chinese population in that borough.
72. *Ibid.*, Oct. 18, 1985.

MICHAEL LAPP

9

The Migration Division of Puerto Rico and Puerto Ricans in New York City, 1948–1969

The late 1940s and 1950s saw the coming of what Daniel Bell has called "the technocratic age," marked by the belief that society could be managed by experts detached from ideologies.[1] A convenient laboratory for the application of this notion was Puerto Rico, where the island's new leaders sought innovative alternatives to economic and political colonialism. In post-World War II Puerto Rico, reformist politicians of the Popular Democratic Party enlisted experts in a campaign to re-make Puerto Rican society. A new elite of Puerto Rican technocrats sought to put some of their findings into practice in order to bring economic growth and social progress to the island.

This article focuses on one aspect of the Puerto Rican government's program, an effort to use expertise to manage mass migration to the United States mainland. This endeavor offers a case study in the application of social science to socio-political problems in post-World War II America. It is also significant in indicating changing popular attitudes among Americans toward a technocratic vision of progress. As the harsh conditions of barrio life persisted in the 1960s, many Puerto

Rican New Yorkers came to regard the Puerto Rican government's efforts
to influence migration and migrant communities as illegitimate. As
Puerto Ricans gained a sense of their own identity on the mainland,
they began to join many others in the United States of the 1960s in
expressing an antipathy toward the efforts of governmental elites to
manage social problems and an insistence on popular participation
in public affairs.[2]

Puerto Ricans began to come to the United States mainland in relatively large numbers after being granted United States citizenship
in 1917. The census counted 53,000 Puerto Ricans in the United States
in 1930. After a long hiatus in migration during the Depression and
extending through World War II, the introduction of inexpensive flights
from the island and the lure of unskilled and low-skilled jobs in New
York City caused a spectacular increase in movement to the United
States with newcomers concentrating in the New York metropolitan
area. In 1946 alone, there was a net migration out of Puerto Rico of
39,900 people, almost as many as had left the island in the entire decade of the 1920s.[3] It appeared likely that prosperity on the mainland,
combined with high rates of unemployment in Puerto Rico, would cause
the numbers of migrants to continue to rise.

This great exodus was taking place at the same time that the new
leaders of Puerto Rico were in the midst of transforming the role of
government on the island. The Popular Democratic Party (PPD) had
come to power in the Puerto Rican legislature in 1940, promising to
give land to the peasants and end the poverty that four decades of United
States occupation had done little to ameliorate. The PPD soon attained
a political dominance that lasted until the middle of the 1960s. After
the United States Congress passed the Elective Governor Act in 1947,
Luis Munoz Marin, the charismatic and forceful leader of the PPD,
became the first elected governor of Puerto Rico, taking office in 1948.
Munoz Marin and the PPD promoted a new governmental activism
in the economy, convinced that the key to economic progress lay in
industrialization. Munoz Marin and other Popular Democratic Party
leaders were confident that Puerto Rico's grave social, economic, and
political problems could be solved in part through the application of
planning and expertise. Thus, their economic development plan, which
came to be known as Operation Bootstrap, envisaged an active government role in encouraging and supervising private investment from the
United States.[4]

The PPD leaders quickly grasped that the continuation of migration to the United States was vital to the success of Operation Bootstrap. The population of Puerto Rico had been rapidly increasing, es-

pecially since 1940.[5] Consequently, even the most optimistic planners predicted that the unemployment rate was likely to remain high on the island for several decades.[6] But they hoped that large-scale emigration, in combination with industrial development, would succeed in reducing the number of unemployed.[7]

The Puerto Rican government was concerned, however, about the possibility that massive and uncontrolled migration would sour the spirit of cooperation and good feeling that was developing between Puerto Rico and the United States.[8] In particular, they worried about the tendency of migrants to settle in New York City, where over 80 percent of the mainland Puerto Rican population lived in the 1940s.[9] Puerto Rican leaders feared that the demands that newcomers would make on New York City government would provoke hostile reactions from local residents and government officials, "The relief, family welfare, housing and educational problems of New York City," wrote Clarence Senior in 1947, "[have] increased to such an extent by the flood of unprepared migrants that serious friction arises."[10] Puerto Rican observers also saw much evidence of the growth of racial discrimination against Puerto Ricans on the mainland. The prospect of heightened social unrest was distressing to Puerto Rican officials not only because it would be likely to lead to greater suffering for already beleaguered migrants, but also because American investment and tourism in Puerto Rico were so important to the island's development strategy; increasing hostility toward Puerto Ricans on the mainland could only hinder such efforts.

The Puerto Rican government had an uncommon opportunity to intervene in the migration process. Puerto Ricans who moved to the mainland were not emigrating across the barrier of a national border; they were migrating from one part of the United States to another. If Puerto Rican leaders sought to supervise the migration, they would not be meddling in the affairs of a foreign government.

It therefore made perfect sense to Puerto Rican leaders to attempt to apply social scientific expertise and bureaucratic "know-how" to the problems of migration, just as such techniques were being applied to the question of economic growth within Puerto Rico. In 1947, Governor Jesus T. Pinero appointed an Emigration Advisory Committee to recommend a migration policy. The committee included several leading planners of the Popular Party's socio-economic programs, including Teodoro Moscoso, Rafael Pico, Clarence Senior, and Fernando Sierra Berdecia. Chairing the committee was Sierra Berdecia, Puerto Rican Secretary of Labor.[11] Teodoro Moscoso headed the Puerto Rican Development Company, the agency primarily responsible for stimulating economic development in the late 1940s. Rafael Pico directed the recently established Puerto Rican Planning Board. Both Moscoso and Pico were American-educated professionals who had been brought into public life in the early 1940s, during the gubernatorial administration of former New Dealer Rexford G. Tugwell.[12] An especially influential member of the committee was Clarence Senior. Senior served in the 1930s as the national secretary of the American Socialist Party.[13] In the early 1940s, he did graduate work in sociology and worked in various positions in federal government. Popular Democratic Party leaders, appreciating Senior's amalgam of technocratic expertise and social democratic sentiment, recruited him in 1946 to serve as the director of the University of Puerto Rico's Social Science Research Center. In that position, Senior conducted research on Puerto Rican migration, and became a knowledgeable advocate of a government role in managing migration.[14]

Senior and the other members of the Emigration Advisory Committee clearly saw the migration of working-class Puerto Ricans in the context of the state-managed economic development program. While the Puerto Rican Economic Development Administration would work to end poverty at home, another government agency could discreetly facilitate migration. The seeds of such an office already existed in New York. Since 1931, a small office of the Puerto Rican Department of Labor in New York City had provided Puerto Ricans with identification cards confirming that they were United States citizens in order to help them obtain work.[15] Consequently, the committee recommended that the Puerto Rican government greatly expand the services of this agency, turning it into a migration office with much broader responsibilities. The office would seek to influence the composition of the migrant population according to the needs of the American labor market, encourage migrants to move to areas other than New York City, and provide services to Puerto Rican newcomers on the United States mainland.[16]

Heeding the Emigration Advisory Committee's recommendations, the Puerto Rican legislature established an agency to assist migrants in December 1947. Originally called the Bureau of Employment and Migration, it was in 1951 renamed the Migration Division of the Department of Labor of Puerto Rico. Under the leadership of Sierra Berdecia, Senior (national director from 1951 to 1960) and Joseph Monserrat (director of the New York office in the 1950s and national director from 1960 to 1969), the agency succeeded in becoming a powerful force in the affairs of Puerto Rican migrants, especially in New York City.[17]

In the eyes of Senior, the new agency constituted a major innovation in the relations between the state and migrants. Experts were now devoted to the problem of making the migration and adjustment processes as smooth as possible. Senior argued in one speech, for example:

> Puerto Ricans and the communities to which they move can count on help the [earlier] immigrants never had. . . . There are now many national, state and local organizations dedicated to the improvement of human relations; they have helped create a much more reasonable and less hostile climate than most of the immigrants of our past had to struggle against. In addition, the Puerto Ricans have the interest and aid of their own government, which few immigrants ever had. These two factors . . . indicate a rapid adjustment process.[18]

The Migration Division itself, he consequently claimed, was "a social invention of first-class importance," utilizing the skills of government administrators to mitigate the problems of migrants.[19] Even the racism that made it so difficult for Puerto Ricans to enjoy harmonious relations with white Americans could be successfully challenged by experts and professionals skilled in the techniques of "human relations."[20]

The Migration Division openly and unabashedly sought to encourage the accommodation of migrants to life on the United States mainland. The chief goals of the agency, according to the legislation which created it, were to "try to reduce to a minimum the natural problems of adjustment that are produced in all migrations of this type," and to "cooperate with city, state, and federal agencies and with private institutions which are sincerely making an effort to resolve . . . those problems of adjustment."[21]

Although understaffed and underfunded, the Migration Division was given a formidable range of responsibilities. Through field offices in Puerto Rico, it was to orient prospective migrants, advising them on job prospects and housing. The legislature directed the agency to find employment for job-seekers and to seek assistance for those with problems ranging from housing and education to health and welfare. It was to encourage city, state, and federal government bureaucracies to meet the needs of the mass of Spanish-speaking newcomers. It was also to exercise a degree of leadership among Puerto Ricans on the mainland. Additionally, in a program that came to be its most controversial, it was to organize the seasonal migration of agricultural workers to the farms of the eastern seaboard.

The Migration Division most directly pursued its strategy of encouraging the adjustment of migrants in its efforts to find jobs for newcomers. The agency operated (and continues to operate in 1990) an employment office which tens of thousands of unemployed Puerto Ricans visited in the 1950s alone. The New York City office was able to place from five to thirteen thousand Puerto Ricans in jobs annually. Most of these jobs were in the secondary labor sector; garment factories, hospitals, and restaurants were major sources of employment. The office also encouraged ambitious job-seekers to take civil service exams by offering preparation courses for the tests.[22]

The Puerto Rican Department of Labor, through the Migration Division and the Puerto Rican Bureau of Employment Security, also organized agricultural labor migration from Puerto Rico, a program which later attracted much controversy. The goal of the project was to lower unemployment among farm workers during the six-month-long *"tiempo muerto"* (dead season) between sugar harvests on the island. East Coast harvests took place during the Puerto Rican off-season. Sending temporarily unemployed farm workers to the mainland for the harvests therefore seemed to Puerto Rico's Labor Department to be a highly rational use of the island's labor force. The Migration Division, in conjunction with the Puerto Rican branch of the United States Bureau of Employment Security, negotiated contracts with farmers on behalf of workers, in theory insuring that wages, provisions for room and board, and transportation arrangements were acceptable to workers. Farmers who did not cooperate with the Puerto Rican government were not permitted to recruit workers on the island, although many ignored the government ban and recruited workers without government authorization.

According to its organizers, the agricultural labor migration program "succeeded" because hundreds of thousands of workers labored on farms in New Jersey, New York, Delaware, Connecticut, and Massachusetts during the 1950s and 1960s. At the peak of the program in the 1960s, approximately 20,000 workers participated annually. The contracts came to include provisions for workmen's compensation and health insurance, and guarantees of regular work during the harvest season. The Migration Division claimed that the program showed "how legislation and social planning . . . combined to help one group attain its dream."[23]

The Migration Division was deeply reluctant, however, to enforce the contracts with sanctions that would antagonize farmers. Considerable evidence suggests that contract violations occurred regularly. Groups investigating the program in the early 1970s found appalling conditions for workers. The Puerto Rican Legal Defense and Education Fund, for example, discovered numerous housing violations.[24] Puerto Rican writer Luis Nieves Falcon, who examined the program in his book, *El Emigrante Puertorriqueno*, found that many workers did not receive the quantity of work they had been guaranteed; he also claimed that Migration Division staff members ignored workers' complaints.[25] Yet never in the history of the program did the Migration Division take legal action against a farmer or farmers' association. Each farmers' association posted a performance bond to guarantee its compliance with the contract. Never did an association lose its bond.[26]

In order to ensure the continued existence of the program, which was vulnerable due to the relatively plentiful supply of unskilled labor on the East Coast, Puerto Rican officials at least subconsciously limited their demands for compliance with the contracts. Rather than stress the need to struggle for better contract terms and stricter enforcement, the Migration Division tended to advocate cooperation among farmers, workers, and the agency, The Migration Division also argued that it was in the farmers' interest to offer adequate working and housing conditions, as satisfied workers would be less likely to leave camp before the end of the harvest. The agency tried to prove this principle to farmers, who clearly did not find it self-evident. For example, it organized an employers' meeting at the end of the 1956 season at which "those employers that provided the worker with the best housing, balanced diets at moderate prices, recreational facilities and religious facilities, kept precise and clear records, and . . . demonstrated a great ability to retain the worker until the termination of the contract, explained to those present the methods they used to attain such good results . . . "[27] Through such activities, the agency revealed its desire to function as a facilitator of harmonious relations between migrants and employers. This approach was most compatible with the Migration Division's preference for accommodation over confrontation.

As well as helping to relieve the problem of rural unemployment in Puerto Rico, the agricultural labor program served as an element of the Migration Division's strategy of dispersing migrants outside of the New York City region. Sierra Berdecia, Senior, and Monserrat soon realized that the New York employment market offered little hope of advancement for large numbers of Puerto Ricans. The growth of the East Harlem barrio and the development of new working-class population centers on the West Side, the Lower East Side, and the South Bronx disconcerted the Migration Division's leaders tremendously; the clustering of the Puerto Rican population in New York City suggested a future at sharp variance with their vision of accommodation and adjustment. They therefore hoped to disperse migrants among other regions of the United States.

To achieve this goal, the agency issued publicity in Puerto Rico announcing the greater supply of jobs in the Midwest.[28] It also attempted, with limited success, to find jobs in the Midwest for unemployed Puerto Ricans living in New York.[29] Senior optimistically wrote in 1954 that "improved machinery for bringing workers seeking jobs together with employers seeking workers has helped speed up the process of dispersion."[30] The activities of the Migration Division and the United States Employment Service were making a haphazard process efficient. Despite Senior's assessment, this project failed to diminish the Puerto Rican population in New York City, although the proportion of Puerto Ricans on the mainland living outside the New York area slowly increased.[31] The Migration Division's efforts to place Puerto Ricans in jobs throughout the United States faltered in part because of insufficient demand from employers and in part because of the agency's lack of staff and money to execute such a program. As was often the case, the Migration Division's plans were grandiose while its resources were limited. The plan, nevertheless, exemplified a vision of a rationalized migration organized by social planners.

The Migration Division tirelessly urged Puerto Ricans to adjust to their new society. According to a 1957 report, one of the Division's chief goals was "to [get] the migrant to understand the need for integration into American life."[32] Joseph Monserrat, reflecting on the work of the agency in 1967, asserted: "We begin by assuming that adjustment means [to] adjust to the middle-class values of the communities in which [the newcomers] live."[33] In pursuit of this goal, the agency broadcast weekly radio programs offering advice to Puerto Ricans over one of the Spanish-language stations in New York. On the programs, Migration Division staff members sought to persuade listeners to learn English quickly in order to get better jobs. They urged migrants to register to vote and to participate in American labor unions. They chastised those who threw their garbage out of tenement windows and in other ways gave New Yorkers an unfavorable impression of Puerto Ricans. They encouraged newcomers to adopt the mores of United States society.[34]

As well as offering services and exhortations directly to migrants, the Migration Division sought to exert influence beyond the barrios of New York. Clarence Senior had noted with concern in 1948 the great reluctance of Puerto Ricans to use New York's employment and welfare agencies.[35] While migrants were alienated from American institutions, city officials, school teachers, and social workers were anxious about how to cope with such a large influx of working class, non-English-speaking migrants. This was a matter of great concern to the Migration Division because its notion of adjustment stressed inserting migrants into an institutional matrix in their new society. It was vital, the Migration Division felt, that schools, welfare agencies, hospitals, and employers absorb migrants as smoothly as possible. The Migration Division's staff consequently worked hard to establish ties with New York City's bureaucracies. They organized, for example, three migration conferences in San Juan, Puerto Rico—in 1953, 1954, and 1958—in which officials of New York City and Puerto Rico discussed what the two governments could to do help migrants adjust to life in New York. The staff advised the school system on programs to teach English to Puerto Rican students. They organized seminars for labor union leaders, hoping to promote the participation of Puerto Rican labor union members in their unions. The Migration Division's social workers consulted regularly with the New York City Welfare Department, Catholic charities, and other social work agencies and also organized annual summer trips to Puerto Rico for social workers, designed to give them a greater understanding of Puerto Rican culture. Monserrat frequently consulted with Mayor Wagner, elected in 1954, about Puerto Rican affairs.[36]

Political scientist James Jennings, in his book *Puerto Rican Politics in New York City*, has argued that the Migration Division so monopolized Puerto Rican political dealings with New York City government that the development of grassroots organizations in the Puerto Rican community was greatly hindered. If city officials had not been able to use the Migration Division as their political link to the Puerto Rican population, they would have had to deal directly with local leaders; this would have stimulated the development of political groups. Whether or not this intriguing argument is true, Jennings is correct to emphasize the Migration Division's dominance of political discourse between Puerto Ricans and New York City government in the 1950s.[37]

The tangible benefits of the Migration Division's relationships with politicians and administrators were usually modest, however. The Migration Division convinced the Board of Education to do an elaborate study, funded by the Ford Foundation, to find better ways to teach English to Puerto Rican students. No perceptible change in educational practices took place because of the study, however.[38] The Mayor's Committee on Puerto Rican Affairs, in which the Migration Division played a role, achieved little of note. Nor did the Mayor's Committee on the Exploitation of Workers, of which Monserrat was a member, or the Labor Advisory Committee on Puerto Rican Affairs, formed because of prompting by the Migration Division, generate much change. While these committees slumbered, actual conditions for Puerto Ricans failed to improve. Slum clearance was driving Puerto Ricans out of their already inadequate apartments; labor unions were often discriminatory.[39] Most seriously, perhaps, the decline in manufacturing jobs in New York City left Puerto Rican workers in a perilous economic position.[40] The Migration Division could not effectively pressure city officials to grapple with these problems. With its leaders clinging to a rosy view of the future for Puerto Ricans in the United States, the migration Division was frequently unable even to articulate the needs of Puerto Ricans in New York.

If the agency failed to shake city institutions out of their apathy toward the problems of Puerto Ricans, it succeeded in attaining symbolic importance for both Puerto Ricans and governmental and private institutions of New York in the 1950s. To Puerto Ricans in New York City, the Migration Division was a representative of the Munoz Marin government and Operation Bootstrap. The Migration Division lost no opportunity to stress its identity as an agent of the Puerto Rican Commonwealth. Officials of the agency publicly called it the "Oficina de Puerto Rico" and the office came to be popularly known by that name. The agency distributed literature in Spanish and English hailing the accomplishments of Operation Bootstrap and the genius of the Commonwealth concept.[41] When political notables from the Popular Democratic Party such as Governor Munoz Marin, San Juan's Mayor Felisa Rincon de Gautier, or Ernesto Ramos Antonini, the Speaker of the Puerto Rican House, visited New York City, they invariably came to the Migration Division's office to praise its work.[42]

The 1950s were years of great optimism and exuberance in Puerto Rico. Every year more factories were built, and the amount of private investment soared. Per capita income on the island shot up.[43] Puerto Ricans in New York with good reason associated the dramatic changes taking place on the island with the PPD and Governor Munoz Marin. This government appeared to many (though by no means all) Puerto Ricans in New York to be attacking the problems of the island in dynamic and resourceful ways. The Migration Division, as an arm of the Commonwealth government in New York, basked in its glory. The connection enabled the agency to gain respect and legitimacy among Puerto Ricans as well as among New York city politicians and administrators.

It is also likely that the agency attracted support among Puerto Ricans because, unlike other bureaucracies in New York City, Puerto Ricans ran it themselves. New York City's employment offices and welfare departments frequently had procedures which seemed byzantine to newcomers from Puerto Rico. Few employees spoke English. Puerto Ricans often felt that they were being treated antagonistically by racist or xenophobic staff members.[44] It is not surprising, then, that thousands would come every year to look for jobs or advice and assistance from the Migration Division's social service section. There they could deal with Spanish-speaking interviewers in familiar and non-threatening cultural milieu. The Migration Division undoubtedly gained some support because it was a bureaucratic agency run by and for a people who were getting little respect from the dominant society in the 1950s. The existence of the Migration Division was a sign of their ability to operate as equals in the bureaucratic world of the United States.

The agency, moreover, performed many useful services for the Puerto Rican population in New York City (as well as in smaller Puerto Rican population centers such as Chicago). The Division found jobs for tens of thousands of mostly non-English-speaking workers. It served as a guide for newcomers to the bureaucracies and institutions of New York City. The Division ran weekly Spanish-language radio programs informing listeners about how to enroll in adult education courses, how to complain about landlords' housing violations, how to register to vote, how to receive social security payments, and many other similar concerns. The Division employed staff members who worked at the New York City airports, providing counseling to newcomers. At its offices in New York and Chicago, trained social workers and education specialists were available to deal with the problems of individuals, and to refer them to other agencies. An identification service provided Puerto Ricans with cards giving proof of their status as United States citizens in order to make it easier for them to get jobs. The fact that thousands of Puerto Ricans took advantage of these services every year is the best evidence that the Migration Division met real needs.

Although the Migration Division was able to assume an authoritative role as a representative of Puerto Ricans in the 1950s and although thousands of Puerto Ricans in New York and elsewhere used its services, the agency was in some ways remote from most Puerto Ricans in New York's *barrios*. Most migrants, for example, did not share the Migration Division's assumption that the majority of Puerto Ricans would remain on the mainland permanently, eventually dispersing into the nation's heartland. Instead, many were keeping one foot on the island. There was a great deal of back-and-forth movement to the island and, in the late 1960s and early 1970s, a substantial return migration.[45]

The fact that so many migrants regarded themselves as temporary residents in the 1950s helps explain why the Migration Division's attempts to mobilize the community were unsuccessful. The agency had a small community organizing staff. The message they brought to Puerto

Rican neighborhoods, however, failed to elicit enthusiastic responses. The community organizers helped to organize annual campaigns to urge Puerto Ricans to learn English. They also played active roles in numerous voter registration campaigns. This was an especially difficult task, because, until the passage of the Voting Rights Act in 1965, Puerto Ricans had to pass an English-language literacy test. Despite the fact that Puerto Ricans voted in overwhelming numbers in Puerto Rico, their participation in elections in New York City continued to be unimpressive.[46] For people who were not often convinced that they were permanent settlers on the mainland neither learning English nor voting were high priorities.

Another problem was the blandness of the Migration Division's community organizing. A major project of the community organizers was to initiate and manage housing clinics staffed by volunteers, operating in various New York City neighborhoods and offering tenants advice on problems with their apartments. They sought to inform tenants about their legal rights and encourage self-help activities. Puerto Ricans in New York, however, were faced with steadily worsening housing conditions, aggravated by massive losses of housing due to the slum clearance projects of city government. New York City slum clearance projects displaced many thousands of Puerto Ricans.[47] It must have struck many tenants that the housing clinics offered little effective assistance in a growing housing crisis.

Although the Migration Division was unable to mobilize Puerto Ricans in the 1950s, no important efforts were made to challenge its authority in that decade, a period called by one student of Puerto Rican New York a "dead season" (*tiempo muerto*) in the political history of New York's Puerto Rican community.[48] In the early 1960s, however, dramatic changes in the United States caused the Migration Division's influence in New York City and other Puerto Rican communities to wane. The black civil rights movement began in the late 1950s and became a model of a popular, grassroots movement for social change. The War on Poverty took shape in 1964, using a new rhetoric of "maximum feasible participation" quite foreign to the milieu in which the Migration Division had been formed. This ideological shift challenged the assumptions on which the Migration Division's work was based. Many in the American public now associated bureaucracy with inefficiency and planning with excessive governmental control. They began to doubt that experts could be relied on to provide solutions for social problems.[49]

Some Puerto Ricans aspiring to leadership roles in New York became discontented with the Migration Division's position in Puerto

Rican public affairs. According to Rosa Estades, author of *Patterns of Political Participation of Puerto Ricans in New York City* and a former Migration Division staff member, "as some Puerto Rican agencies developed, they resented the principal role of the Division . . . claiming that their role was co-opted by the government agency."[50] James Jennings has put forward a similar argument. He cites one Puerto Rican active in a Brooklyn anti-poverty program, who said: "I don't think that any government office should play the role of institutional leader for the community. I'm opposed to that."[51] Such activists objected to a bureaucratic organization which appeared to be imposing direction from above.

The initiation of the federal War on Poverty in 1964 was in some ways a government reaction to increasing public antagonism to unresponsive bureaucracies. Initially prompted in part by the civil rights movement, the War on Poverty came to include as a major element in its strategy a plan for increasing the "participation" of the urban poor in politics. Bureaucracies would not make policies for the poor; the poor would themselves gain the tools to effect social change. The programs were aimed especially at blacks. After a period of struggle, some War on Poverty funds were directed to new Puerto Rican organizations. The Puerto Rican Community Development Project was a notable example of a program run by and for New York Puerto Ricans.[52] The Community Development Project and other new agencies put much more emphasis on mobilizing Puerto Ricans to assert political power than had the Migration Division, arousing community support for such causes as bilingual education programs and improved social services.[53] Ironically, as Jennings has argued, in their relationship to the state the anti-poverty programs in many ways followed the patterns established by the Migration Division. In both, Puerto Ricans held posts in which they ultimately had to answer to other government officials rather than to their Puerto Rican constituencies.[54]

In the middle and late 1960s, signs of the Migration Division's decline were abundant. As jobs in anti-poverty programs and federal, state, and city government became available to blacks and Puerto Ricans, many of the Migration Division's staff left their relatively low-paying jobs for new positions. Herman Badillo, Ramon Velez, Gilberto Gerena Valentin, and others became important Puerto Rican spokesmen, so that Monserrat ceased to be a dominant figure.[55] The decline of faith in bureaucratic solutions affected the Migration Division's sponsors in Puerto Rico as well. The shiny surface of prosperity which Operation Bootstrap had given to Puerto Rico began to tarnish; the economy began to slump and popular dissatisfaction grew.[56] The pro-statehood

New Progressive Party defeated the PPD and assumed power in 1968. This party lacked sympathy with the goals of the Migration Division. Soon after the new government took office, a Puerto Rican Controller's office report claimed to have found a pattern of misuse of government funds at the Migration Division.[57] Monserrat, who was closely linked to the successes of the agency, left in 1969 to become a member of the New York Board of Education. The Migration Division came under fire from groups trying to organize farm workers in the 1970s for its continuing participation in the agricultural labor migration program, which began to send fewer and fewer workers to the mainland. When a brash, young reformer named Marco Rigau briefly took charge of the Migration Division in the spring of 1973, he found a dispirited, moribund organization.[58]

The Migration Division continues to survive as of 1990, albeit with a greatly diminished role in the affairs of New York Puerto Ricans. Some Puerto Rican activists in New York have continued to raise questions about the appropriateness of having appointees of the Commonwealth of Puerto Rico involved in the political affairs of the New York community.[59] The agency, however, no longer wields enough influence to arouse fervent opposition.

The spirit of the Migration Division had withered by the late 1960s. By that time, the persistent economic and political marginality of Puerto Ricans supplied ample cause for activists to question promises of quick economic and social progress. Furthermore, for Puerto Rican activists, as for many others in the United States, it no longer seemed plausible to bring about the adjustment of a group of people to life in another social system simply through the application of expertise. Indeed, as a mood of cultural nationalism gained strength in Puerto Rican New York, the Migration Division's emphasis on encouraging Puerto Rican migrants to adjust to life on the mainland appeared to many to be an example of repressive assimilationism rather than liberal cultural pluralism. In a 1967 speech, Monserrat himself recognized the weaknesses of a strategy based on promoting adjustment to American culture, complaining that "the psychic costs [of pressuring Puerto Ricans to adjust to American middle class values] have never been measured."[60]

The Migration Division was established in a period of great optimism about the power of social scientists and other technocratic decision-makers to correct social ills. Hamstrung by its limitations as an arm of the Puerto Rican government and its inability to mobilize an ethnic constituency, the agency was never able to fulfill the expectations of its creators. Nevertheless, it exerted substantial influence during the early years of the post-World War II Puerto Rican diaspora. When, in the 1960s, an indigenous leadership emerged in New York's Puerto Rican community, the Migration Division suffered a rapid decline.

Notes

1. Daniel Bell, *The Coming of Post-Industrial Society: A Venture in Social Forecasting* (New York, 1973), 341–367; Edward A. Purcell, Jr., *The Crisis of Democratic Theory: Scientific Naturalism and the Problem of Value* (Lexington, Kentucky, 1973), 235–272.
2. Three studies that have considered the role of the Migration Division in the Puerto Rican community of New York are Rosa Estades, *Patterns of Political Participation of Puerto Ricans in New York City* (Rio Piedras, Puerto Rico, 1978); Judith F. Herbstein, "Rituals and Politics of the Puerto Rican 'Community' in New York City" (Ph.D. dissertation, City University of New York, 1978); and James Jennings, *Puerto Rican Politics in New York City* (Washington, D.C., 1977).
3. Stanley L. Friedlander, *Labor Migration and Economic Growth: A Case Study of Puerto Rico* (Cambridge, Mass., 1965) 170
4. Henry Wells, *The Modernization of Puerto Rico* (Cambridge, Mass., 1969) 135–136.
5. Friedlander, *Labor Migration and Economic Growth*, 46–63.
6. Planning Board of Puerto Rico, Economic Division, *The Economic Development of Puerto Rico, 1940–1950 and 1951–1960* (San Juan, Puerto Rico, 1951), 43.
7. Clarence Senior, *Puerto Rican Emigration* (Rio Piedras, Puerto Rico, 1947).
8. This cooperative spirit was reflected in the creation of a new status for Puerto Rico. In the new system — proposed by the PPD, approved in a referendum of the Puerto Rican people and ratified by the United States Congress in 1952 — Puerto Rico theoretically was fully in control of its own domestic affairs but remained an integral part of the United States. Its architects hoped that a new permanent bond was being established with the mainland, one which would nevertheless permit the retention of a distinct cultural identity in Puerto Rico.
9. José L. Vázquez Calzada, "Demographic Aspects of Migration," in Centro de Estudios Puertorriquenos, *Labor Migration Under Capitalism: The Puerto Rican Experience* (New York, 1979), 227.
10. Senior, *Puerto Rican Emigration*, 49.
11. Manuel Maldonado Denis, *The Emigration Dialectic: Puerto Rico and the U.S.A.* (San Juan, Puerto Rico, 1976; reprinted, New York, 1980), 86–87.
12. Henry Wells, *The Modernization of Puerto Rico*, 380–381.
13. W. A. Swanberg, *Norman Thomas: The Last Idealist* (New York, 1976), 115–116, 210.
14. Telephone interview with Ruth Senior, December 1986. Works published by Senior during this period were *Puerto Rican Emigration* and *The Puerto Rican Migrant in St. Croix* (Rio Piedras, Puerto Rico, 1947).
15. Lawrence R. Chenault, *The Puerto Rican Migrant in New York City* (New York, 1938; reprinted, 1970), 74–76.
16. Annette B. Ramirez de Arellano and Conrad Seipp, *Colonalism, Catholicism, and Conception: A History of Birth Control in Puerto Rico* (Chapel Hill, 1983), 78–81.
17. Major sources for the study of the Migration Division were the monthly and annual reports of the agency to the Puerto Rican Department of Labor and other papers in the possession of the Migration Division of the Department of Labor of Puerto Rico, 304 Park Avenue South, New York, New York 10010; the archival collection of the Migration Division has yet to be organized. Also extremely useful were interviews with the following former Migration Division staff members: Luis Cardona, Bethesda, Maryland, August 1984; Joseph Monserrat, New York, New York, January 1985; Jose Morales, New York, New York, February 1986; Matilde Perez de Silva, New York, New York, October 1984; Alan Perl, Croton-on-Hudson, New York, June 1985; Tony Vega, New Brunswick, New Jersey, August 1985.

18. Senior, "Dispersion of Puerto Rican Migration," speech delivered at the annual conference of the Welfare and Health Council of New York, May 7, 1953. A copy is in the possession of the Migration Division of the Department of Labor of Puerto Rico.

19. Senior, radio broadcast of July 25, 1954, station unidentified; tape recording in the possession of the Migration Division, New York.

20. Senior, *The Puerto Ricans: Strangers—Then Neighbors* (2nd. ed., Chicago, 1965), 61-64.

21. Legislature of Puerto Rico, Law Number 25, December 5, 1947.

22. Migration Division Annual Reports, 1954-1969 (unpublished reports in the possession of the Migration Division, New York).

23. Petroamérica Pagan de Colón, transcript of untitled, undated speech before the American Public Welfare Association, New York City (copy in the possession of the Migration Division, New York).

24. For reports on the charges of the Puerto Rican Legal Defense and Education Fund, see *New York Times*, December 20, 1972 and November 20, 1975.

25. See Luis Nieves Falcón, *El Emigrante Puertorriqueno* (Rio Piedras, Puerto Rico, 1975), 127-136.

26. Interview with Alan Perl, former legal consultant to the Department of Labor of Puerto Rico, June 1985.

27. Migration Division Annual Report, 1956-1957, pp. 44-45.

28. See, for example, Department of Labor of Puerto Rico, Programa de Orientacion, "Información sobre ciudades importantes do los Estados Unidos" (undated leaflet in the possession of the Migration Division, New York).

29. See, for example, Clarence Senior, Migration Division Monthly Report to the Department of Labor of Puerto Rico, November 1955, p. 3.

30. Senior, "Dispersion of Puerto Rican Migration," 3.

31. 1960 U.S. Census, "Puerto Ricans in the United States," PC (2) 1D, table A, p. viii; 1970 U.S. census, "Persons of Spanish Ancestry," PC (SI) 30, February 1973, table 1, p. 1; both cited in Kal Wagenheim, *A Survey of Puerto Ricans on the U.S. Mainland in the 1970s* (New York, 1975), 37.

32. Migration Division budget, 1957-1958 (in the possession of the Migration Division, New York).

33. Joseph Monserrat, untitled speech, April 9, 1967 (copy in possession of the Migration Division, New York).

34. Transcripts of Migration Division radio broadcasts, 1954-1958 (in possession of Migration Division, New York City). See, for example, transcripts of January 13, 1954 and September 12, 1956.

35. Clarence Senior, *The Puerto Ricans of New York* (New York, 1948), 20.

36. See Migration Division Monthly and Annual Reports, 1951-1964.

37. Jennings, *Puerto Rican Politics in New York City*, 75-85.

38. See Angela Jorge, "The Puerto Rican Study: Its Character and Impact on Puerto Ricans in New York City" (Ph.D. dissertation, New York University, 1984).

39. See Herbert Hill, "Guardians of the Sweatshop," in Adalberto Lopez and James Petras, eds., *Puerto Rico and Puerto Ricans* (New York, 1974), 384-416.

40. Clara E. Rodriguez, "Economic Factors Affecting Puerto Ricans in New York," 208.

41. Senior notes, for example, in the Migration Division Monthly Report, January 1955, p. 4, that the agency was publicizing and distributing copies of Earl Parker Hansen's highly enthusiastic account of Operation Bootstrap, *Transformation*.

42. See, for example, Migration Division Monthly Report to the Department of Labor of Puerto Rico, July 1952, p. 10; Migration Division Annual Report, 1959-1960, p. 14.

43. Raymond Carr, *Puerto Rico: A Colonial Experiment* (New York, 1984), 205-206.

44. Elena Padilla, *Up From Puerto Rico* (New York, 1958), 249-274.

45. Centro de Estudios Puertorriquenos, *Labor Migration Under Capitalism*, 225-228.

46. Elena Padilla, *Up From Puerto Rico* (New York, 1958), 255-256; Dan Wakefield, *Island in the City* (New York, 1959; reprinted, New York, 1960), 274-275.

47. Robert Caro, *The Power Broker* (New York, 1974; reprinted, New York, 1975), 967–968; Terry Rosenberg, *Residence, Employment and Mobility of Puerto Ricans in New York City* (Chicago, 1974), 46–50.
48. Sherrie Baver, "Puerto Rican Politics in New York City: The Post-World War Two Period," in James Jennings and Monte Rivera, eds., *Puerto Rican Politics in Urban America* (Westport, Conn., 1984) 43–56.
49. Thomas Haskell, ed., *The Authority of Experts: Studies in History and Theory* (Bloomington, 1984), pp. xii-xvii.
50. Estades, *Patterns of Political Participation*, 41–42. See also Jennings, *Puerto Rican Politics in New York City*; Joseph Fitzpatrick, *Puerto Rican Americans: The Meaning of Migration to the Mainland* (Englewood Cliffs, N.J., 1971), 64–65.
51. William Rodriguez, Director of Williamsburg Community Corporation, quoted in Jennings and Rivera, eds., *Puerto Rican Politics in Urban America*, 85.
52. Judith Herbstein, in "Rituals and Politics of the Puerto Rican 'Community' in New York City," describes in detail the growth of Puerto Rican involvement in poverty programs. See also Estades, *Patterns of Political Participation of Puerto Ricans in New York City*, 53–59.
53. Monte Rivera, "Organizational Politics of the East Harlem Barrio in the 1970s," in Jennings and Rivera, eds., *Puerto Rican Politics in Urban America*, 43–56.
54. Jennings, *Puerto Rican Politics in New York City*, 80–85.
55. Baver, "Puerto Rican Politics in New York City: The Post-World War Two Period," in Jennings and Rivera, eds., *Puerto Rican Politics in Urban America*, 43–56.
56. Arturo Morales Carrión, *Puerto Rico: A Political and Cultural History* (New York, 1983), 312–315.
57. Office of the Controller, Commonwealth of Puerto Rico, *Report Number DB-71-9*, The New York Office, Migration Division, Department of Labor, Puerto Rico, August 1969.
58. See *El Tiempo*, July 4, 1973; *San Juan Star*, July 2, 1973.
59. In May 1986, for example, it was reported that a new Migration Division director, Nydia Velazquez, had been appointed in order to organize a voter registration drive among Puerto Ricans designed to assist the political campaign of Herman Badillo, a Puerto Rican candidate for New York State Comptroller. The New York Spanish-language newspaper, *El Diario*, printed complaints from Puerto Rican New York activists who attacked the Migration Division for allegedly seeking to interfere in the politics of New York. The Migration Division subsequently denied that the voter registration drive was designed specifically to help Badillo. See *El Diario*, May 15, 16, 18, 1986.
60. Monserrat, untitled speech, April 9, 1967 (copy in possession of Migration Division, New York).

10

Portal of Portals:
Speaking of the United States
"As Though it Were
New York"—And Vice Versa

A few years ago an Italian immigrant, responding to an inquiry about his decision to migrate to the United States, replied, "I did not choose America. I chose New York." While thousands did immigrate to Nieu Amsterdam/New York during the colonial period, it was not until the third decade of the nineteenth century that the lure of that city became so great that newcomers were beginning to equate New York with America. So positive was its reputation that immigrants were often refusing to land elsewhere. In the 1840s and 1850s, the city and state expanded upon the port's reputation by initiating a series of unprecedented measures to process newcomers efficiently, safely, and honestly.[1]

Castle Garden, opened in 1855 at the tip of Manhattan, immediately became the principal immigrant port of entry to the United States. By the time it was closed in 1890, 7.8 million persons—70.6 percent of all immigrants (1855 to 1890)—had passed through its gates. Thus, well before the federally run station on Ellis Island opened its doors in January 1892, New York City had already been, for more than half a century, America's undisputed portal of portals. During the next three and a half decades approximately 70 percent of all newcomers continued to enter through it, despite dramatic changes in the volume and sources of American immigration. Even in the following quarter century of restrictive quota laws, depression, war, and Ellis Island's declining role and physical deterioration (1929 to 1954), three out of five immigrants first arrived in New York City.[2]

What happened after Ellis Island closed in November 1954? To what extent did New York City retain its position as the nation's leading port of entry? This essay attempts to answer this question using data from Immigration and Naturalization Service (INS) annual reports and public-use computer tapes (the latter covering the 1972 to 1985 period).[3]

The findings detail the extent to which New York City and New York State have survived at the center of American immigration history throughout all the changes in the homelands and the numbers of newcomers. The state has long possessed a great magnetism, for two out of five newcomers entering Castle Garden and three in ten among all those passing through Ellis Island and the Barge Office in lower Manhattan remained in New York State.[4] Surviving as well have been New York City's mystique among foreigners and its intrinsic appeal as one of the world's most dynamic meeting, eating, and competing metropolises. Underlying and anchoring that ubiquitous image has been the widespread conviction that it is a place where "practically everyone is alien [and therefore] no one is alien." This atmosphere of anonymity and toleration and the promise of abundant opportunities continue to beckon tens of thousands of immigrants. Not atypical were the remarks of two recent newcomers: a Honduran woman's observation that in New York "nobody cared who my father was" and a Soviet Jewish émigré's description of the city as "the capital of immigrants."[5] Even after the legislative reforms of 1965 precipitated a profound transformation in the nation's composition of immigrants, the attraction of the city (and the state) endured.

I. New York and the Changing Immigration Patterns

The latest shift in the sources of American immigration began after 1950. The number of persons from the Caribbean, Mexico, Asia, and the Middle East crept upward, and this country's Southern and Pacific rims became more prominent as entry points. When the quota system was abolished in 1965, Europe's share of American immigration already had fallen from a peak of nearly 93 percent at the turn of the century to 53 percent, and by the first half of the 1980s only 11 percent of all immigrants had been born in Europe[6] (see Table 1).

The more general causes for these shifts have included over-population; unemployment and under-employment; political instability and political oppression; civil war, revolution, and outside military intervention; business, professional, and educational opportunities; and the prospect of family reunification. Additional factors explaining the shifts in the sources of immigration include the postwar economic prosperity in much of Western Europe, which dissuaded many potential migrants from leaving; the political barriers in Eastern Europe; the stationing of American troops in several Asian and Pacific nations, which led to many intermarriages; the enormous psychological and cultural impact of American exports, American television programs, movies, and magazines; migrants returning to their homelands with all the trappings of American materialism and tales of ample jobs and comparatively good wages; and the millions in remittances sent home. All these have added fuel to the imaginations of those still in their homelands and to their determination to migrate. At the same time, in recent years speedier transoceanic jets and cheaper air fares have heightened that determination by further easing long distance travel. The airline routes themselves, coupled with the prior migrant routes, have channeled many to New York City's airports.

According to historian David Reimers, behind these many general and specific elements has been a key, underlying, unintended factor: the reforms of 1965, which provided equal opportunities for persons in all nations in the Eastern and, later, the Western Hemispheres to apply for admission. Specifically, the 1965 act, by eliminating the quota system, permitted more equal access to United States visas in the Eastern Hemisphere. A 1976 act extended the annual visa limits of 20,000 per country as well as the preference system to the Americas. And legislation in 1978 combined the allotments of the Eastern and Western Hemispheres into one uniform system. The acts of 1976 and 1978 especially benefitted non-Mexican migrants from independent countries in the Americas (particularly Jamaicans and Dominicans) by enabling them to apply under their own, separate 20,000 person quota limits instead of under the previous limit of 120,000 persons from the entire Western Hemisphere. At the same time, while these various American reforms reinforced certain existing migration patterns, some alternative or competing pathways out of the Caribbean were substantially reduced by England's legislative changes, which in 1962 tightened the admission laws with respect to its former colonial peoples. Finally, the extraordinary liberalization of our refugee admission laws between 1965 and 1980 was an additional factor accelerating both this transformation of our foreign-born population and the equally profound changes in the choices of ports of entry into this country.[7]

The details of these causes for the newest wave of immigration have already been drawn innumerable times in books and articles, particularly by Reimers, Roy Bryce-Laporte, Thomas Archdeacon, Tricia Knoll, and Joan Moore. By focusing the discussion on New York State and New York City, my objective is to provide greater concreteness than the many sensational articles that cite questionable estimates of foreign populations. However, because we are not dealing here with the issue of undocumented aliens, clearly the hidden factor in any determination of the complete composition of the foreign-born population, we cannot offer actual population totals. In addition, because Puerto Ricans are citizens, their extraordinary movement back and forth between their island and the mainland (still principally New York City) constitutes a migration akin to that of American Indians to and from their reservations and not a true immigration. To be sure, Puerto Ricans remain an important factor in the city's expanding Latino/ Hispanic population and they are a major variable in any discussion of the socio-economic, political, educational, and cultural issues of the city. Because numerous persons in the Caribbean try to pass themselves off as Puerto Ricans in order to enter the country illegally through Puerto Rico, the Puerto Rican migration does have some effect on immigration. Still, Puerto Ricans are not central for an analysis of the legal immigration into New York.[8]

Legal immigration has included a substantially new population, significantly different in language, culture, and even color, and one rapidly supplanting the "new" southern and eastern immigrants of the early twentieth century. The extent to which this has been particularly true in New York can be gauged by noting at the outset three interrelated facts for the period between 1972 and 1979. First, one-fifth of all the nation's newcomers indicated that they were planning to reside in New York State, and over 80 percent of them specifically listed New York City. Second, from another angle, three out of ten of the nation's immigrants were actually processed in New York State, and some 60 percent of them were going to, or remaining in, New York City. Third, and even more relevant, almost nine-tenths of those processed in the city itself and planning on living in the state were staying in New York City. In other words, immigrants indicating that they intended to live in New York State more than likely specified New York City and most often they made it a point to arrive directly there. Thus, whether one looks at the city, the state, or the nation, New York City continues to hold a dominant place in American immigration history. If we add the greater metropolitan region, that is the adjacent suburbs, the enduring importance of the city is still more firmly and indisputably established. The 1970 and 1980 censuses, which found nearly 70 percent of the state's foreign born in New York City, also reenforce that conclusion.[9]

Nonetheless, New York's position was undergoing a change due to the alterations in the nation's immigration patterns, patterns that had begun in the 1950s and had accelerated with the huge influx of Southeast Asian refugees in the late 1970s and early 1980s. During these decades the West emerged as a chief portal and destination of immigrants. California passed New York in 1960 in the number of aliens registering; in 1976 in the number of newcomers designating it as their intended residence; in 1978, 1980, and since 1983 in the number of persons naturalized; and in 1980 in the total number of foreign born. While between 1955 and 1979 22.5 percent of all immigrants still regularly designated New York State as their intended destination, during the period 1982 to 1985 (no data are available for 1980 and 1981), only about one in six of those admitted or adjusted to permanent residence said they were bound for (or were remaining in) New York; one-fourth listed California (17.2 percent v. 26.2 percent).[10]

New York State may no longer be the leading state of intended residence for immigrants, but New York City remains the foremost port of entry in the nation. Its share of all immigrants admitted has fallen by more than two-thirds since the great eras of Castle Garden and Ellis Island, but in the early 1980s 22 percent of all immigrants were still processed there, while the second leading center, Los Angeles, handled under 14 percent of the total. Furthermore, it now appears that New York City remains securely the portal of immigrants, for two out of five of those granted permanent residence in Los Angeles in fiscal year (f.y.) 1984 were refugees and others already in the country, whereas four-fifths of those admitted in New York City (nearly 112,000) were actually newcomers: 32 percent of the national total for new arrivals.[11] Thus, just as New York retained its leadership when the sources of immigration shifted to southern and eastern Europe a century ago, it has done so again as those sources moved to Mexico, the Philippines, Cuba, Korea, China/Hong Kong/Taiwan, India, Vietnam, the Dominican Republic, and Jamaica. And it has held that lead despite economic setbacks and a 10.4 percent drop in total population during the 1970s.[12]

How dramatic the impact of the new groups will be has frequently been a matter of debate. Leon Bouvier, of the United States Census

Table I: Immigration to the United States: Changing Regional Origins, Fiscal Years 1951 to 1985*

Regions	Admissions 1951–1965 A 1) Total 2) Pct. of U.S. Total		Admissions 1966–1980 B 1) Total 2) Pct. of U.S. Total		1) Pct. Change[a] (B/A) in Avg. Annual No. 2) Change in Proportion	Admissions 1981–1985 C 1) Total 2) Pct. of U.S. Total		1) Pct. Change (C/B) in Avg. Annual No. 2) Change in Proportion
Total United States		3,965,791		6,364,679	57.86%		2,864,406	37.26%
Asians	1) 2)	263,053 6.63%	1) 2)	1,956,577 30.74%	1) 631.30% 2) 363.65%	1) 2)	1,376,299 48.05%	1) 114.54% 2) 56.31%
Europeans	1) 2)	2,106,404 53.11%	1) 2)	1,443,571 22.68%	1) −32.59% 2) −57.30%	1) 2)	321,855 11.24%	1) −32.00% 2) −50.44%
North & Central Americans	1) 2)	1,095,763 27.63%	1) 2)	1,276,607 20.06%	1) 14.59% 2) 9.90%	1) 2)	514,190 17.95%	1) 22.85% 2) −10.52%
South Americans	1) 2)	190,211 4.80%	1) 2)	397,015 6.24%	1) 105.29% 2) 27.40%	1) 2)	144,908 5.06%	1) 11.33% 2) −18.91%
West Indians	1) 2)	266,627 6.72%	1) 2)	1,125,455 17.68%	1) 315.19% 2) 163.10%	1) 2)	371,532 12.97%	1) −.69% 2) −26.64%

* Source: Dept. of Justice. *Annual Report of the Immigration and Naturalization Service*, 1951–78. Table 14; *Statistical Yearbook*, 1979–85, Table IMM 1.6; & "Immigration Statistics: Advanced Report, 1985."
   [a] Percentage change for U.S. total is the change in the average annual numbers for each period. For the regions, the figures are the percentage change in (1) the average annual number and (2) the proportion of the total held by each region. The 1966–1980 period includes 15.25 fiscal years because of the transitional quarter, Fall 1976, when fiscal years shifted from July 1 to October 1.

Bureau, for one, sees the nation "on the verge of being transformed ethnically and racially." On the other hand, several prominent historians surveyed by Barry Siegel, of the *Los Angeles Times*, concluded that "America, as it always has, will have a greater impact on today's immigrants than they will have on it." Oscar Handlin, for example, finding many similarities with earlier episodes and foreseeing "no major change from the past," concluded that "in fifty to sixty years this will look like just another wave on the graph." Likewise, Stephan Thernstrom commented, "I certainly don't think the shift from Poles and Slavs to Koreans and Vietnamese is all that significant . . . nothing now portends what the country went through in the mid-nineteenth century and the start of the 20th century." In fact, as demographer David North pointed out, the current influx is "less dramatic than in the early 1900s. They are being absorbed into a far more populous society." Indeed, in fiscal years 1906 and 1907 alone, 762,952 persons said they were bound for New York State, more in only those two years than the 751,517 who so indicated between 1972 and 1979, when the state's overall population was almost twice as large. The general public, however, appears not to be comforted by the scholars' long-term view; in 1984 a Gallup Poll found that 53 percent of those polled thought too many immigrants were coming from Latin America and 49 percent felt the same about those from Asia.[13] These concerns have considerable relevance for New Yorkers because of their city's continuing central role as the nation's principal port of entry. Also, for the first time, the profile of those who have been specifically entering and remaining there is different from the composition of the nation's leading immigrant groups.

II. New York's Newest Immigrants

Table II readily reveals that New York, the historic portal for Europeans, has become the gateway for peoples from the Asian subcontinent, the Caribbean, and South America, along with a smaller mix of British and southern and eastern Europeans. Nonetheless, between 1972 and 1979 New York was not the chief entryway for nine of the country's fifteen leading immigrant groups. Most notably, Mexicans were at the top nationally but too few were admitted via New York City to be among a list of its foremost 23 groups processed. Indeed, the sample used here includes 23 nationalities only because the nation's second most numerous imigrant group, the Filipinos, ranked twenty-third there.

The 23 leading groups entering via New York City accounted for three-fourths of the 1,022,479 immigrants who entered the United States via New York City (or had their status adjusted there) between 1972 and 1979. Their national totals included 22 percent of all who were legally admitted to the entire United States during that period. Among them, the five major West Indian groups (Dominicans, Jamaicans, Haitians, Trinidadians, and Cubans) represented nearly one-quarter of all New York's admissions, and if the three South American peoples (Guyanese, Colombians, and Ecuadorans) are added to the West Indians, the total equals one-third. Another one-fourth came from eight European counties, and 15 percent from seven nations in Asia, the Pacific, and the Middle East.

New York's location and economic opportunities obviously explain much of its ability to draw this distinct admixture of recent immigrants. Additionally, chain migration — particularly the long tradition of people migrating from the Caribbean to New York (except for Bahamians and Cubans) — is quite central to the current great influx. In fact, many in the Caribbean region view present-day migration to New York as but one facet of an ongoing process of more than a century's duration, a migration made easier by the changes in American immigration laws in 1965, 1976, and 1978.[14] But other factors have also played a role for certain groups. One illustration is the Asian Indians, for whom it is as easy to fly from Bombay to New York as from New Delhi to Los Angeles. Because of their professional and commercial backgrounds, many Indian immigrants view New York, with its myriad business possibilities, as the more desirable destination. As a consequence, during this period 49 percent of these newcomers came through New York, and the 1980 census found the northeast had proportionally more Indians than any other major Asian nationality. Thus, the technology of travel and the knowledge of the city's economic opportunities worked in tandem to draw this group to the New York area, just as similar elements had enhanced the city's appeal for other groups since the early 1800s.

Yet in 1980 one Asian group considerably more numerous than the Asian Indians lived in New York City, namely the Chinese (124,372 vs. 46,708). Although nearly three times more Indian immigrants were first processed in the city during the 1970s than were Chinese (1972 to 1979: 68,908 vs. 23,596), almost twice as many Chinese were going to remain in (or make their way to) New York during that period (42,711 vs. 23,056). Rather than creating new paths, as the Indians were doing, these Chinese were now following by air those routes carved by their predecessors across the Pacific and North America over the past 130 years.[15]

Table II: Rank Orders of Key Immigration Indices:
U.S., New York State, New York District, 1972 to 1979[a]

	Rank Order Pct. of Total Immigration to U.S. 1972-1979		Rank Order Pct. of Total to U.S. Via N.Y. Dist. 1972-1979		Rank Order Designating N.Y. State, Pct. of Total 1972-1979		Rank Order Designating N.Y. Dist. Pct. of Total 1972-1979		Rank Order Pct. of Group's U.S. Total Designating N.Y. State	
1)	Mexican	14.7	Dominican	8.3	Dominican	11.2	Dominican	12.7	Guyanese	74.2
2)	Filipino	8.0	Italian	7.1	Jamaican	8.1	Jamaican	8.5	Dominican	71.0
3)	Cuban	6.7	Indian	6.7	Chinese[b]	6.4	Chinese[b]	6.7	Haitian	70.4
4)	Korean	6.3	Jamaican	6.7	Italian	5.8	Italian	4.7	Russian	67.8
5)	Chinese[b]	5.6	Greek	4.9	Haitian	4.2	Haitian	4.6	Ecuadoran	62.0
6)	Indian	3.9	Trinidadian	4.0	Indian	4.0	Trinidadian	4.4	Trinidadian	60.3
7)	Vietnamese	3.7	Ecuadoran	3.4	Trinidadian	4.0	Guyanese	4.1	Jamaican	55.9
8)	Dominican	3.3	Haitian	3.1	Guyanese	3.7	Indian	3.6	Israeli	42.7
9)	Jamaican	3.0	Guyanese	3.1	Ecuadoran	3.2	Ecuadoran	3.6	Italian	41.9
10)	Italian	2.9	Portuguese	3.0	Colombian	3.2	Russian	3.4	Colombian	40.2
11)	British	2.7	British	3.0	Greek	3.2	Colombian	3.3	Greek	32.4
12)	Canadian	2.7	Cuban	2.8	Cuban	3.1	Cuban	3.1	Yugoslavian	30.6
13)	Portuguese	2.4	Russian	2.8	Korean	2.8	Greek	3.1	Polish	26.3
14)	Greek	2.0	Colombian	2.5	Russian	2.9	Filipino	2.4	Chinese[b]	24.1
15)	Colombian	1.7	Chinese[b]	2.3	Filipino	2.6	Korean	2.2	Indian	21.5
16)	German	1.4	Yugoslavian	2.0	British	2.0	British	1.6	British	15.6
17)	Trinidadian	1.4	Israeli	1.9	Yugoslavian	1.4	Yugoslavian	1.4	Iraqi	13.4
18)	Haitian	1.2	Polish	1.9	Polish	1.3	Israeli	1.3	Iranian	12.2
19)	Ecuadoran	1.1	German	1.7	Israeli	1.2	Polish	1.2	German	9.8
20)	Japanese	1.1	Iraqi	1.5	Portuguese	.9	Portuguese	.5	Cuban	9.6
21)	Guyanese	1.0	Iranian	1.1	German	.7	Iranian	.5	Korean	9.4
22)	Thai	1.0	Korean	.8	Iranian	.5	German	.5	Portuguese	8.4
23)	Polish	1.0	Filipino	.7	Iraqi	.3	Iraqi	.4	Filipino	6.6
24)	Yugoslavian	1.0								
25)	Iranian	.9								
TOTAL		3,592,197		1,022,479		751,517		637,196		. . .

[a] Data based on Country of birth.
[b] Includes Mainland China, Taiwan & Hong Kong.
* Source: INS *Annual Reports*, Tables 5, 12, 44 and INS public use tapes.

Besides the Chinese and Indians, numerous other groups specifically designated New York City as their destination or residence. As Table II indicates, the list is not simply the same as that of those entering via New York. Instead, in addition to the Chinese, those particularly intent on remaining in the city or going there from other ports of entry (in terms of percentages of the total) include Dominicans, Jamaicans, Italians, Haitians, Trinidadians, and Guyanese. "Remaining" is important to mention, because, with only five exceptions (Filipinos, the Chinese, Koreans, Ecuadorans, and Colombians), from 87 percent (among Haitians) to 99 percent (among Iraqis) of those 23 groups in the sample who were planning to reside in New York City (or were already present there) were admitted or adjusted in that INS district. Among those others, only about one-third of the Asians (excepting the Indians) and 70 percent of the South Americans who landed at Kennedy Airport — the principal entry and processing center — were going to live in the city.[16] Likewise, although Italians, Greeks, and "Russians" (mostly Soviet Jews) were also among the top one dozen groups intent on residing in New York City, their percentages of the total were small, and, overall, the Europeans in the sample used here had the lowest proportions of those processed in New York who were remaining there. Moreover, the number of these Italians and Greeks entering New York and the United States actually began falling steadily in the 1970s (as was true for Germans, too — traditionally another important group in New York). Not only did those declines continue in the first half of the 1980s but a remarkable and dramatic shift also occurred in the destination of Soviet Jews from New York to California, and especially to Los Angeles.[17]

In sum, leaving aside the tourists and students who came and "forgot" to leave and other undocumented persons in the 1970s, among just the 23 groups sampled more than three-fifths were from the Caribbean, South and Central America, Asia, and the Middle East — and not from the traditional European sending nations whose successive waves of immigrants had shaped the city, the state, and the nation. These newest New Yorkers most often directly migrated to the city and, while their total average annual immigration dipped in many cases during the economic troubles of the mid 1970s, their numbers began rising sharply during the late 1970s and early 1980s.[18]

Although the national totals for arriving immigrants and the patterns of their state destinations do not necessarily shift or change in the same directions, the data presented in Table III suggest several trends that probably affected New York City and state in the 1980s. First, the "traditional" sending countries were, as noted above, not sending as many people. For example, in the period 1982 to 1985 (no data exist for 1980 and 1981) there were sharp drops in the average number of Greeks, Italians, Yugoslavians, and Portuguese admitted. Second, even though the average annual number of immigrants intending to reside in New York State actually rose almost 7 percent during the early part of the decade, that was far below the national average jump of over 29 percent. As a result, there was nearly an 18 percent shrinkage in the proportion of newcomers headed toward (or remaining in) New York State; proportionally, more persons were going elsewhere. Third, only three of the 23 groups sampled had an increase in the average number going to New York State compared with the years of 1972 to 1979, and the average drop for all 23 groups was close to one-quarter for the period 1982 to 1985. Nevertheless, because New York State's share of all intended residences did rise in 1984 and 1985, it is possible that some of the declines in 1982 and 1983 may have been short term and that by the middle of the decade the state was recovering some of its ground.[19]

III. Immigration and Remigration: An Hypothesis

The immigration and settlement patterns described here are, of course, only part of the newcomers' story. How well they integrate, the nature and extent of their ties with their homelands, how many acquire citizenship, and what percentage choose to return to their native lands are other important, overlapping chapters. For instance, the strength of the bonds that are preserved with the homeland and of those that are forged here are subject to many variables beyond the scope of this essay, but some of those factors are particularly relevant to the key decision whether to remain here or return home. Remigration, as the return move is now termed, is not a new phenomenon by any means. Given the relatively low costs and ease of travel nowadays, it is, in particular, usually neither too formidable nor too expensive. The degree to which it occurs, ranging from permanently to cyclically, has a significant impact on ethnic communities both here and in the homelands in terms of family ties, occupational gains, accumulation of economic resources, religious institutions, educational programs, and political clout at the ballot boxes, to name but a few areas. Consequently, some notion of the extent to which the groups remain and become naturalized can give a clearer perspective on the net effect of the recent, extraordinary immigration trends we have observed.

The consequences of remaining here and becoming United States citizens might be minimal (although emotionally difficult) for such

Table III: U.S. Total Immigration and Immigration to New York State: Selected Nationalities, Fiscal Years 1982 to 1985, Compared with Fiscal Years 1972 to 1979[1]

Country of Birth	Total Immigration 1982-1985		U.S. Total Avg./Yr. 1971-1980	U.S. Total Avg./Yr. 1982-1985	Percent to N.Y. State 1972-1979	Percent to N.Y. State 1982-1985	Percent Difference in Pct. to N.Y. State 1972-1979 vs. 1982-1985	Percent Difference in U.S. Avg. No./Yr. 1971-1980 vs. 1982-1985
	To U.S.	To N.Y. State						
China[2]	176,537	38,242	24,393	44,134	24.06%	21.66%	-9.98%	80.93%
Colombia	41,268	12,604	7,566	10,317	40.16%	30.54%	-23.95%	36.36%
Cuba	48,120	1,994	27,003	12,030	9.62%	4.14%	-56.96%	-55.45%
Dominican Republic	86,443	56,663	14,441	21,611	70.97%	65.55%	-7.63%	49.65%
Ecuador	17,016	11,480	4,894	4,254	61.90%	67.47%	9.00%	-13.08%
Germany	27,895	2,170	6,438	6,974	9.80%	7.78%	-20.61%	8.33%
Greece	11,913	3,603	9,146	2,978	32.37%	30.24%	-6.67%	-67.44%
Guyana	35,982	20,417	4,637	8,996	74.16%	73.42%	-1.00%	94.00%
Haiti	37,207	21,594	5,727	9,302	70.42%	58.04%	-17.58%	62.42%
India	98,179	15,526	17,245	24,545	21.46%	15.81%	-26.33%	42.33%
Iran	51,355	3,756	4,503	12,839	12.22%	7.31%	-40.18%	185.12%
Iraq	10,329	387	2,328	2,582	13.41%	3.75%	-72.04%	10.91%
Israel	12,774	4,421	2,595	3,194	42.71%	34.61%	-18.97%	23.08%
Italy	13,213	4,300	12,696	3,303	41.94%	32.54%	-22.41%	-73.98%
Jamaica	76,991	40,801	13,853	19,248	55.89%	52.99%	-5.19%	38.94%
Korea	133,358	13,560	26,337	33,340	9.36%	10.17%	8.65%	26.59%
Philippines	177,394	8,164	35,143	44,349	6.61%	4.60%	-30.41%	26.20%
Poland	31,231	4,858	4,252	7,808	26.31%	15.56%	-40.86%	83.63%
Portugal	14,301	1,476	10,195	3,575	8.38%	10.32%	23.15%	-64.93%
Trinidad	12,419	6,646	5,341	3,105	60.19%	53.51%	-11.10%	-41.86%
United Kingdom	56,726	7,424	12,053	14,182	15.63%	13.09%	-16.25%	17.66%
U.S.S.R.	30,285	5,596	4,216	7,571	68.27%	18.48%	-72.93%	79.58%
Yugoslavia	6,031	1,615	4,109	1,508	30.56%	26.78%	-12.37%	-63.30%
U.S. Total	2,267,806		438,372	566,952	20.92%	17.20%	-17.78%	29.33%
N.Y. Total[3]		390,003	91,243	97,501				6.68%

[1] Source: Public use tapes from INS, 1972-1985, INS *Statistical Yearbooks*, 1982-1984, and "Immigration Statistics: Advanced Report, 1985."
[2] Includes Taiwan, Hong Kong, and Mainland China.
[3] New York State average is for 1971-1979. No data exist for 1980-1981.

groups as the Israelis and Dominicans, whose countries recognize dual citizenship. India, on the other hand, rejects the concept; Indians choosing to be naturalized are compelled to give up their property in India and seriously jeopardize any future efforts to resettle there.[20] In any case, regardless of the legal consequences, many persons are so attached to their native land that they cannot imagine surrendering their loyalty to it, or they fear becoming stateless if adverse conditions develop here or if negative experiences compel them to renounce their American citizenship. A Peruvian woman, dismissing the idea of switching citizenships, said that the man suggesting it "doesn't understand what it means to change citizenship. I feel Peruvian." A Jamaican girl emphasized that "I am not an American citizen. I don't plan to become one and I'd rather go back to Jamaica where they don't have this big thing about color." Many others, though, balance the economic, political, and social benefits of American citizenship against the emotional appeal and/or the preplanned intentions of returning home.[21]

One gets the general impression from discussions about remigration earlier in this century and from the fact that the INS ceased keeping emigration data after 1957 that such return migrations have ceased. Except for Warren and Peck's study of the 1960s, Glen Hendrick's on Dominicans, and references to Mexican patterns, it is infrequently mentioned with respect to current immigrants. Yet, any assessment of the impact of the recent waves of immigrants must take into account the reality of the strong desire to return among many who have come here during the past two decades. In one recent collection of essays, William Stinner, Klaus de Albuquerque, and Roy Bryce-Laporte focused on Caribbean return migration. They emphasized that for many the decision to come here often is linked with the intent to go back and that even those who later find themselves unable to return continue to act as if they will, making the process more accurately one of circulation rather than migration. The authors found many concrete reasons why people return, such as completion of studies, retirement, family ties, homesickness, changing societal conditions (and fortunes) here, and maladaptation (simply not liking the American lifestyle), and they stressed that non-economic motives were predominant.[22]

One illustration bearing out these observations is the Dominican Republic's own 1974 survey, which found that 39 percent of its emigrants returned home.[23] That the return sentiment in general is so strong among so many who may never actually resettle in their homelands may be highly significant, for that mind-set undoubtedly affects their integration into American society and their ultimate impact upon that society and upon New York City in particular. For example, in preparation for David Vidal's excellent four-part series on Hispanics/Latinos in the city (May 11-14, 1980), the *New York Times* interviewed 566 persons, 90 percent of whom were foreign born.[24] Vidal reported that "most were reluctant to wean themselves from the past." Among the "non-Puerto Ricans interviewed, none mentioned citizenship as a personal goal. However, the goal is *'la residencia,'* the right to permanent residence in this country . . ."[25] Similarly, Dr. Elsa Chaney, an expert on Colombian migration, described a key neighborhood in Queens as " 'more like a remote province of Colombia than an ethnic barrio of New York City' because so many people dream of going home." She noted the selective acculturation of these immigrants, who were "preserving a strong cultural identity in which the myth of the return to Colombia plays a large part," and, she added, as a result, they were "avoiding involvement in United States politics or community affairs."[26]

During the 1960s and early 1970s, Glen Hendricks also found that "few Dominican immigrants who are eligible become citizens" because "the universal expectation is that [they] will move back to the Republic," especially when they retire. One priest in New York lamented that it was hard to get Dominicans to contribute to the church because they were either sending so much money back home "or [were] saving for their own return." Hendricks acknowledged some increase in naturalizations, but the return sentiments remained powerful.[27]

Perhaps the best general assessment is that of Hymie Rubenstein, who wrote that "return migration is an extremely significant part of the Caribbean migration phenomenon." Indeed, he added, a study in the mid 1970s found "that most West Indians in New York intend ultimately to return to their homeland societies." And he concluded, as had Chaney regarding Colombians, that even where the intent is "an empty dream," for immigrants who "continue *to act* as if they will eventually return to their homelands," the consequences are "significant." [Italics are author's.][28]

All of these observations point to the importance of determining just how much remigration has occurred. If we calculate the proportion of a given year's arrivals who acquire citizenship over a set period of time, we cannot only assume that the remainder stayed in the city (or in the United States) but chose not to change nationalities.[29] That assumption would suggest the scenario of a great pool of alien residents remaining and growing larger by the year because the proportion of those made citizens is usually far below the total number of arrivals. On the other hand, if many of the unnaturalized immigrants actually leave while others come, we are dealing with a highly visible and a highly dramatic situation but one less portentous to some native-

born Americans and perhaps one less likely to support the wild specu-
lations about the number of foreigners that some journalists have put
forth. Furthermore, if the latter scenario is true, as our sources have
suggested, the pool of newcomers is expanding fitfully but less rapidly,
and the challenge to the particular ethnic communities and the general
community is a much different one in terms of the absolute (viz., total)
numbers being simultaneously processed, or absorbed. Hence, a specific
group might be experiencing the social effects of a sizable population
turnover, but because the group's total net number is increasing only
gradually, the impact of that growth on it and on the general society
may well be less severe than if all the newcomers were actually remaining.

The hypothesis that follows is grounded in this latter perspective
for it is based on findings that indicate important "gaps" between the
1980 census figures for many nationality groups and the totals one would
derive based on INS figures for persons arriving from those homelands.
My hypothesis is that any attempt to account for these gaps must consider an extraordinary out-migration of legally admitted foreign-born
residents (especially West Indians and Latinos) to eastern New Jersey and other nearby communities and, more often, back to their
homelands. Any effort to "guesstimate" the number of undocumented
aliens involved in this same process is not the focus here, for others,
such as Frank Bean and Jeffrey Passel, have concentrated on that matter.
I will acknowledge that during the period from 1972 to 1979 over 2.4
million visitors came to the United States from just the eight West In-
dian/Latin American nations sampled here (Jamaica, Haiti, Dominican
Republic, Trinidad, Guyana, Colombia, and Ecuador)—nearly half
of them Dominicans and Colombians—and an unknown but not inconsequential number of them apparently never returned home.[30]

Testing my hypothesis involves a four-way comparison of the data
in Table IV on the number of aliens who registered in January 1972
and January 1980, the number of persons naturalized in New York
State, and the number of immigrants who gave New York State as their
intended residence when they were first processed during this period.
This is a somewhat rough test because it does not compensate for: a)
underregistration by aliens in each January; b) those who never went
to or did not stay in the state they designated at the time of their admission; c) those who died; and d) those immigrants who arrived between July 1 and December 31, 1971 (the first half of fiscal year 1972,
which should be excluded from a survey confined to calendar years
1972 to 1979), and those who came between October 1 and December
31, 1979 (the first quarter of fiscal year 1980, which should be included).

As Table IV shows, 724,492 aliens registered as permanent residents

Table IV: Estimate of "Gap" Between Immigration and Resident Alien Population: New York State: 1972 to 1980[1]

Country of Birth	Permanent Aliens Registered N.Y. State Jan., 1972	Permanent Aliens Registered N.Y. State Jan., 1980	Numerical Difference 1980–1972	Natural-izations N.Y. State[3] 1972–1979	Total No. of Immigrants Designating N.Y. State 1972–1979	Estimated Net "Missing"[4]	Estimated Gap: "Missing" as Pct. of Total Designating N.Y. State
China[2]	25,646	30,514	+4,868	19,152	37,318	13,298	35.6%
Colombia	22,970	27,871	+4,901	4,696	24,028	14,431	60.1%
Cuba	46,712	21,158	−25,554	15,313	23,108	33,349	144.3%
Dominican Republic	50,465	81,785	+31,320	9,950	83,851	42,581	50.8%
Ecuador	17,975	27,646	+9,671	3,323	24,170	11,176	46.2%
Germany	29,871	17,721	−12,150	5,409	5,085	11,826	232.6%
Greece	23,198	14,339	−8,859	14,220	23,667	18,306	77.4%
Guyana	4,556	14,658	+10,102	4,270	27,469	13,097	47.7%
Haiti	16,736	12,618	−4,118	10,295	31,492	25,315	80.4%
India	9,734	19,685	+9,951	4,639	30,010	15,420	51.4%
Iran	1,687	2,203	+516	857	4,073	2,700	66.3%
Iraq	184	220	+36	554	2,616	2,208	84.4%
Israel	8,813	7,382	−1,431	3,503	9,115	8,094	88.8%

Italy	104,906	59,697	−45,209	28,138	43,003	60,074	139.7%
Jamaica	45,215	40,493	−4,722	16,514	60,578	48,876	80.5%
Korea	4,596	15,159	+10,563	6,064	21,094	4,467	21.2%
Philippines	7,576	10,357	+2,781	7,081	19,135	9,273	48.5%
Poland	20,602	12,094	−8,508	7,041	9,461	10,955	115.8%
Portugal	5,924	7,881	+1,957	2,217	7,073	2,899	41.0%
Trinidad & Tobago	16,468	17,877	+1,409	4,196	29,778	25,627	86.1%
United Kingdom	54,378	44,579	−9,799	5,170	15,206	19,835	130.4%
U.S.S.R.	7,204	14,676	+7,472	2,353	21,812	11,987	55.0%
Yugoslavia	8,632	5,501	−3,131	6,033	10,375	7,473	72.0%
Total	724,492	690,383	−34,109	248,214	751,517	537,412	71.5%

[1] Sources: Immigration & Registration data from *Annual Reports:* 1972, Table 34; 1980, Table 18; 1972–1979, Table 12A, and public use tapes from INS.

[2] Figures includes China and Taiwan only.

[3] Total naturalizations for 1972–1979 based on *Annual Reports* and public use tapes.

[4] a. If decrease in registrations was *greater* than the number of persons naturalized, latter was subtracted from that decrease and difference was *added* to immigration figure to determine estimated number "missing."

b. If decrease was *less* than naturalizations, the decrease figure was *subtracted* from naturalizations and that figure was deducted from total immigration to determine estimated number "missing."

c. If registrations *increased,* net gain added to naturalizations and that figure was then *subtracted* from total immigration to determine estimated number "missing."

Estimates are not adjusted for migration, mortality, under-registrations or persons not going to designated states, all of which might cancel out each other (I assume most legal residents registered).

in 1972. Eight years later, only 690,383 registered, for a drop of 34,109. To that 34,109 we add the 751,517 new arrivals who said they were bound for, or were planning to remain in, New York State (fiscal years 1972 to 1979) and then we deduct from that sum the 248,214 persons who were naturalized between fiscal years 1972 and 1979 and who would no longer have been required to register as aliens.[31] What remains is an unexplained "gap" of well over a half million persons—a figure equal to 70 percent of the total number of immigrants who gave New York State as their intended residence during most of the 1970s.

The table provides specific calculations for the 23 groups sampled. In the most noteworthy cases, we find the unexplained gap in the number of Germans, Italians, British, Poles, and Cubans to exceed by far the total numbers of persons arriving and/or being adjusted to permanent, resident status who had said they were residing in, or planning to re-side in, New York State during the period studied. At least half of the newcomers from most groups apparently were not present in the state in 1980, and the smallest unexplained difference was for Koreans, among whom fully one-fifth were "missing." Even if the many variables noted at the outset could be computed and deducted from these estimates, a considerable number of foreign-born persons would remain unaccounted for in New York State and especially in New York City. Although, many legally resident aliens undoubtedly moved out of the city and state to other locations in the United States (particularly Cubans and other refugees who could not return home and those from older sending nations for whom dispersal patterns here are well established), the literature supports the hypothesis that far more of them emigrated (usually remigrating homeward) than has been detailed by previous observers of current immigration patterns. A 1984 Census Bureau estimate that some 133,000 foreign-born legal residents are emigrating annually lends much credibility to this hypothesis.[32]

In other words, the phenomenon of remigration—so common among many earlier immigrant groups, such as the French Canadians, Greeks, Poles, Italians, and Chinese, that it prompted observers to label many of those newcomers as sojourners or "birds of passage"—never really ended. We have indeed opened our doors to ten million more immigrants and refugees since 1965, but many of them have chosen not to remain, or never came with that intention. Whether this has been more true for those going to New York City than elsewhere remains to be determined. But it has not been inconsequential there and its impact on the city's expanding array of ethnic communities has been significant.

IV. Conclusion

This essay used a variety of INS materials to document more closely some of the dramatic demographic changes in immigration to New York City that journalists and scholars have been describing since at least 1970. (Space limitations preclude detailing more of the specific characteristics of these newcomers, such as the age, sex, marital status, and occupational distributions.) It is apparent that, while New York lost ground both as a port of entry and as an intended destination, the sources of those entering or being adjusted there simultaneously underwent a significant swing to the South, the Pacific, and the Middle and Far East for a host of economic, political, social and legislative reasons. New York thus became the principal gateway for West Indians, many Central and South Americans, Asian Indians, peoples from the Middle East, and Soviet Jews.

Between 1980 and 1985, the number of newcomers among many of the European groups that had long been prominent in the city diminished after the initial surges of backlogged applicants in the late 1960s and early 1970s. Likewise, the average annual number coming from the West Indies also dipped in the early 1980s but soon returned to the level of the 1970s. In addition, while many groups were arriving in greater numbers during the 1980s, smaller proportions of most of those populations sampled were intending to reside in New York. As a result of those trends during the period from 1982 to 1985, New York State's percentage of total designated residences fell to 18 percent, and New York City's share of admissions dropped to 22 percent — despite an increase in the average annual number admitted there to over 100,000 in fiscal years 1984 and 1985.

Certainly, the 642,083 Asian refugees admitted to permanent residence throughout the United States between 1980 and 1983 skewed the totals for this period. It is also possible that the serious loss of jobs and the general economic difficulties that have besieged New York combined with difficult living conditions and the high cost and scarcity of housing to discourage immigrant decisions to reside in New York City. These factors were likely compounded as well by increasing job opportunities outside the state, the deepening paths cut by Asian-Pacific-Middle Eastern immigrants towards California, and changing conditions in the Caribbean and Latin sending nations.[33]

The fact that by the mid 1980s we find over 100,000 immigrants per year indicating that they were planning to live in New York State does not nullify the hypothesis offered here, based on the evidence for the 1970s, nor does it suggest that the emigration process has stopped, or even significantly changed. Rather, the data and literature support the hypothesis that there was, *and continues to be*, a considerable, perhaps an incredible, circulatory flow of many new immigrants arriving and others moving on to other states or back to their homelands, in all creating a picture of extraordinary flux among the newer ethnic communities of New York.

The census of ancestry taken in 1980 offers a moment's snapshot of New York's fluid ethnic scene. In the state were 326,516 persons with at least one Asian ancestor, another 1,872,421 from the Caribbean and Latin American countries, and 194,815 from Africa and the Middle East. In New York City, the census counted 239,300 Asian/Pacific Islanders (with 124,000 Chinese), 1.4 million persons of Spanish origin (including 462,000 who were neither Cuban, nor Mexican, nor Puerto Rican — the "others"), and 1.2 million of mixed European ancestry (one ancestor was English, or French, German, Irish, Italian, or Polish) as well as 802,000 Italians, 317,600 Irish, 215,700 Russians (mostly Jews), 195,500 Poles (Jews and non-Jews), 181,700 Germans, and 82,000 Greeks, etc. New York was still a city predominantly European in ethnic origin; it is also a city in the midst of a most significant ethnic transformation.[34]

The evidence points to a city receiving a multitude of new peoples, many with the sojourner mentality. They hold tenaciously to their cultures, send enormous sums home, save more for their own return, and regularly welcome new members into their communities. Many newcomers are also finding an Asian, or a Latino/Hispanic, or a Caribbean culture that has begun both to incorporate and to transcend the cultures of their individual groups. This "supra-subculture" is fostering a bicultural, bi-ethnic experience that is, at least for the time being, pan-Asian Indian, or pan-Asian/Pacific, or island ethnic and Caribbean, as in the term "Dominican-Caribbean" rather than Dominican-American. The constant immigrant exchanges (many coming, others going) intensify the visibility of these various groups. It appears to be, as Barry Levine described it, that many have gone to New York not to make it but to learn how to make it — back home.[35]

The literature and data also reveal that within each of the newer communities, some of which are already a generation old, there is a growing nucleus of people who have become citizens and who will remain here, intentionally or not. They are the immigrants most likely to proceed with the traditional integration into American society. Very much like New York's Puerto Ricans, they remain part of bi-polar ethnic communities whose roots here and at home are constantly reinforced by their members' regular migrations and visits and by the continuous exchanges of people, products, and cultural media. The proximity of homeland in many of these instances and the ease with which cheaper air travel enables modern migrants to bridge ever greater distances are profoundly affecting the patterns of adaptation in New York.[36]

The literature on ethnic-group assimilation confirms the observations noted here: where such bi-polarism exists, the native language, culture, customs, and identity of immigrants persist — not indefinitely, just longer. That has been the experience in New York many times and, in all likelihood, will be the experience now. Clearly, as this paper has shown, the players have changed. Some of the variables have also changed; possibly even the time factor has changed; and certainly the languages are changing. But the powerful assimilative forces that have permeated the New York experiences in the past continue to operate, for the impact of our media-dominated mass culture is far stronger and more pervasive than it was half a century ago, and the economic advantages of fitting in too irresistible. The changes in immigration described here have certainly begun to change the portrait of New York City (its face, its foods, its festivals, its chatter), but in the long term, the integrative encounters of the current immigrant groups will more closely approximate those of their predecessors than not.

Historian John Higham may have summed up the whole process best when he told reporter Barry Siegel, "Old immigrants always respond to new immigrants by co-opting them. The future will resemble the past more than be a departure." That most likely will be the case for America's portal of portals, its home for millions of newcomers, for, in Thomas Kessner and Betty Boyd Caroli's words, "New York . . . is not America, but it is New York."[37]

Notes

1. The quote in the title is from Glen Hendricks, *The Dominican Diaspora: From the Dominican Republic to New York City* (New York, 1974), 25. The quotation in this paragraph is from Thomas Kessner and Betty Boyd Caroli, who also wrote that "for most Islanders, the United States meant New York City." Kessner and Caroli, *Today's Immigrants: Their Stories* (New York, 1981), 182 and 189. The early period is described more fully in Elliott R. Barkan, "New York City: Immigrant Depot, Immigrant City," in Gail Stern, ed., *Freedom's Doors: Immigrant Ports of Entry to the United States* (Philadelphia, 1986), 1–12.

2. Based on William J. Bromwell, *History of Immigration to the United States* (1856; reprinted, 1969); Jesse Chickering, *Immigration Into the United States* (1848; reprinted, 1971); Friederich Kapp, *Immigration and the Commissioners of Emigration of the State of New York* (1870; reprinted, 1969); Felice Jo Lamden, "Statistical Information on Immigra-

tion, 1820–1931" (unpublished tables, prepared for the Balch Institute, 1985); and unpublished tables on New York, Ellis Island, and ports of entry (1982–1985), furnished by the Immigration and Naturalization Service (INS).

3. The many calculations done for this paper were based on the published *Annual Reports of the Immigration and Naturalization Service*, 1951–1978; the *Statistical Yearbook of the Immigration and Naturalization Service*, 1979–1984; INS computer tapes of all applications for admission and adjustment of immigrants, 1972–1985; tapes of all naturalization applications for 1972–1983; INS "Immigration Statistics: Fiscal Year [hereafter F.Y.] 1985 Advance Report" (June 1986); and other unpublished tables furnished to the author by the statistical section of the INS (with great thanks to Michael Hoefler and Margaret Sullivan). Tables 12, 12A, and 14 were specifically used here as well as tables 13 in the 1979 report and IMM 1.3 and IMM 5.3 in the 1983 and 1984 *Statistical Yearbooks*. Because the 1980–1985 records have only just become available, the focus of this paper was principally on the 1972–1979 period.

4. The Barge Office was located in lower Manhattan and was used to process immigrants during the interim between the closing of Castle Garden and the opening of Ellis Island and during the 1897–1900 period, when Ellis Island was closed due to a fire. It is important to point out that steerage passengers were checked on Ellis Island, whereas first and second-class passengers were usually checked on board their ships and could then proceed on their way if no problems were found. See Ann Novotny, *Strangers at the Door: Ellis Island, Castle Garden, and the Great Migration to America* (1971; abridged ed., 1974), 103–104 and 108.

5. Kurt Andersen, "New York. 'Final Destination.' " in *Time*, July 8, 1985, 46–49. See also, Robert Lindsey, "The New Asian Immigrants," *New York Times Magazine*, May 9, 1982, 22–28+; and Samuel G. Freedman, "The New New Yorkers," *ibid.*, November 3, 1985, 24–29+. The two immigrant quotes are from Kessner and Caroli, *Today's Immigrants*, 29 and 182, respectively.

6. Sources are given in note 3, notably table 6 in the *Annual Reports* prior to 1980. The figure for the 1980s includes 1980–1985.

7. David Reimers pinpointed the fact that the extraordinary changes resulting from the legislative revisions in 1965 were largely unanticipated. See Reimers, *Still the Golden Door: The Third World Comes to America* (New York, 1985), 75, 77, 85. Just as the Korean War had profoundly affected immigration from Asia, so, too, would the Vietnam War, which escalated the same year as the new immigration law was enacted (see p. 99). The effects of the 1980 Refugee Act were similarly underestimated. See also, pp. 35–37, the charts on pp. 95, 97–99, 104, 108, 110–112, 117–120 and Reimers' chapter, "Recent Third World Immigration to New York City, 1945–1988: An Overview," in this volume.

8. In addition to Reimers and Bryce-Laporte, already cited, see Tricia Knoll, *Becoming Americans* (Portland, 1982); Thomas Archdeacon, *Becoming American: An Ethnic History* (New York, 1983); and Joan Moore and Harry Pachon, *Hispanics in the United States* (Englewood Cliffs, N.J., 1985). Many news stories have focused on the return migration of Puerto Ricans during the 1970s, which was not novel but only proportionally greater in volume to the flow of migrants in the 1950s and 1960s. We are not focusing on them here because they are citizens. However, on this matter, see Barry Levine, "The Puerto Rican Circuit and the Success of Return Migrants," in William F. Stinner, Klaus de Albuquerque, and Roy Simon Bryce-Laporte, eds., *Return Migration and Remittances: Developing A Caribbean Perspective*, RIIES Occasional Paper No. 3 (Washington, 1982) 157–181; Guy Gugliota, "Neoricans' Reverse Migration Changes Puerto Rico," *Los Angeles Times*, January 2, 1977; William Stockton, "Going Home: The Puerto Ricans' New Migration," *New York Times Magazine*, November 12, 1978, pp. 20–22; Angela and Ceferino Carrasquillo, "Unwelcomed in Two Worlds: The Neorican," *Migration Today*, November/December 1979, pp. 12-17; and Joan Moore and Harry Pachon, *Hispanics in the United States*, 35, 54–55.

Jeffrey Passel and Karen Woodrow, "Geographic Distribution of Undocumented

Immigrants: Estimates of Undocumented Aliens Counted in the 1980 Census by State, *International Migration Review* 18 (Fall 1984), 642–671, have estimated that the 1980 census included over two million undocumented persons nationwide, 234,000 of them in New York State (the second such populous state after California). They calculate that 15,000 in New York were from Cuba and the Dominican Republic, 113,000 from other Caribbean and Central American nations, 37,000 from South America, 26,000 from Europe, and 22,000 from Asia. These figures, of course, do not include those still uncounted, but they do indicate how profoundly the immigrant population is changing. Such immigration and census data can give us only a strong sense of the basic populations and a partial insight into the shifts underway. It is, after all, well known that the illegal or undocumented very often follow the paths etched first by those legally able to enter and whose apparent success encourages the others on and whose own nascent communities have frequently become a haven for those others. They may, however, use different means of entry; for example, see "Northern Border Faces Alien Problem," *New York Times*, April 20, 1986.

See, too, Frank D. Bean, Allan King, and Jeffrey S. Passel, "The Number of Illegal Migrants of Mexican Origin in the United States: Sex Ratio-Based Estimates for 1980," *Demography* 20 (February 1983), 99–109. The INS' 1980 Alien Registration table reported 801,411 for New York, but these authors adjusted for underrepresented persons and they estimate that a closer figure *at the time of the census date*, April 1, 1980, rather than on January 1, was 832,000. However, it is not broken down by country. They do suggest that 377,000 came between 1975 and 1980 and that 229,000 arrived between 1970 and 1974.

With regard to some of the figures bandied about but impossible to confirm (they tend to get repeated once published), see M. A. Fisher, "Million Illegal Aliens in Metropolitan Area," *New York Times*, December 29, 1974 and his "Unlawful Aliens Use Costly City Services," *ibid.*, December 30, 1974; and "750,000 'Illegals' in City is 'Credible,'" *ibid.*, September 4, 1977. Also see Sheila Rule, "For Hispanic Americans: A Diversity of Cultures," *ibid.*, November 22, 1977; David Vidal, "Hispanic Newcomers in City Cling to Values of Homeland," *ibid.*, May 11, 1980; Michael Goodwin, "Immigrants Revitalize City, but Strain Its Resources," *ibid.*, May 6, 1981; "It's Your Turn in the Sun," *Time*, October 16, 1978, p. 55; Carlo De Rege, "Dominicans are coming to New York," *Migration Today*, July 1974, p. 1; Philip M. Kayal, "The Dominicans in New York, Part I," *ibid.*, June 1978, p. 17; Andersen, "New York," 47; and, for contrast, Freedman, "The New New Yorkers," 24.

Other scholars have made broad "guesstimates," too, such as that by Thomas Morrison and Richard Sinkin, "International Migration in the Dominican Republic: Implications for Planning," *International Migration Review* 16 (Winter 1982), 821. Bryce-Laporte also referred to a study estimating 500,000 to 1.5 million in the city alone (which is quite a spread): Roy Simon Bryce-Laporte, "New York City and the New Caribbean Immigration: A Contextual Statement," *International Migration Review* 13 (Summer 1979), 220.

9. On the average, another 10.8 percent of those entering New York were going to New Jersey, 2.4 percent to Pennsylvania, and 2.9 percent to Connecticut. Thus, three-fourths were remaining in the four-state area. Regarding the census figures and population shifts, see Edmund Burks, "Drop in Europeans Found in City as Latins Increase," *New York Times*, July 31, 1972; Irvin Molotsky, "Census Indicates a Sharp Decline in Whites in City," *ibid.*, April 6, 1981; John Herbers, "Census Finds That New York's Pot is Still Melting," *ibid.*, April 25, 1982; Department of Commerce, Bureau of the Census, *1970 Census of the United States, General Social and Economic Characteristics, Vol. 34, New York* (Washington, 1973), tables 141–142, and *1980 Census of Population: Characteristics of Population, General Social and Economic Characteristics, U.S. Summary*, PC80-1-C1 (Washington, 1983), tables 236, 238, 246–250; and Leon Bouvier, "International Migration: Yesterday, Today, and Tomorrow,"

Population Bulletin, September 1977 (and updated in August 1979), p. 27. Totals calculated for 1971–1980 from the INS 1980 *Annual Report*, table 13.

10. Computed from INS tables 19 (prior to 1955), 5, 12, and 12A, for 1955–1979, IMM5.1 in 1981 and IMM5.2 in 1983, along with unpublished tables from the INS for 1982–1985 ports of entry; the Advanced Report for 1985; the data in Kapp, pp. 234–235; and the tables in Elliott Barkan, "Evermore the Golden Gate: Recent Immigration and Naturalization Trends in California" (paper presented at the American Studies Association meeting, San Diego, November 3, 1985.)

11. See Elliott Barkan, "New Origins, New Homelands: Immigration into Selected Sunbelt Cities Since 1965," Raymond Mohl, ed., *Searching for the Sunbelt* (University of Tennessee Press, 1990) and table IMM 1.5 in the 1984 *Statistical Yearbook*. This was the first year in which the INS published a table enumerating new arrivals rather than all persons processed, as was usually the case. That suggests the extent to which the adjustments of status of aliens who were already present (particularly refugees) had become even more significant than they previously had been, when they accounted for one-fourth of all persons "admitted" (1966–1979).

12. For example, see Office of Statistical Coordination, New York State Division of the Budget, *New York State Statistical Yearbook, 1974*, pp. 75–76, and *1977*, pp. 71–72, 99, 107, 110, 114.

13. The quotations are from Barry Siegel, "Immigrants: Sizing Up the New Wave," *Los Angeles Times*, December 12, 1982, pp. 1 and 23. The Gallup Poll was done for *Newsweek* (with a plus or minus 3 percent margin of error) and reported by Tom Morganthau in "Closing the Door?," June 25, 1984, p. 21. My data were calculated from the unpublished INS tables for 1892–1932 and the *1979 Annual Report*, table 12. In addition, see Reimers, cited above, note 7, and Bryce-Laporte, below, note 14.

14. More Colombians came to the United States than Ecuadorans, but 9,000 more of the latter went to New York. The 23 peoples sampled were the principal groups arriving in and remaining in New York State during these years. They accounted for 76.5 percent of that total number (449,971 out of 588,480), 45.3 percent of all those entering via New York City, and 77.5 percent of all those giving the city as their destination upon arrival there (400,103 out of 516,490). In fact, 83 percent of the national total of the sample groups had come in through New York City. While they, therefore, represented the vast majority of New York entries, there were also sizable numbers of Barbadians, Pakistanis, Turks, Peruvians, and Grenadans, along with somewhat smaller groups of Canadians, Hungarians, Czechs, Spaniards, Rumanians, Japanese, Egyptians, Jordanians, Lebanese, and Yemenites. By the late 1970s, the Central Americans—Panamanians, Hondurans, Salvadorans, and Guatemalans in particular—were more visible. Africans made up no more than 2.5 percent of the total, aside from Egyptians; Ghanaians and Burundians were most numerous.

    What is so dramatic is that there was scarcely a sending country in the world that did not have at least a few arriving each year in New York City. One is reminded of Glen Hendricks' account of the first man from the village of Aldea, in the Dominican Republic, who came to the city in 1939 and brought his sister seven years after; she, in turn, initiated a tidal wave of emigrants: Hendricks, *Dominican Diaspora*, 24 and 73.

    For a relatively short but informative treatment of Central and South Americans, see Ann Orlov and Reed Ueda's "Central and South Americans," in Stephan Thernstrom and Ann Orlov, eds., *Harvard Enclyclopedia of American Ethnic Groups* (Cambridge, Mass., 1980). Also see Reed Ueda's essay "West Indians," Glen Hendricks' "Dominicans," and Michael Laguerre's "Hatians" in the same volume. A wide range of essays were collected by Bryce-Laporte and Delores M. Mortimer in *Caribbean Immigration to the United States*, RIIES Occasional Paper No. 1 [1976] (Washington: Research Institute on Immigration and Ethnic Studies, the Smithsonian, 1983). See, too, Reimers, *Still the Golden Door*, particularly ch. 5 on migration from the

Caribbean and South America, and Hendricks, *Dominican Diaspora*, 23, 25, 38-40, and 45. Hendricks stressed that the village he studied, Aldea, had become "an economic and social appendix of New York and vice versa." Many "have lived, are living, or hope in the near future to be living *alla*"—there, in New York City (p. 25). Going there, in fact, had become an "almost universal assumption among the children" (p. 38).

Bryce-Laporte wrote in 1979 that "New York remains the leading target and *entrepot* for Carribean peoples to the United States," notwithstanding the geographic and transportational advantages of Miami ("New York City," p. 215). Michael Laguerre, in documenting the successive waves of Haitians, quoted a study that found that 73 percent of all Caribbean migrants in the United States were residing in New York City: Laguerre, *American Odyssey: Haitians in New York City* (Ithaca, 1984), p. 25n. Laguerre adds that "almost every Haitian living in the United States has a relative or close friend in New York" (p. 31). He also emphasized the concept of a "migration ideology" operating there, and in many other places, whereby an individual perceives the possibility of attaining personal goals by moving. In the mid-1970s, when he was in Haiti, New York was a "very popular topic of conversation" in Port-au-Prince. Equally important, while the Duvaliers were still in power, migration was also "a symbolic form of resistance" (pp. 35 and 45), for an atmosphere existed there wherein "one need not be an overt opponent of . . . Duvalier" to be in danger. In 1980, concerning the returnees, a Haitian priest observed that "you never know if you're involved in Haitian politics or not"—until you step off the plane in Port-au-Prince. Quoted by Jerry Adler in "The New Immigrants," *Newsweek*, July 7, 1980, p. 31.

Among other studies providing related background information, see Hymie Rubenstein, "Return Migration to the English Speaking Caribbean. Review and Commentary," Stinner, et al., eds., *Return Migration and Remittances*, 14-16; Antonia Ugalde and Thomas Langham, "International Return Migration: Socio Demographic Determinants of Return Migration to the Dominican Republic," *ibid.*, 79, Guy Poitras, "Return Migration from the United States to Costa Rica and El Salvador," *ibid.*, 115; Kessner and Caroli, *Today's Immigrants*, 95-96 and 293; Franck Laraque, "Haitian Emigration to New York," *Migration Today*, September 1979, pp. 28-31 (noting $80 million in remittances in 1977 alone); James Allman, "Haitian Migration: 30 Years Assessed," *ibid.*, X, 1 (1982), 7-12, which describes Haitian migration to the United States as part of a larger, on-going process of out-migration; Dawn Marshall, "Emigration as an Aspect of the Barbadian Social Environment," *ibid.*, VIII, 4 (1980), 6-14, which noted, among other points, that more West Indians came here between 1961 and 1970 than between 1891 and 1950; Philip Kayal, "The Dominicans in New York-Part II," *ibid.*, 1978, pp. 10-15; and Robert L. Bach, "Caribbean Migration: Causes and Consequences," *ibid.*, X, 5 (1982), 7-13, for an excellent summary of causative factors behind migration. Bach stresses that "U.S. politicians and academicians may see silent invasions and surreptitious, underground floods, but the people in the Caribbean see it [migration] as a fact of life" (p. 10).

Other works of note are: Douglas S. Massey and Kathleen Schnabel, "Recent Trends in Hispanic Immigration to the United States," *International Migration Review* 17 (Summer 1983), 212-244; Fernando Urrea Giraldo, "Life Strategies and the Labor Market: Colombians in New York in the 1970s," *Migration Today*, X, 5 (1982), 28-32; Thomas Morrison and Richard Sinkin, "International Migration"; the special issue devoted to "Caribbean Migration to New York," *International Migration Review*, edited by Elsa M. Chaney and and Constance L. Sutton, 13 (Summer 1979); and Raymond Mohl, "Cubans in Miami: A Preliminary Bibliography," *Immigration History Newsletter* 16 (May 1984), 1-10, which has a useful introductory essay and cites many general works. Likewise, see his second piece there, "The New Haitian Immigration: A Preliminary Bibliography," *ibid.*, 17 (May 1985), 1-8.

Several related journalistic accounts are: Gary Hoenig, "The Poor and Hud-dled Now Come From South America," *New York Times*, August 18, 1974; Cowan, "For Hispanos It's Still the Promised Land," *New York Times Magazine*, June 22, 1975; and Bella Stimbo, "Haiti: Land of Poverty and Fear," *Los Angeles Times*, December 15, 1985, part of a three-segment in-depth study of contemporary Haiti just prior to the fall of Duvalier.

15. Reimers, *Still the Golden Door*, pp. 101, 114–116, and Maxine Fisher, *The Indians of New York City: A Study of Immigrants from India* (New Delhi, 1980), 11, 17-19. For a brief description of how Asian Indians perceive themselves here with respect to their professional backgrounds and minority status, see Robert J. Fornaro, "Asian Indians in Americas Acculturation and Minority Status," *Migration Today* XII, 3 (1984), 28–32. Regarding the Chinese in Manhattan, see see Glenn Fowler, "Planner, Citing Population Rise in Chinatown, Urges Help by City," *New York Times*, November 26, 1979, and "Chinese largest group in Lower Manhattan," *Asianweek*, December 9, 1982.

16. Inspector Tom Spellman, of the Chief Examiner's Office, INS New York District Office, confirmed this in a telephone interview, January 12, 1987.

17. In fact, during the 1970s the *number* of Italians, Greeks, and Yugoslavians going to New York City fell (and Russians, too, after a peak in 1976), while that of the Portuguese, Germans, and Poles remained relatively the same; only the British increased in 1978–1979. Moreover, significant downward fluctuations occurred among Koreans and Chinese in the mid-1970s and among Indians and Cubans in the late 1970s. Only Colombians, Jamaicans, and especially Dominicans recorded sizable increases during the eight years. For example, whereas almost 7,000 Dominicans were bound for New York City in 1972 (78 percent entering directly in New York), over 13,200 were heading there in 1978 and 11,900 in 1979 (with 93.3 percent now coming directly). Apparently, the 1976 legislative changes, extending the prefer-ence system and the 20,000 per country limits to the Western Hemisphere, worked to the benefit of those peoples who had been eagerly waiting to migrate. (Similarly, 7,125 Jamaicans went to the city in 1972 and 9,851 in 1979.) In addition, and rather curiously, more than 19,000 persons from the Caribbean and South America made their way into the United States by crossing the Canadian border into New York State (or by flying into Buffalo) during the eight years under review (based on figures for Jamaicans, Bardadians, Trinidadians, Dominicans, Haitians, Guyanese, Peru-vians, Colombians, and Ecuadorans).

With respect to arrivals and residence intentions, the unique pattern here can also be appreciated from the fact that in 11 of the 23 cases, a majority of those ad-mitted in New York City were planning to reside in the city. Six of them registered over 70 percent, with Dominicans (the leading group going to the city and the state) having 86 percent admitted and remaining in New York City. Seven of those eleven were Caribbean or South American, three Asian, and only one (mostly Jews from the Soviet Union) European. The lowest percentages arriving/remaining were uni-formly among the Europeans, including only 10 percent of the Portuguese and 15 percent of the Germans; in fact, only the Russians had a majority any longer going to New York City and that abruptly changed during the early 1980s. On the av-erage, about one-third of the Europeans stayed in New York City, whereas three-fourths of the West Indians processed were intending to remain there. For the census sources, see note 9, above. On Europeans, also see items cited in the same note. Regarding the shift to California, see table IMM5.3 in 1982–1984 *Statistical Year-books* and table 5 in the 1985 *Advance Report*.

A fascinating study of the impact of these immigration changes on the school population is Robert Scheer's "Bronx Revisited: Old Schools Survive and Thrive," *Los Angeles Times*, July 10, 1986, pp. 1+. Commenting on his old school, P.S. 96, he wrote that "The Jews and Italians together now make up less than 20% of en-rollment, whereas only ten years ago they numbered more than 90%, mostly Jewish."

Their place has been taken by blacks, Puerto Ricans, Yugoslavians, Cubans, Vietnamese, Afghans, and representatives from virtually every South American and Caribbean country. At least ten languages are used in informal cafeteria conversation along with English" (p. 18).

18. See INS, 1983 *Statistical Yearbook*, table IMM 3.1.

19. Derived from 1982, 1983, and 1984 *Statistical Yearbook*, tables IMM 2.6, IMM 3.1, IMM 5.3, and REF 4.1 on refugees, and INS computer tapes for 1982–1985.

20. See Maxine Fisher, *The Indians*, 17 and 96; Hendricks, *Dominican Diaspora*, 54–56; Elliott Barkan and Nikolai Khokhlov, "Socio-Economic Data as Indices of Naturalization Patterns in the United States: A Theory Revisited," Ethnicity 7 (1980), 159–180; Barkan and Robert O'Brien, Naturalization Trends Among Selected Asian Immigrants, 1950–1976," *Ethnic Forum* 4 (Spring 1984), 91–108; Barkan, "Whom Shall We Integrate? A Comparative Analysis of the Immigration and Naturalization Trends of Asians Before and After the 1965 Immigration Act (1951–1978)," *Journal of American Ethnic History* 3 (Fall 1983), 29–56.

21. The quotes are from Kessner and Caroli, *Today's Immigrants*, 112 and 202, respectively; and see p. 21 about the "tentative commitment to remain" that "many immigrants—both legal and illegal—come with . . ." For other motives, see *ibid.*, 252, 269, and 281; Maxine Fisher, *The Indians*, 96; Ueda, 1024–1025; and Nancy Foner, "Jamaicans in New York City," *Migration Today* (1984), 6–12.

22. Stinner, Albuquerque, and Bryce-Laport, *Return Migration and Remittances*, pp. xlvi, lv–lvi.

23. Cited by Antonia Ugalde and Tom Langham in *ibid.*, 73.

24. David Vidal's four part series was entitled: "Hispanic Newcomers in City Cling to Values of Homeland." New York Times, May 11, 1980; "Hispanic Residents Find Some Gains Amid Woes," May 12, 1980; "Study Shows Hispanic Residents in Favor of Bilingual Way of Life," May 13, 1980; and "For Hispanic Migrants 'Home' Is Elusive," May 14, 1980.

25. Quoted by Vidal, *New York Times*, May 11, 1980.

26. Quoted by Vidal, *New York Times*, May 14, 1980.

27. Hendricks, *Dominican Diaspora*, 54, 85–86, and 118.

28. Rubenstein, "Return Migration," 20, 22–23.

29. This was most recently done by Alejandro Portes and Rafael Mozo, "The Political Adaptation Process of Cubans and Other Ethnic Minorities in the United States: A Preliminary Analysis," *International Migration Review* 19 (Spring 1985), 35–63, particularly in tables 3a to 3c. See the tables on naturalization in my essay, "Whom Shall We Integrate?"

30. Data on non-immigrants are derived from table 17 in the *Annual Reports* of the INS. See, too, Hendricks, *Dominican Diaspora*, table on p. 154. Note that immigrants are registered only once upon formal admission to the United States and do not appear in immigration tables again when they return after a temporary departure.

31. The actual number of immigrants would probably be somewhat lower were we to drop the first half of F.Y. 1972 and add the first quarter of F.Y. 1980, and, given the rising volume of naturalizations, the number of new citizens would be slightly greater were the same adjustments made.

32. See Kessner and Caroli, *Today's Immigrants*, 21 and 25, and Hendrick's table in *Dominican Diaspora*, 153.

One recent story on the movement out of the city is by Elizabeth Kolbert, "More Asians, Seeking Strong Schools, Choose the Suburbs," *New York Times*, June 13, 1986. More importantly, in 1984 the Census Bureau reported in its estimate that "the number of legal residents who emigrate each year is more like 160,000, about 27,000 of whom are American born. The number would be even higher if Census could get a handle on the number of illegal aliens leaving the United States," *Newsweek*, June 25, 1984. This figure is also cited in the INS' *1987 Statistical Yearbook*, p. xxiii. Sometimes the emigration of such persons does attract attention, particularly when it involves politically sensitive matters. The decision of a large group of Soviet-born persons, including a number of Jews, to return to the Soviet Union in late 1986 was a good example of this. "50 Soviet Emigres Gather in New York to Return Home," *Los Angeles Times*, December 29, 1986, and the *Times'* editorial on the episode, "Freedom's Price," on January 2, 1987.

33. See tables IMM 5.3 and REF 4.1 in the 1982–1984 *Statistical Yearbooks* as well as table 5 in the *Advance Report* for 1985.

34. U.S. Department of Commerce, Bureau of the Census, *1980 Census of Population: Ancestry of the Population by State: 1980. Supplementary Report PC80-S1–10* (Washington, 1983), table 3, pp. 25 and 31. Gurek and Kritz cite a 1980 study that found 119,965 Dominicans and 42,986 Colombians among those 462,000 "Other Hispanics" (p. 59). Note also, the percentages given on the city in *Migration Today* 12 (1984), 1. Dominicans were 8.5 percent of Hispanics, Cubans 4.3 percent, Colombians 3.1 percent, and Puerto Ricans 61.2 percent.

35. Barry Levine, "The Puerto Rican Circuit," 173–174. For a good short statement describing the split sentiments among Jamaicans, see Nancy Foner, "Jamaicans in New York City," 11-12.

36. See Elliott Barkan, "Proximity and Commuting Immigration: An Hypothesis Explored via the Bi-Polar Ethnic Communities of the French Canadian and Mexican Americans," Jack Kinton, ed., in *American Ethnic Revival* (Aurora, Ill., Social Science and Sociological Resources, 1977), 163–183. The prior study was broader: Barkan, "Commuting 'Immigrants': Puerto Ricans, Mexicans, Amerindians, and French Canadians in the United States During the Past Century" (paper presented at the Organization of American Historians Meeting, Denver, April 1974).

37. Higham, quoted by Barry Siegel, *Los Angeles Times*, December 12, 1982, pt. 1, p. 25; and Kessner and Caroli, Today's Immigrants, 29.

Contributors

ELLIOTT R. BARKAN is Professor of History, California State University, San Bernardino.

SELMA BERROL is Professor of History, Baruch College, City University of New York.

MARY ELIZABETH BROWN is Adjunct Professor of History, Kutztown University, Pennsylvania.

JAMES H. DORMON is Professor of History and American Studies at the University of Southwestern Louisiana.

ANTHONY GRONOWICZ is Assistant Professor of History, Pennsylvania State University, Hazelton Campus.

MICHAEL LAPP is a Doctoral Candidate in History at the Johns Hopkins University.

DAVID MAUK is a Doctoral Candidate in American Civilization at New York University.

RANDALL M. MILLER is Professor of History at St. Joseph's University.

STANLEY NADEL is Assistant Professor of History, Austin Peay State University.

WILLIAM PENCAK is Associate Professor of History, the Pennsylvania State University, Ogontz.

DAVID M. REIMERS is Professor of History, New York University.

LEONARD R. RIFORGIATO is Associate Professor of History, the Pennsylvania State University, Shenango Valley.

ANDREW P. YOX is Assistant Professor of History, University of Texas/Pan American.

Index

Abolitionists, 42, 71
Abramovich, Max, 155
Addams, Jane, 117
Adler, Jacob, 155, 169n26
Afgans, 185-86
Africa, 234
Agricultural workers, 110, 203-4, 211
Albany Regency, 31
Albuquerque, Klaus de, 227
Aleichem, Sholom, 154
American Celt, 42, 44-45
American Federation of Labor, 77
Americanization: and ethnicity, 166, 169n30; movement, 131-36, 145. *See also* Assimilation
American National Reform Association, 62
American Republican Party, 8, 10
American Socialist Party, 201
Amerikanische Arbeiterbund (American Workers' League), 73-76
Annals of the New York Stage (Odell), 150
Anti-Semitism, 84
Apollo Hall, 15, 25n52
Arbeiterbund (Workers' League), 68-69, 72-73
Arbeiter Zeitung, 142
Archdeacon, Thomas, 218
Arrighi, Antonio, 122n16
Artisans, 9, 15, 28, 36, 90; German, 56-80
Asians, *xiv*, 180, 182-83, 188-91, 193, 197nn, 216, 217, 221, 222, 224, 234, 237n8
Assimilation, *xiv*, 4, 5, 85; and benign stereotypes, 84; and bipolarism, 234-35; by Irish, 28, 30, 37, 39, 49, 52-53; and Italian Catholic church, 120; by Puerto Ricans, 205-6, 211; and remigration, 178
Astoria, 183
Aurora, 130, 133, 136, 142

Babeuf, 60, 62, 66
Bach, Robert L., 239n14
Baden Legion, 69
Badillo, Herman, 210, 214n59
Bahamians, 222

Baltimore Council, 31
Barat settlement house, 115, 116, 120
Barkan, Elliott, 178, 197n68, 215-42
Barth, Frederick, 149
Bauer, Henrich, 60
Bayes, Nora, 170n35
Bayley, Bishop James Roosevelt, 50-51
Bean, Frank, 229
Befreiungsbund (Liberation League), 63
Bell, Daniel, 198
Belletristisches Journal, 72
Bernard, Sam, 166
Bernstein, Iver, 24n40
Bernstein, Michael A., 24n40
Berrol, Selma, 83-85
Besser, Ernst, 128
Bethelship Norwegian Methodist Church, 90
Beyond the Melting Pot (Moynihan and Glazer), 179
Big Winner, The (Gordin), 154
Billings, John S., 105n8
Blacks, 22n15, 167, 176, 179, 180, 181, 183, 187, 191, 192, 193, 210
Blanc, Louis, 59, 66, 70
Blanqui, August, 60
Blumin, Stuart, 21n11
Bookman, The, 151-52
Boston *Pilot*, 42, 44, 48
Boundary markers, 149, 165-66, 167n3, 171n78
Bouvier, Leon, 219-21
Boys clubs, 111-14
Brandt, Dorothy Chin, 193
Breckinridge, Rev. John, 32
Bridges, Amy, 22n21
Brighton Beach, 185
Brill, Friedrich, 137, 138, 139
British, 221, 232, 240n17
Bronx, 110, 176, 183, 186, 204
Bronx Science high school, 189
Brooklyn, 35, 83, 110, 180, 182, 183, 185, 187, 188; Norwegians in, 86-108
Brown, Mary Elizabeth, 83, 84, 109-25

Brownson, Orestes, 37, 38, 43
Bryce, James, 19
Bryce-Laporte, Roy, 218, 227, 237n8, 239n14
Buck, George, 138, 139, 140, 142
Budget, 161
Buffalo, *xiii*, 4; Catholic Church, 27, 31;
    Colonization Convention (1856), 42,
    44–54; German Americans, 126–47; Irish,
    35–37;
Buffalo Academy of Medicine, 141
Buffalo *Catholic Sentinel*, 48
Buffalo, *Commercial Advertiser*, 43
Buffalo *Courier*, 135, 138
Buffalo *Express*, 132, 135, 138
Buffalo Medical College, 31
Buffalo News, 129, 132, 134, 135, 137, 138
Buffalo *Times*, 139
Buffalo und Sein Deutschtum, 128
Buonarroti, 66
Burkhardt, Karl H., 141, 143, 145
Businessmen, 9, 10, 17, 28, 30, 75, 189;
    Indian, 190–91, 222; Korean, 190;
    Norwegian, 88, 91, 108n26
Business and Slavery (Foner), 24n35
Butler, Edward H., 132
Butt-End Coon Hunters, 9, 14
Butterfield, Fox, 197n66

Cabet, Etienne, 59, 65, 66
California, 176, 185, 219, 224, 233, 240n17
Calvin, Alva Fedde, 106n12
Cambodians, 191–92
Canada, 47, 48, 183, 240n17
Cantor, Eddie, 167, 170n35
Capitalists, 21n11, 22n19, 23–24n31
Caribbean immigrants, 175, 176, 180–83,
    186–88, 192–93, 195n10, 196n37, 216–18,
    221–22, 224, 227, 228, 234, 237n8, 239n14,
    240n17
Caroli, Betty Boyd, 235, 235n1
Carr, Thomas, 13–14
Carroll, Bishop John, 39
Carroll Hall, 33
Carter, Leslie, 170n35
Castle Garden, 215, 216, 236n4
Catholic Charities, 121, 206
Catholic Church, 3, 5, 8, 84; and Germans,
    130, 133, 138; and Irish, 4, 27–55; and
    Italians, 109–25
Catholic Emigration Society of Ireland, 41
Census, 95–96, 108n35, 110, 145–46n5, 176,
    184, 186, 188, 199; of ancestry, 234; gaps,
    229–32, 237n8
Central Americans, 181, 187, 224, 233, 237n8,
    238n14

Central Schuetzen Verein of Sharpshooters,
    142
Chain migration, 178, 222
Chaney, Dr. Elsa, 228
Chants Democratic (Wilentz), 56, 70
Chen, David S., 196n41
Chicago, 127, 139
Children of Mary, 114–15
Chi Luu, 192
Chinese, 180, 182, 188–89, 190, 191, 192, 194,
    196n41, 197n71, 219, 222, 224, 232, 240nn
Chinese Exclusion Acts, 182
Chisholm, Shirley, 193
Christian: socialists, 65; symbols, 147n36
Church of the Nativity, 115–16
Church property bill, 32
Ciambelli, Benniemino, 152
"Circolo Filodrammatico Italo-Americano,"
    151, 168n13
Citizenship (naturalization), 178, 182, 193,
    197n68, 199, 227, 228, 241n29
City Reform Club, 25n52
Civic officials, 9, 21n10, 22n13, 25n56, 26n69;
    elected, 13, 18, 193
Civil liberties groups, 185
Civil rights, 183, 209, 210
Civil service exams, 203
Clay, Henry, 10, 13, 15
Cleveland, Grover, 8, 17
Cleveland clubs, 17, 25n52
Colombians, 181, 186–87, 222, 224, 228, 229,
    238n14, 240n17
Commedia dell'arte, 151
Committee of 53 on City Reform, 25n52
Committee of One Hundred, 132
Committee of Seventy, 17
Committee on Americanization, 132
Communia, Iowa, colony, 68–69
Communist League, 60
Communist Manifesto (Marx), 60
Communists, 60–63, 64–66, 75
Community: boards, 193; organizers, 209
"Compagnia Comico-Drammatica Italiana,"
    151, 152
"Compagnia Napoletana, La," 151
Concerned Citizens of Queens, 193
Condition of the Working Class in England
    (Engles), 61
Congedo, Guiseppe M., 118
Connecticut, 237n9
Conried, Heinrich, 150
Constitution Day, 92, 106n16
Conzen, Kathleen Neils, 108n26
Cooke, Walter P., 132
Cooperative workshops, 64–68

Corriere Italiano, 134
Corrigan, Archbishop Michael Augustine, 111, 113
Council of Sachems, 8
County Democracy, 15, 17, 25*n*52
Cubans, 185, 186, 219, 222, 232, 237*n*8

Daily Plebeian, 10, 11, 13–15, 20*nn*
Danforth, Brian, 24*n*35
Davis, Hartley, 165
Day-care nurseries, 112, 115, 117–18, 119, 120, 124*nn*
"Decline of Protestantism and Its Causes, The" (Hughes), 33
Debs, Eugene, 134, 139
De Lancey, William, 30–31
Dell, Robert, 156, 157
Democratic (Democracy) Party, 4, 5, 15, 25*n*52, 33, 35, 61, 71, 94; Corresponding Committee, 11; decline of labor within, 7–26; General Committee, 8–9, 10, 25*n*52; sub-organizations of, 23*n*27; ward committees, 9–10, 18, 20–21*nn*, 22*nn*, 24*n*44
Democratic-Republican Party, 8
Democratic Review, 24*n*44
Demokrat, 142
Denison, T. S., 170*n*35
Depression: of 1837, 39, 40–41; of 1850s, 76; Great, 180, 199
Deutscher Arbeiter Verein (German Workers Union), 63, 74
Deutscher Humoristen club, 142
Deutsche Volksverein, 60, 61, 62
Deuther, Charles G., 54*n*54
DeWitt, Clinton, 13
Die Aströa, 66
Dilerenso, Giovanni, 135–36
Dinkins, David N., 193
Discrimination, 183; vs. Asians, 180, 182; vs. Catholics, 32, 33, 37, 42; vs. Germans, 135–36, 140–41; vs. Italians, 110; vs. Irish, 37, 43; racial, 12, 187, 188, 192, 200, 202, 207–8
Divine, Robert, 195*n*14
Dobrowski, Michael N., 171*n*67
Dockhorn, Robert, 21*n*11
Dolan, Jay P., 121
Dominguez, Virginia, 195*n*10
Dominicans, 181, 186–87, 190, 195*n*10, 217, 219, 222, 224, 227–28, 229, 237*n*8, 238*n*14, 240*n*17
Dorman, James, 83–84, 148–71
"Draft Riots of 1863 and the Industrial Revolution in New York, The" (Bernstein), 24*n*40
Dubois, Bishop John, 29, 38

Dutch, 179
Dutch Act, 156–57, 170*n*38
Duvalier regime, 181, 187, 239*n*14

Eastern Europeans, *xiii,* 4, 83, 135, 154, 160, 183, 217, 221
East Harlem, 118, 119, 204
Eccleston, Archbishop Samuel, 37
Echo, 133, 141, 142
Eckert, Mendel, 135
"Economic Exchange-Association," 67
Ecuadorans, 222, 224, 229, 238*n*14
Education, 187–93, 197*n*66, 206, 208, 210
Efrahem, 59
Egyptians, 191
Elections, 9, 10–15, 20*n*9, 209, *See also* Voting
Elective Governor Act (1947), 199
Elites, 40, 88, 91, 97, 108*n*32, 189; government, 198–99
Ellis Island, 215, 216, 236*n*4
Emerson, School Superintendent, 141
Emigrante Puertorriqueno, EL (Nieves Falcon), 204
Emigrant Industrial Savings Bank, 41
Emigration from Russia (play), 155
Emmaus Lutheran Church, 130
Employment, 193–94; of Asians, 189–91, 192; of Middle Easterners, 191; of Puerto Ricans, 202–5, 207–8; of Third World immigrants, 187, 188, 192, *See also* Occupations; Unemployment
Empire Club, 12
Engles, Friedrich, 61
Episcopalians, 29, 30–31
Ernst, Robert, 77*n*3
Estades, Rosa, 210
Ethiopians, 191
Ethnicity: affirmation of, *xiv;* and bi-polarism, 234–35; and Democracy party, 10, 22*n*17, 25–26*nn;* hidden 132–33; maintenance of, 178–80
Ethnic stereotypes, 149, 156–67, 171*nn;* benign, 84, 166
Ethnic theater, 148–55, 167
Ethnic Theatre in the United States (Seller), 148–49
Europeans, 237*n*8
Evangelical Churches, 130, 138
Evangelium der armen Sünder (Weitling), 65
Evans, George Henry, 61
Family unification, 183
"Farfariello," 151, 158
Farley, John Cardinal, 111, 116
Fearnot Club, 9
Fedde, Gabriel, 92, 106*n*12, *n*16

Federalists, *xiv*, 8
Fields, Lew, 156–57, 166
Filipinos, 182, 190, 191, 219, 221, 224
Fillmore, Millard, 31, 42, 43
Filodrammatica Italiana di New York, 151
Fiske, Jim, 16
Five Points, 24*n*37
Florida, 176, 185, 187
Flushing, 188
Folkestad, Sigurd, 91, 93, 99, 107*n*19
Foner, Philip, 24*n*35
Ford Foundation, 206
Fordham University, 114
Försch, Dr., 74
Fourier, 60, 64
Franklin, Benjamin, 66
Freeman's Journal, The, 40, 41, 48
Freethinkers' Society, 74, 75
Freiheit lodges, 142
French Canadians, 232
French Huguenots, 179
French Revolution, 58, 59, 60, 70, 75
Fuhrmann, Louis, 128, 133–34, 137–38, 140

Gaertner, Wilhelm, 129, 132, 135, 144
Gallitzen, Demetrius Augustus, 39
Gallup Poll, 221, 238*n*13
Garment industry, 67, 84, 187, 192, 203
George, Henry, 17
Gerena Valentin, Gilberto, 210
German-American Bund, 126, 127, 129, 132–34, 137, 140, 142–43
German-American Plot, The (Wile), 135
German Central Verein, 133
German Conspiracies in America (Skaggs), 135
German Day celebrations, 129–30, 133, 135, 136
German Hospital (Buffalo), 132
Germania Theater, 150
German Revolutions of 1848, 63, 69
Germans, *xiv*, 3, 5, 179, 182, 232, 234, 240*n*17; in Buffalo, 36, 83, 84–85; Catholics, 31, 34, 35; demise of culture, in Buffalo, 126–47; and Democratic party, 8, 10, 11, 15, 16, 18, 22–23*nn*, 25*n*64; and ethnic theater, 149, 150–51, 168*n*7; and labor radicalism, 56–80; in mainstream theater, 156–57; and political culture, 3, 4
Gerter, David A., 171*n*66
Geschichte der Deutschen in Buffalo and Erie County (1898), 128
Giocometti, Paolo, 151
Girls, Italian, 111, 114–15
Gjerdrum, Jørgen, 87–88
Glazer, Nathan, 179
Goethe, 150

Goldfadn, Avram, 153, 171*n*80
Gompers, Samuel, 77
Gordin, Jacob, 154, 169*n*26
Gould, Jay, 16
Grant, Ulysses S., 16
Greeks, 183, 224, 227, 232, 234, 240*n*17
Greeley, Andrew, 53, 54
Greeley, Horace, 13, 68
Greene, Finley H., 132
Greenhorns, The (Lateiner and Mogulesko), 155
Green Shoemaker, The (Abramovich), 155
Greenwich Village, 119
Griffen, Clyde, 21*n*11
Gringnon, 59, 63
Gronowicz, Anthony, 3–4, 7–26
Grün, Karl, 70
Guatemalans, 186, 187
Gurney, Marian, 123*n*39, 124–25*n*61
Guyanese, 222, 224, 229

Haas, Frederich, 133
Haitians, 181–82, 185–88, 192–93, 195*n*11, 196*n*38, 222, 224, 229, 239*n*14
Handlin, Oscar, 221
Hansen, Earl Parker, 213*n*41
Hapgood, Hutchins, 151–54, 168*n*17, 169*n*26
Hard to Be A Jew (Gordin), 154
Harlem, 180
Harrigan, Edward, 157–58
Hart, Tony, 157–58
Harugari lodges, 142
Hawgood, John, 131
Hayes, Patrick Cardinal, 111
Hays, Samuel P., 26*n*72
Hecker, Rev. Isaac, 37
Heisler, Martin, 142
Hendricks, Glen, 195*n*10, 227, 228, 235*n*1, 238–39*n*14
Hendricks clubs, 17, 25*n*52
Hershberg, Theodore, 21*n*11
Herwegh's Legion, 69
Hexamer, Charles, 143
Hibernians, 134
Higham, John, 235
Hispanics, *xiv*, 176, 181, 186–87, 192, 193, 196*n*31, 218, 228, 234
Hitzel, Gustav, 132–33, 134, 135, 136, 137, 143
Homestead Law, 61
Hondurans, 186, 216
Housing crisis, 209
Howe, Irving, 162
Hughes, Archbishop John, 4, 27–30, 32–34, 40–45, 48, 50–54, 55*n*65
Hughes, Patrick, 29
Hurwitz, Moshe, 154

Ibsen, 154, 169*n*26
"Immigrant church," 121
Immigrant/ethnic theatre, 83–84, 148–71
Immigration: changing patterns, 216–25, 233; early twentieth-century, 83–85; lure of NY city and, 215–42; old, 3–5; post-WW II, 175–78; rank order of recent, 224; Third World, 179–97
Immigration and Naturalization Service (INS), 183–88, 192–94, 216, 233
Immigration Commission of 1911, 97
Immigration laws, 178, 180–83, 187–89, 191, 196*n*37, 216–17, 222, 236*n*7
Indians (Asian), 180, 182, 190–92, 219, 222, 227, 233, 240*nn*
Indians (North American), 33, 218
Indochinese, 185, 191–92
Industrial Congress, 67
Industrialization, 11, 18, 199
Industry, decline of, 175, 176
Investigation, The (Harrigan), 158
Involuntary exiles, 30, 35
Iranians, 185, 191
Iraquis, 224
Irish, *xiii, xiv*, 3, 5, 67, 84, 132, 134, 138, 167*n*4, 179, 234; colonization, 27–55; and Democratic party, 8, 10, 11, 12, 15, 16, 18, 22–23*nn*, 25*n*64, 33, 35; and Italian "problem," 110–11; political machine, 3–4, 36
Irish Emigrant Associations, 40
Irish Emigration Society, 40–41
Irish Immigrant Aid Society Convention of 1856, 44–54
Irving Hall, 15, 25*n*52
Irving Place Theater, 150
Isolationism, 134
Israelis, 191, 227
Italian Padrone, The (play), 157
Italians, *xiv*, 84, 122*n*5, 127, 134, 138, 179, 234; and ethnic theater, 149, 150–51; and Irish, 83; immigration after 1965, 183, 195*n*15, 224, 227, 232, 240*n*17; in mainstream theater, 157–60, 171*n*79; Northern, 117; youth during Progressive era, 109–25
Italians in Chicago, 1880–1930 (Nelli), 122*n*5

Jackson, Andrew, 13, 19, 26*n*71
Jacobins, 58, 75
Jacobson, Charlotte, 106*n*12
"Jahn, Father," 69
Jamaicans, 187, 217, 219, 222, 224, 227, 229, 240*n*17
Japanese, 180
Jefferson, Thomas, 8, 66
Jennings, James, 206, 210

Jesuits, 112–13, 114, 116, 120
Jewish King Lear, The (Gordin), 154
Jewish Priest, The (Gordin), 154
Jews, 179, 192; and ethnic theater, 149, 152–55, 157; German, 84; in mainstream theater, 160–65; Russian, 84, 127; Shylock stereotype, 171*nn*; Soviet, 185, 216, 224, 233, 234, 240*n*17, 242*n*32
Johnson, Christopher, 59
Johnson, Lyndon, 183
Jolson, Al, 167, 170*n*35
Jones Act (1917), 181

Kahler, Friedrich, 129, 137, 147*n*36
Kalisch, Bertha, 155
Kapor, Bawnesh, 191
Kapor, Suesh, 191
Katz, Michael, 21*n*11
Kazer, Arthur, 159
Kennedy, John F., 182
Kenrick, Bishop Francis P., 33
Kessler, David, 155
Kessner, Thomas, 106*n*8, 235, 235*n*1
Kier, A. N., 88
Kim, Illsoo, 189–90, 197*n*47
Kindergartens, 112, 115
King Bill (1918), 142–43
Kinkel, 66
Kirwin, Rev. Dean, 44–46, 48, 52
Knoll, Tricia, 218
Know-Nothings, 32, 36, 37, 42–43, 48, 53
Koch, Edward, 184, 194
Kommunisten Klub, 75
Komp, Albert, 75
Koreans, 182, 189–92, 197*n*47, 219, 224, 232, 240*n*17
Korean Produce Association, 190
Kotzebue, 150
Kriege, Hermann, 61–62, 63, 76

Labor Advisory Committee on Puerto Rican Affairs, 206
Laborers, 30, 57; low-cost, 193–94
Labor market, 197*n*70, 201
Labor movement, 4; decline of, in Democratic Party, 7–26; radicalism, German artisans and, 56–80
Lamennais, 60, 65, 66
Land reform, 61
Lang family, 128
Language, 188, 189, 206, 208, 209; bilingualism, 129–30, 194, 210; German, 130, 140–41, 156
Languerre, Michael, 195*n*11, 196*n*38, 239*n*14
Lapp, Michael, 177, 198–214
Lateiner, Joseph, 154, 155

Latin Americans, 221, 229, 234
League of Exiles, 60, 75
League of the Just, 60, 61
Lebanese, 191
Leif Erikson Day parade, 92
Lessing, 150
Levine, Barry, 234
Liberty Loan program, 137, 138, 143
Lievre, Eugen, 63
Lifson, David, 152, 153
Little India, 191
Little Italy, 188
Literacy, 97
Loras, Bishop Jean Mathias Pierre, 41, 42, 45, 48, 50, 52, 55n65
Lord, Rev. John C., 31
Loreto Club, 113
Loretto, Pennsylvania, colony, 39
Los Angeles, 176, 183, 224
Lower East Side, 112-13, 117, 118, 153, 188, 204
Lutherans, 34, 86, 89, 91, 99, 106n12, 130, 137

McCarran-Walter Immigration Act (1952), 181, 183
McCloskey, John Cardinal, 111
McCormick, Richard L., 20n1
McGee, Thomas D'Arcy, 43-45, 49, 50-53
McNally, William, 170n35
Madison, James, xiv
Madison, James (comedy author), 170n35
Madison's Budget, 156, 170n35
Madonna House, 117
Maguire, James, 75
Majori, Antonio, 152
Manhattan, 110, 176, 181, 183, 186, 187, 191; Norwegians, 86-89, 90, 99, 105n3
Mann, Evelyn, 184
Manufacturing, 12, 207
Marcos, Ferdinand, 190
Marshall, Dawn, 239n14
Marx, Karl, 20n7, 60, 65, 66, 70, 72, 74
Marxism, 69, 72-73, 74, 75, 76
Maryland, 34, 39
Mayor's Committee on Puerto Rican Affairs, 206
Mayor's Committee on the Exploitation of Workers, 206
Mauk, David C., 83, 84, 86-108
Meehan, Thomas, 112
Merchants, 12, 24n35
Methodist Bethelship mission, 88
Metropolitan, The, 50
Mexican American war, 62
Mexicans, 190, 196n37, 216, 219, 221, 227
Mezzogiorno region, 110-11, 117
Miami, 176, 185

Middle class, 84, 86, 149, 166, 182, 187, 189-90; flight, 176-77; values, 205, 211
Middle East, 216, 222, 224, 233, 234
Midwest, 205
Migration: "ideology," 239n14; of Puerto Ricans to NY, 198-214
Migration Division of the Department of Labor of Puerto Rico, 201, 202-12, 214n59
Miller, Kerby, 28, 30
Miller, Randall M., 175-78
Milwaukee, 127, 139
Minna (Gordin), 154, 169n26
Mogulesko, Sigmund, 155
Moll, Karl Joseph, 60
Monroe, NY, summer camp, 115, 116
Monserrat, Joseph, 201, 204, 205, 206, 210, 211
Moore, Ely, 10, 22n18
Moore, Joan, 218
Moscoso, Teodoro, 200, 201
Moynihan, Daniel, 179
Mueller, Rev. Edwin, 130
Müller, Father, 67
Municipal Reform Committee, 25n52
Munoz Marin, Luis, 199, 207
Mystères de Paris (Sue), 61
Mysteries of Mulberry Street, The (Ciambelli), 152
Mysteries of New York, The, 155

Nadel, Stanley, 3, 4, 56-80
Nadir, Mosche, 153
Nation, The, 44
National Bank, 14
National parishes, 111, 121
National Reform Association, 61
National Security League, 141
Native American Movement, 3. See also Know Nothings
Native-born Americans, 36, 43, 57, 77n2
Nativists, 4, 10, 36-40, 42-43, 53, 83, 84, 128, 131
Nazis, 147n66
Nelli, Humbert, 122n5
Neo-minstrel roles, 167
Neue Rheinische Zeitung, 66
Neue Stadttheater, 150
New Jersey, 185, 229, 237n9
New Progressive Party of Puerto Rico, 211
Newspapers: ethnic, 20n3, 141-42, 145, 194, 197n71; party, 11
Newton, Harry, 158
New Urban Immigrants (Kim), 197n47
New York City: Board of Education, 206, 211; Common Council, 9, 14; Irish in, vs. Buffalo, 35-37; mayoral elections, 9, 10-11, 17; populated by immigrants, xiii, 3; as

"portal of portals," 215–42; post-WW II, 175–78; Puerto Rican migrations to, 198–214; Third World immigration to, 179–97, 218; Welfare Department, 206

New York City Baptist Mission Society, 112

New York City Mission and Tract Society, 112

New Yorker Staats-Zeitung, 60–61, 62, 63, 65–69, 71, 72, 74, 79n69

New York *Herald*, 67–68

New York Jewish Repertory Company, 166

New York State: immigrants remaining in, *xiii*, 216, 218–19; legislature, 9

New York Taxi Drivers Institute, 191

New York *Telegraph*, 160

New York *Times*, 51, 72, 228

New York *Tribune*, 68

New York Workingmen's Alliance, 20n7

Nicaraguans, 185, 186, 187

Nieves Falcon, Luis, 203–4

Nordiske Blade, 87, 91–93, 107n19

Nordiske Tildende (*NT*), 91–93, 95, 96, 97, 99, 106nn, 107nn

Nordmandenes Sangforening, 87

North, David, 221

"Northern Labor Finds A Southern Champion" (Bernstein) 24

Norwegian-American Historical Association Archives, 106n12

Norwegian-American Seamen's Association, 90–91

Norwegian Lutheran Deaconesses' Home and Hospital, 89, 97

Norwegian Lutheran Synod, 89, 106n16

Norwegian National League, 94

Norwegian Relief Society, 89

Norwegians, *xiv*, 83, 84, 86–108

Norwegian Singing Society, 91, 92, 106n12

Norwegian Society, 87, 88, 90, 91, 92, 106n16

Norwegian Trinity Lutheran Church, 91, 92, 106n16

Occupations: of Hispanics, 187; of Norwegians, 100–4, 107–8nn; and politics, 21n12. *See also* Employment

O'Connell, Daniel, 41

O'Connor, Michael, 45, 50

Odell, 150, 152, 155

Old German Society, 142

Old Stock Americans, 10, 11, 18, 22–23nn, 25n64

Olsen, Ingolf, 106n12

Operation Bootstrap, 199–200, 207, 210, 213n41

Order, Capt. John, 14

O'Reilly, Rev. Bernard, 31

O'Sullivan, John, 24n44

Our Lady of Loreto mission, 113–17, 123n22, 124n56

Our Lady of Mount Carmel parish, 118, 120

Our Savior's Norwegian Lutheran Church, 87, 88, 90, 91, 106nn

Owen, 64, 66

Paine, Thomas, 66

Pakistanis, 190, 191

Palestinians, 191

Panic: of 1837, 40; of 1854–55, 75, 76; of 1857, 75, 76; of 1873, 16

Pan-Scandinavian institutions, 87, 105n3

Parochial schools, 31, 33, 113, 114, 119, 120–21

Parole power, 182

Partisan Society of the Rights of Man, 59

Passel, Jeffrey, 229

Passeri, Ruggero, 119

Pastor, Tony, 161

Patterns of Political Participation of Puerto Ricans in New York City (Estades), 210

Peck, 227

Pencak, William, *xiii-xiv*, 3–5

Pennsylvania, 34, 237n9

People's Theater, 153

Peruvians, 227

Pico, Rafael, 200, 201

Pinero, Jesus T., 200

Pius X, Pope, 114

Plunkitt, Boss, 19

Poles, 127, 132, 135, 138, 185, 232, 234, 240n17

Polish Boy, The (play), 155

Political: clubs, 94; events, 21nn, 23n25, 25nn; exiles, 182; machine, 4; organizations, hierarchy of, 20–22nn, 25–26nn

Politics: Catholics and, 32–34; Irish and, 36, 53; Norwegians and, 107n20; Puerto Ricans and, 206, 209–11, 214n59; Third World immigrants and, 193, 194, 228

Polk, James K., 10, 14, 15

Popular Democratic Party of Puerto Rico (PPD), 198, 200–1, 207, 211, 212n8

Population: classification of 1844, 21n; German, 77nn, 127–28, 132, 145–46n5; Norwegian, 95–96, 105nn, 107n24; recent data, 178; Puerto Rican, in NY, 199, 205; Third World immigrants, 184, 188, 196nn. *See also* Census

Population Office of New York City Planning Department, 184

Portuguese, 227, 240n17

Poverty: Chinese, 189; Haitian, 187–88; Hispanic, 187; Irish, 35–36, 38, 40, 47, 49;

Italian, 110, 118–19; Norwegian, 88–90, 92–93; post-WW II, 177; Puerto Rican, 198–99, 206–7, 214n52
Power, Rev. John, 40
Preference system, 183
Preparedness Parade committees, 132
Professionals, 9, 10, 17, 21n11, 25n63, 28, 30, 36, 96, 108n26, 182, 187, 189, 190, 192, 194, 222; women, 97
Progressive Era, 109–25
Progressives, 3, 19, 110
Prohibition, 143–44
Proletarierbund, 72
Protestant, The, 32
Protestants, 8; and Germans, 135; and Irish Catholics, 30–34, 38, 40, 45; and Italian Catholics, 112, 118–19, 122n16
Proudhon, Pierre-Joseph, 59, 64, 65, 66
Public policy, 177–78
Public schools, 4, 31, 32–33, 113, 114, 128–29, 140–41, 188–89, 192, 206, 240–41n17
Public School Society of New York, 32–33
Puerto Rican Bureau of Employment Security, 203
Puerto Rican Community Development Project, 210
Puerto Rican Department of Labor, 201, 203
Puerto Rican Legal Defense and Education Fund, 203–4
Puerto Rican Development Company, 200–1
Puerto Rican Economic Development Administration, 201
Puerto Rican Emigration Advisory Committee, 200–1
Puerto Rican Planning Board, 201
Puerto Rican Politics in New York City (Jennings), 206
Puerto Ricans, xiii n, 176–78, 181, 186, 193, 196n31, 218, 236n8; and ethnicity, 179, 234; migration, to NY, 198–214
Puerto Rico, University of, Social Science Research Center, 201
Purcell, Bishop John, 38
Putting-out system, 67

Queens, 110, 181, 183, 186, 187, 188, 190, 193
Quota restrictions, 180–83, 187, 196n37, 216–17
Quinn, Daniel J., 116, 123n34

Rabinovitch, Solomon, 154
Race. See Discrimination, racial
"Racial comic," 169n33
Radicalism, 3, 4, 5, 56–80
Ramos Antonini, Ernesto, 207
Rankin, Jeannette, 138

Rapone, Pasquale, 152
Red Hook-Gowanus district, 89
"Reflections and Suggestions on what is called the Catholic Press in the United States" (Hughes), 50
Reformed Churches, 130
Reformists, 10, 18
Reform schools, 32, 35
Refugee Act (1980), 185, 218, 236n7
Refugees, 182–88, 195–97n24; Indochinese, 192, 219, 233
Reimers, David M., 179–97, 217, 218, 236n7, 238–39n14
Remigration, 177, 178, 183, 186, 192, 208–9, 218, 227–32, 234, 236n8
Republicans, 4, 8, 16, 17, 71, 94
Republik der Arbeiter, Die (The Workers Republic), 64, 68, 74
Revolution, die, 72
Reynolds, Abe, 165
Richmond, Dean, 31
Richter, Erhard, 63, 74
Ridder, Herman, 134
Riforgiato, Leonard, 3, 4, 27–55
Rigau, Marco, 211
Rincon de Gautier, Felisa, 207
Robespierre, 60
Romano, Aloysius, 113
Roosevelt, Theodore, 16, 19, 26n71
Rosenfeld, Lulla, 155
Rose, Julian, 165, 166
Rossi, Louise, 114
Rubenstein, Hymie, 228
Russians. See Jews, Soviet
Russo, Nicholas, 112–14, 116, 117, 120
Rygg, A. N., 106n10
Rynders, Capt. Isaiah, 12

Sacred Hearts of Jesus and Mary, 118
Sacred Heart School (Buffalo), 31
St. Aloysius Club, 113–14
St. Ann's parish, 118
St. Anthony of Padua parish, 111, 117–19
St. Francis Xavier Preparatory School, 114
St. Joachim's parish, 117
St. Joseph's Cathedral (Buffalo), 32
St. Joseph's parish, 117
St. Joseph's Summer Institute, 118
St. Louis Church (Buffalo), 32
St. Lucy's parish, 118
St. Patrick's Cathedral, 34
St. Patrick's Old Cathedral, 115
St. Sebastian's, 119
Saint-Simon, 60
St. Stanislaus Club, 114
Salesians, 118

Salvadorans, 185, 186, 187, 188
Salvation Army, 94
Sans culottes, 58, 60
Sargent, Epes, 160-61
Sartz, R. S. N., 89-90
Scheer, Robert, 240n17
Schiff, Jacob, 164
Schiller, 150, 154
Schlüter, Wilhelm, 79n58
Scholer, Dr., 79n7
Schramm, Dr., 74
Schülter, Hermann, 73
Schwab, Frank, 138
Seamen, 88-91, 94, 97, 101, 105n5, 108n35
Seamen's Association, 91, 92, 96, 99, 106nn
Seamen's Church, 91, 93, 98, 107n19
Seamen's Mission society, 89, 91, 93, 107nn
Select schools, 31
Seller, Maxine, 148-49
Senegalese, 184-85, 195n22
Senior, Clarence, 200-2, 204-5, 212n14, 213n41
Service sector, 12, 181, 187
Settlement houses, 112, 115, 117-18, 123n39
Seward, William H., 42, 43
Shaw, Richard, 44
Shields, James, 41-42, 45
Shopkeepers, 30, 36, 190-91, 194
Siberia (Gordin), 154
Siegel, Barry, 221, 235, 238n13
Sierra Berdecia, Fernando, 200, 201, 204
Sigel, Franz, 79n71
Silver Gray faction, 42
Simpson-Mazzoli bills, 184
Simpson-Rodino Act (1988), 184
Sinatra, Frank, 175
Sisters' Hospital (Buffalo), 31
Skaar, Sigmund, 99
Skaggs, William, 135
Skilled workers, 9, 10, 17, 21n11, 23n31, 25n63, 36; Norwegian, 96-97, 102; and radicalism, 57, 74
Slaughter, The (Gordin), 154
Slavery issue, 11-12, 15, 16, 18-19, 24nn, 42; German radicals and, 71, 75, 79n69
Small business, 96, 192, 194
Socialistischen Turnverein, 69-70
Socialists, 60, 64, 66, 69-70, 72, 76-77, 94, 129; in Buffalo, 134, 137, 138-39, 142
Social Reformers, 62, 63
Social services, 34, 177, 178, 210
Societies for the Promotion of Actual Settlements, 49
Society of the Seasons, 60
Sodalities, 113
Sollors, Werner, 167n1, 169n30
Sorge, Adolf, 69, 75

South Africans, 191
South Americans, 176, 181, 186, 187, 221, 222, 224, 233, 237n8, 238n14, 240n17
South Bronx, 204
Southeast Asians, 219
Southern Europeans, xiii, 83, 183, 221
Sozialreformassoziation (Social Reform Association), 61-62, 67, 69-73, 76
Spartan Club, 12
Spellman, Tom, 240n16
Spirit of the Ghetto (Hapgood), 153
Stadttheater, 150
Staten Island (Richmond), 110, 183
Steffens, 64
Stinner, William, 227
Strikes, 64, 66-68, 72-73, 74
Struve, Gustave, 75
Stuyvesant high school, 189
Sue, Eugène, 61
Summer camps, 112, 115-16, 118, 120
Sung, Betty Lee, 196n41
Survey, The, 160
Statue of Liberty, xiv
Sweatshops, 189
Swedish-Norwegian consul, 89
Syrians, 191

Tailors strike, 67-69
Tammany Hall, 8, 10, 15, 16, 17, 25n52
Teatro Italiano, 152
Technocrats, 198-99, 201, 211
Tenant farmers, 29, 30
Texas, 29; annexation, 12, 13-14
Thalia Theater, 150, 153-54
Theater, 84, 148-71
Thernstrom, Stephan, 108n26, 165, 221
Third World immigrants, 179-97
Thomashevsky, Boris, 155
Thompson, Bill, 137-38
Tilden, Samuel J., 8, 19
Timon, Margaret, 28
Timon, James, 28
Timon, Bishop John, 4, 27-32, 34-35, 37, 43, 45, 48-54, 55n65
Tobago, 187
Tobier, Emanuel, 195n19
Tocqueville, Alexis de, 19
Tomasi, Silvano, 121
Tompkins Square Riot, 76
Trade-Exchange Bank, 64, 65, 66, 67, 68, 128
Tradesmen, 9, 15, 21n11, 88, 128
Trecy, Rev. Jeremiah, 41, 50, 51-52
Tribun de peuple, 62
Trinidadians, 187, 222, 224, 229
Trinity through the Years 1890-1965 (Olsen), 106n12
Tucker, Sophie, 167

Tugwell, Rexford G., 201
Turner, Jack, 165
Turngemeinde (Gymnastics Society), 69
Turnverein (Gymnastics Union), 57, 69–73, 79*n*55, 141
Turn-Zeitung, 70, 72, 79*n*55
Tweed scandals, 4, 16, 25*n*50

Uhl, Jacob, 60–61, 65–66
Ulbrich, Otto, 128
Undocumented immigrants (illegal aliens), 184–85, 187–88, 192–94, 218, 237*n*8, 241*n*32
Unemployment, 74–76, 88, 89, 176, 199, 200, 203, 205, 233
Unions: and German radicals, 62, 64, 66–67 68, 71–74, 76; and Puerto Ricans, 205, 206, 207
U. S. Bureau of Employment Security, 203
U. S. Congress, 9, 40, 141, 142–43, 180, 182, 183, 184, 196*n*37, 199, 212*n*8
U. S. Employment Service, 205
United Trades, 67, 68
Unskilled workers, 9, 10, 17, 21*n*11, 25*n*63, 36, 42, 96, 103, 110, 204
Upper classes, 17, 19, 75, 90
Upper West Side, 186, 204
Utopian: colonies, 68, 69; socialists, 75

Vambrana, Haydee, 193
Van Buren, Martin, 12
Van Buren Associations, 12
Vanderbilt, Cornelius, 16
Vaudeville, 156–65, 169*n*35, 170*n*58
Velazquez, Nydia, 214*n*59
Velez, Ramon, 210
Vidal, David, 228
Vietnamese, 191, 219
Volksfreund, 130, 135–36, 137, 140, 141–42
Voluntary departure status, 185
Voting, 9, 19–20*n*1, 205, 209, 214*n*59; fraud, 20*n*8, *See also* Elections
Voting Rights Act (1965), 209

Wagner, Mayor, 206
Walsh, Mike, 12, 19, 62
Walsh, William H., 114–16, 117, 120
War Brides Act, 182
Ware, Caroline, 119
War on Poverty, 209, 210
Warren, 227
Washington, George, 66
WASPS, 4, 166

Weber, Joe, 156–57, 166
Weed, Thurlow, 42
Weismann, Henry, 143
Weitling, Wilhelm, 58, 60, 62–69, 73, 74, 76
Welfare, 177, 178, 205, 206, 207
Welsh, Joe, 161, 165, 166, 170*n*35
Western Europeans, 217
West Indians, 180, 181, 183, 186, 187, 192, 193, 222, 228, 229, 233, 239*n*14
"We-they" polarity, 149, 155–56, 166
Weydemeyer, Joseph, 20*n*7, 72–76
Whelan, Richard, 45, 50
Whig Party, 8, 10, 13, 33, 35, 42
Whiskey Ring scandals, 16
White collar workers, 9, 10, 17, 25*n*63, 96
Whites, 176, 191, 193
Wild Man, The (Gordin), 154
Wile, Frederic, 135
Wilentz, Sean, 22*n*21, 56–57, 70, 77*n*1
Williams, Eva, 165
Wilson, Woodrow, 133, 135, 136, 137
Windsor Theater, 153
Winter, Frederick, 135–36
Wittner, Judge Bonnie, 195*n*22
Women, 22*n*15; Italian, 111, 112, 114–15; Norwegian, 97–98, 104, 108*nn*
Women's Branch of the New York City Mission and Tract Society, 112
Women's clubs, 97
Worker's Hall, 68–69
Working class, 86; Norwegians, 92–96; Puerto Ricans, 201, 204; and Progressive Era, 112; and radicals, 63; role of, in Democratic Party, 7–26; *See also* Labor
Workingmen's Parties, 4
World War I, 126, 127, 129–30, 132, 136–40, 144–45
Wynn, Ed, 170*n*35

Yiddish theater, 152–54, 166
Young Hickory association, 12–13
Young Ireland movement, 44
Young Man's Heart, A (play), 168, 171*n*79
Young Men's Central Hickory Association, 13
Young Men's Democratic Club, 25*n*52
Young Men's Democratic Committee, 8, 10, 17
Young Tammany Democrats, 17, 25*n*52
Youth, Italian, 109–25
Yox, Andrew, 83, 84–85, 126–47
Yugoslavians, 227, 240*n*17